LET SOMEONE
HOLD YOU

LET SOMEONE HOLD YOU

The Journey of a Hospice Priest

Paul F. Morrissey

CROSSROAD · NEW YORK

1994

The Crossroad Publishing Company
370 Lexington Avenue, New York, NY 10017

Copyright © 1994 by Paul F. Morrissey

Printed in the United States of America

Library of Congress Cataloging-in-Publication Data

Morrissey, Paul F.
    Let someone hold you : the journey of a hospice priest / Paul F. Morrissey.
      p. cm.
    ISBN 0-8245-1408-4 (pbk.)
    1. Morrissey, Paul F. 2. Catholic Church—New York (N.Y.)—Clergy—Biography. 3. Church work with the terminally ill—Catholic Church. I. Title.
BX4705.M7244A3   1994
259'.4—dc20   93-45874
                                             CIP

*For nurses everywhere, especially
"the midwives to the heavenly spheres"
who care for the terminally ill
and
for Tom and Nora,
who showed me by example
the pearl of great price*

Disclaimer

Although the experiences recounted in this book are real, the names, descriptions, and other identifying characteristics of individuals have been disguised to protect their privacy. Any resemblance to actual persons is purely coincidental.

~ Contents ~

~ Foreword ~

THE FIRST TIME I sat beside a dying patient, I think I was closer to death than she. I mean I was scared to death. Fifteen years of spiritual practice had not prepared me to be quite this "real." But the confrontation offered unmistakable potential. At a dying person's bedside, theories about death are not enough, only the open heart of Jesus, only the clear mind of our essential Buddha nature.

There is a teaching in Zen Buddhism: "Your spiritual practice is fit for calm, but is it fit for disturbance?" For me to be with this dying woman was a test for all that had gone before. I could not think the moment; I had to *be* it. Only the truth would do, only mercy and awareness. Nothing I had learned up to that moment quite prepared me for the immediacy required, the simplicity needed to enter the consciousness of one who no longer could use "time" as a denial of the present moment. This is what happens when someone dies: there is no time. For her, the future and past had dissolved in the reality of a body burning with leukemia.

Seeing my dismay, the woman was very kind. She let me *be* and gave me my first great teaching in service to the ill and injured: simply be, that you may touch the disheartened with your heart. But that is precisely what can frighten us. One's heart can feel too small to handle the collapsing heart of another. But what if this dying one isn't just "another"? To hold with mercy and awareness what we have for so long withdrawn from in fear and judgment may only be possible if we see each patient as the Beloved.

This is the teaching that Father Paul has so deeply integrated in his service to the dying in the homes and hospitals of New

York City. From the stillness of the monastery he has moved into the noisy commotion of the streets with Jesus just over his left shoulder. As he travels on subways and expressways into the homes of hospice patients, the reader is invited along with him.

It is suitably ironic to his broad expression of heart that when I search for a word to describe this man, only a word in Yiddish seems to suffice — this priest is a "mensch," a whole human being. It is easier to be a saint than a whole human being. Indeed, many of the saints were a bit neurotic and one-sided, but Paul is a whole human being. A rare phenomenon. There is a wholeness in his book too, which will draw you into it and empower you with your own ability to hold others who are hurting.

Mother Teresa speaks of gently peeling into her arms the body of a fellow baked to the pavements of Calcutta, a man who had been dying for days as people stepped around or over him with indifference. She says she does not become lost in the fears or even the fragile sentimentalities that might arise in such circumstances. Instead, she recognizes this fellow as "Jesus in his distressing disguise." She sees him as the Beloved on its way to the heart of completion.

The hospice patients Paul introduces to us in *Let Someone Hold You* will not soon be forgotten. They are Jesus in his distressing disguise today: a person with AIDS, a Hispanic, Jewish, Irish, black, poor, or rich person. They are of different faith traditions, but their common mortality unites them.

These are stories of the spiritual healings and physical deaths occurring at this very moment. If you attend carefully to the next beat of your heart, you can sense this call for mercy from every corner of the universe.

Those who read this book will find in it a call to service that resonates in the cells. This is the yoga of compassion. This is more than just the often spoken of "path with a heart." This is the path *through* the heart to the truth that remains when all that blocks the truth has been offered up for the benefit of other sentient beings.

My teacher used to say, "Don't be a Buddhist, be Buddha. Don't be a Christian, be Christ." Whatever your religion or even aversion to it, this loving presence is what will stir in you as you read these pages.

I know Paul won't care for this, but if ever there was an angel of mercy, he is it. His wings are his heart. His ability to fly is his willingness to stay with the earthbound suffering of so many. He seems to have the gift to "keep the heart open in hell." This is a heroic journey, but, amazingly, Paul describes the learning of skillful mercy and deeper listening as coming to him from his patients. It is they who "hold" him, he says. Thus to his readers who are caregivers, as well as to those who are patients, he urges, *Let Someone Hold You.* As you read this book about people you never knew, they will come alive and hold you with their love and courage. From then on, death and dying will no longer scare you out of living to the fullest.

STEPHEN LEVINE
Chamisal, New Mexico

~ Acknowledgments ~

I THANK GOD for all who helped me give birth to this book. I want to thank all of my Augustinian brothers, especially John Shea and Tom Casey, who were my readers and advisors, and Harry Cassel and Joseph Duffey, who were my superiors and "padrones." I am deeply grateful for the Marianist Community in West Hills, California, who provided such a warm and prayerful space during my sabbatical year, and for my terrific family who believes in me and my writing and encouraged me to go for it. I thank my team members at Visiting Nurse Service in New York City, who taught me how to be a priest in the secular city, and every patient and family I was privileged to meet in this ministry; by allowing me to get close to them in their most vulnerable state, they taught me to be less afraid of death and thus to live more fully now.

I owe special thanks to a friend, Dr. Fred Schwartz, who provided advice on the medical references in this work; to Rev. Richard Friedrichs, who critiqued the pastoral interactions; to Bobbie Moulton, RN, who assisted with the appendix on hospice criteria; to my sister, Honora Freeman, whom I consulted about family references; and to Emilio German, my advisor on the musical entries. For all of my counselors I am grateful, especially Aelred Shanley, Gail De Maria, Frances Datz, Carl Sword, Bob Gunn, and the members of my priest' support group.

Three people especially were an inspiration from the beginning of this book sixteen years ago: Norbert Brockman, an African missionary; Dick Hite, a hermit in the hills of West Virginia; and Jeff Pick, a beloved friend who has since died from cancer, but who told me years ago when I spilled out the story of my mother's death to him, "Paul, you've got to write this down for many others." Well, I finally did it, Jeff! Thank you.

It takes two people to conceive a baby. A book too, I believe. My editor, Judy Warner Scher, conceived the initial idea for the book from collections of my writing she had seen. All through the process, Judy's special combination of clear-sighted direction and warm-hearted encouragement has been the indispensable ingredient without which this book would never have become a reality. I thank Judy with all my heart for her co-creativity, but especially for her spiritual support.

I am very grateful for Barbara Bowen, my agent, who helped me shape this manuscript into its final form. She guided me through the labyrinths of the publishing world and with her wry humor provided sparks of hope until the book was published. To all of those who helped in the publishing process, especially to John and Mary Ellen Eagleson, I give thanks.

Finally, I have been encouraged by a kind word or inquiry about the book's progress made by many dear friends through the years. To each I wish to share the joy of this accomplishment and offer my heartfelt gratitude.

PAUL F. MORRISSEY
Bronx, New York
Summer 1993

~ Introduction ~

THE VISITING NURSE SERVICE of New York City, founded by Lillian Wald over one hundred years ago, is one of the pioneers in home health care in the United States. An average of sixteen hundred visits *a day* are made by these dedicated visiting nurses to the apartments and homes of sick or dying people in New York City alone. It seems to me that the city would gasp its last breath if the bandaging and suctioning, medicating and touching that these nurses offer daily under the most excruciating circumstances of travel and security were to cease. Why there are monuments to generals and business geniuses in the city squares and none to the visiting nurses is beyond my comprehension. I intend this book as a monument to them, a celebration of their lives and the people they serve.

I am a Roman Catholic priest. Having been trained as a pastoral counselor as well, I prayed to God to help me use this training to heal some of those suffering from the AIDS epidemic ravaging our city. Strangely, perhaps as a result of my prayers, I was led to a job in a nonreligious agency; I was hired as Pastoral Care Coordinator for the Hospice Program of the Visiting Nurse Service. My job was to provide spiritual/pastoral care to the patients and families of the terminally ill in our program, mostly cancer patients of many different religious traditions. It was not a matter of giving them my faith, but of helping them discover and claim their own faith, whatever it was, so that their spiritual roots could provide them sustenance in their dying.

As a priest I was used to people coming to me in a church or classroom so that I could minister to them. It was an unusual and challenging shift for me to go where the people were, that

1

is, into their homes — their bedrooms mostly — and meet them on their "turf."

Formally established only in the past few years, the Hospice Program of the Visiting Nurse Service focuses specifically on caring for people who are terminally ill and who want to die at home. Foregoing any more aggressive care, these patients wish to be in familiar surroundings for their last days, as pain-free as possible, with their families and loved ones if they are able to care for them.

The poignant relationship between the primary care persons — the family members we call PCPs — and the patient who is dying is a manifestation of how a particular couple or family deals with death. Some PCPs attempt to protect the patient from knowing the full extent of his or her illness, believing the sick person will give up on hearing the bad news. The PCPs may really be protecting themselves. Do they really think the patient does not know by bodily feeling or all the secretive talk what is actually going on? On the other hand, "denial" by either the family members or the patient seems intimately connected to hope and may even contribute to a patient's living longer.

Patients themselves may put on a good face for their family members or even the hospice personnel so they do not become a burden, but it may also be to protect themselves from owning publicly what is happening to them and having to express the very vulnerable and often "not nice" feelings they may have at such a time. Medicines and food become tools in this game. Prayer and one's relationship with God can too. There is an awesome spectrum of meanings we humans find in suffering, from "I'm being punished for something" (which I may or may not feel is just) to a sublime offering of oneself as a "victim" for the sins of the world. Some don't even bother to search for a meaning, expressing frustration or silent endurance: "It's just the way it is."

Into the midst of this complex web of needs and motives, loves and fears, walks the hospice team — the nurses, doctors, social workers, nutritionists, home health aids, volunteers, and pastoral caregivers — carrying the baggage of our own needs, motives, and fears. Why do we do this? Do we get a sense of power from others' helplessness? Does it make us put our own ailments and losses in perspective? Along with genuinely wanting to alleviate suffering, do we also have motives that are less altruistic, such as wanting to be needed or needing to deal with our own fear of pain and death? Are we best at short-term, quick-and-intense relationships? If so, the six-month prognosis required for a hospice patient may match our needs perfectly.

To realize that many of these mixed motives are present and not be paralyzed by them as we proceed in our patient care is the challenge. After all, if we see less beautiful sides of ourselves and are not blown away by them, we are more likely to really convey through our acceptance of our patients and their families that they are free to be themselves with us. This is good for them, the best medicine. If they have an image of God and can be themselves more honestly in that relationship as well, it can only result in better health, deeper faith.

During my hospice ministry I met many patients who showed me these dynamics graphically. Interestingly, many were in their forties and fifties, younger than I imagined terminally ill people would be, but that made it easier to identify with them. They were extraordinary in the way they related to their family members and to me, though not always in what we might judge to be healthy ways. Death certainly cuts through the charades. When people ask me about my work in ministering to those who are close to death, they often seem to assume it is depressing, as though one can have only sad stories to relate about another's death, another's loss. What a hellish job, right? Well, sometimes and some days, but generally it is otherwise. Getting close to death — if done in faith — can give one eyes to see the preciousness of life, how precious each moment is. *Seize life now! Live your dreams now!* — this is the lesson to be learned from the experience.

Working with a hospice team was a new experience for me. No longer was I with fellow Catholic priests; now I had to learn the arcane language of nurses and doctors talking about Duoderm or Halcion and social workers describing Borderlines and Enmeshed Family Systems. Also, these Jewish, Protestant, and Catholic colleagues — sometimes looking at me with glazed eyes — had to figure out what I might mean by anointing the patients with "holy oil" or suggesting that the patients might need forgiveness more than Tylenol and that *they*, my co-workers, might be the ones who could offer it.

We have had an extraordinary experience learning to work together. Never have I felt such loving solidarity among people I've worked with! Probably we were driven to it by facing the crisis of death: our patients' deaths and, in them as in a mirror, our own. The stories will offer this mirror for you too. May they touch your heart with the incredible courage and love we humans can rise to. May they help you discover life, even God, in death.

The story of my own mother's sudden death over seventeen years ago was the original book I wanted to write. "Oh, so *this* is what death is like!" I discovered in shock at that time. As a priest for almost ten years then, I had buried many people and given many sermons on death to the grieving loved ones. But death became real for me — with the questions and doubts about God and the meaning of life — only when my mother died. Ever since then I have wanted to help others encounter this greatest of human challenges with a little more preparation than my family had.

Nora was the mother of fourteen children of whom I am the second oldest and, according to some of my siblings, "Mama's favorite." If her story occasionally tumbles into the other ones I present here, it is because the experience of her death enabled me to relate to the hospice patients with more heart. Moreover, though I hardly noticed at first, these patients were helping to heal me of my long-buried grief. Yes, those you must care for can do this for you too. All you have to do is "let someone hold you."

I hope you enjoy the unforgettable people you're about to meet. Some will appear in these pages as barely a snapshot, an image of a figure in a bed or a face with a crooked smile — that's all I got of them too. Many I knew only briefly. They came into the program too late for us to do anything but help them prepare for their funeral. Some lived longer, from three months to two years, time enough to have a much deeper relationship with them, with all the pain and sweetness that could bring. Yet each of them brings out an important piece of the puzzle of dying and living in a way that no one else can. It brought tears of joy to me when I met them again in the writing.

~ Isha ~

B Y THE TIME I FIRST SAW HER, Isha had been in our hospice program for over three months. She was a forty-nine-year-old Ethiopian woman with end-stage cancer of the liver. She had come to the United States in 1979 on a work visa to provide house care for an Ethiopian diplomat and was stranded in New York City when the Ethiopian government was overthrown in a military coup. When her work visa expired, she became an undocumented person. Isha's husband had remained in Ethiopia, hoping to join her when she was established here. Their only child, Lilianne, at that time thirteen years old, had accompanied Isha.

When I met them they were living in a two-room efficiency apartment in a drug-infested area of Manhattan. Lilianne, now nineteen years old and an engineering student on scholarship at a local college, had recently quit her sophomore year to get a job and care for her mother, who had become sick the year before. Isha's husband had never been able to get out of their homeland.

As originally explained at our hospice team meeting, Isha had a large abdominal tumor, which was growing and causing increasing pain. The cancer had spread to her lungs and had been unaffected by two rounds of chemotherapy. Ruby, her nurse, had until then not felt that morphine should be prescribed, but it was becoming increasingly necessary to consider it, given the severity of the pain.

Many patients believe that morphine is the end of the line, the sign that they are so far gone that it doesn't matter if they are drugged into a stupor as long as it stops the pain. Many want to hold this medication off as long as they can because of what it symbolizes. Taking morphine is like saying goodbye to hope.

5

Isha was one of these, preferring Tylenol and other milder pain killers.

Isha was also concerned about Lilianne, her only child, who would be alone in this vast, bewildering country and in the wilds of New York City. She wanted to live for her daughter, to stay strong and communicative as long as she could.

Lilianne was described as being in denial about the seriousness of her mother's illness. The hospice team had decided that Beverly, our social worker, would focus on this aspect of Isha's care, while I would pay attention to the patient's spiritual needs. Isha belonged to the Orthodox Church and was open to a pastoral care visit, so I phoned Lilianne and introduced myself as the pastoral care director of the hospice program.

"What religion are you?" she asked. A very young voice.

"Catholic," I responded, "but we serve people of all faiths."

"I haven't wanted to ask the pastor of the Orthodox church. My mother doesn't speak much English," she said. "Also, we had a bad experience with him in the past."

"I could pray..."

"Yes, my mother would like you to come." We arranged for a visit the next week at a time when Lilianne would be there to help translate.

When I arrived at the first-floor apartment on 112th Street off First Avenue, I rang the buzzer and waited, noticing the black and Hispanic men of all ages lounging on the steps and in the doorways along the street. After a second ring and a long wait, the door squeaked open, and I saw a pair of eyes peeking out of a dark room. It was the patient herself in her nightgown. Smiling shyly, she fumbled at the lock until the vestibule door opened, and then walked with some difficulty in her bare feet ahead of me into the room.

Despite the language barrier we introduced ourselves and touched hands. She showed me a sofa in the tiny room with barely enough leg room for me to sit while she got herself back into her bed right next to it. The drapes were drawn, but in the shadows I noticed a red, green, and black map of Africa taped to the wall. A button with a picture of Haile Selassie was fastened in the middle of it.

Removing the plastic bag I had tried to protect it with, I produced a large, salmon-colored dahlia to present to Isha, which at this point was flopping over, its stem bent from the subway ride.

"Ohhh!" A bright smile lit her face. "Me?"

"Yes." I apologized for the broken stem with more hand-gestures than words, sounding to myself as though I were talking to a baby.

Isha produced a small vase and asked me to put some water in it. When I had done so, she carefully placed the flower in it, stroking the injured part with such gentleness that it seemed like a pet animal or even human.

I settled back into the cushions and relaxed, taking off my jacket because of the heat. A big yellow tabby cat bounded up from under her bed and jumped on my lap. "No!" Isha commanded. "No, Patrick!" But she scolded with a loving tone. Spotting the little switch in her hand and the look of devilment in her eyes, the cat waved its tail and disappeared again into the shadows. A game they played. I knew I would enjoy this visit.

We glanced at each other, gazing across the culture gap, I suppose. Ethiopia, what did I know of it? It is a country in Africa, with huge numbers of starving people. Pictures of children with bloated bellies came to mind. Deserts and camels. Nomadic tribes. Fighting. What did I have in common with this lady looking at me out of her gaunt black face with its high cheekbones, the frizzy hair, a flimsy nightgown hung on her bony shoulders?

And her? She saw a white clergyman in a dark suit and Roman collar, with a slim build and blue eyes, like so many other conquerors her people had known. Rich, compared to her, stuck in this little steaming flat. Educated and free, healthy and surrounded by a network of family and friends. Christian, yes, but of a different church. A celibate priest, with all of the mysteries of the priesthood.

"How are you? How do you feel today, Isha?" I pronounced the words slowly and carefully.

"Me good, me nice."

"I spoke to Lilianne last week. She said she'd be here."

"Lilianne work." She pointed toward the street.

"Yes . . . "

She stared at me calmly. Oh, boy, this was going to be a trip. Maybe we would be able to communicate a little, but it wouldn't go too far. My Ethiopian was rather rusty.

Glancing around the room, I spotted a small bookcase underneath a TV. "You have a Bible?" I was making exaggerated gestures like a mime artist.

"Bible, yes," she nodded. Then like a magician she produced with a flourish an old book from under her pillow.

"Bible . . . Lilianne me read." She opened it carefully and I saw what looked like hieroglyphics.

"Oh, it's in your language! Will you read it for me?"

"Me no read." Announcing this with a smile, she held her fingers next to the page and then up to her eye.

"Ohh, too small . . . the print's too small."

"Yes." She understood. It felt like we were on a TV game show.

"Isha, maybe you would like it if I read you a Scripture story in English?"

"Okay."

I wondered if she knew what I was saying. In any case, I'd be doing something that would give me a sense of accomplishment. I hadn't yet learned that I could just be with a patient, not do anything.

I read the passage about Jesus as the Good Shepherd, that he knew the voice of his sheep and they knew his. "The Good Shepherd lays down his life for the sheep . . ." (John 10:11).

Spotting the crucifix on a side wall I went on, "Jesus loves us," swirling my hands around to include her and me.

"Me sheep?" she asked with a faint smile, pointing at the large tumor in her belly. "God love sheep." I laughed. Yeah, but I wonder where God is in your life. Does God even know Ethiopia exists?

About forty-five minutes passed. Surprised and happy at the communication we had managed without knowing each other's language, I looked for a way to make an exit on this upbeat note.

"Isha, could we say a prayer before I go?"

She agreed, and I opened my palms in front of her and held them upward. Isha placed hers downward on top of mine while I said the Lord's Prayer slowly with my eyes closed. This felt good, and we remained in this position for a few silent moments.

When I opened them at the conclusion I thought I noticed her wince in pain, but she said in a sweet voice, "God, thank you," pointing her hands toward me and looking up. "You come again?"

"Certainly, Isha. How about two weeks from now?"

"Two weeks?" She looked perplexed.

"I'll call Lilianne and let her know."

"Okay," Isha nodded. "You nice."

Then, with obvious strain, she arose to let me out the door. Before leaving, I went over to the window sill where Isha had placed the flower in the vase and carefully stroked the bent stem with the tips of my fingers as she had done. A grin of understanding passed between us. Patrick emerged to rub my leg when I leaned to embrace Isha goodbye. Yes, for all our differences I liked this place, this little lady with the bright eyes and the dark, dark face. This was the first of over forty visits I would make to her.

On the way home I remembered back to when I was first ordained. It was 1967 and I was serving as a chaplain at Queens General Hospital. Priests are supposed to take death in stride, but it felt like I spent that entire summer anointing bodies they found on the expressways around New York City. So my introduction to dealing with the crisis of death began many years before I joined a hospice team. I used to get phoned out of bed in the middle of the night at the Augustinian parish where I lived, a nurse's voice calling "Critical on Sixth North!" into my dream-fogged brain.

I would drag my body to attention, slip on my black suit, and walk swiftly through the cool and silent shadows to another injury, another death, another human being who needed me. They would be brought into the emergency room with the ever-present sirens screaming in the background. It was spooky, that baptism, and I was unprepared for it. I wasn't ready to have young Hispanic kids dying on an overdose crunch my hand for support and scream for Jesus Christ while half-dazed interns jammed needles into their already ravaged arms. Caught off guard to see a leg amputated, a tear rolling down a rough guy's cheek while I said something stupid like "It'll be all right." Revolted to encounter cold, gray bodies in the morgue or old, wheezing ladies lying in their own waste, babbling some phrase from a long-lost conversation as they strained to get out of their steel cribs.

One early morning after the Fourth of July I arrived to see

the flashing lights of an ambulance at the back of the emergency ward. "He's in the back," said a cop by the door. He grinned knowingly.

Half groggy with sleep, I climbed up on the back bumper of the ambulance and stooped into the dimly lit rear section. A heavy-set man — like my father — was strapped to a chair, his head thrown back, mouth open. Dead.

"Run!" a voice whispered inside of me. "Get away from all this sickness and death!" I opened the holy oils, quickly reaching for his forehead. The flesh was clammy and limp to the touch. I made the sign of the cross with the oil.

"You can smell it!" the voice inside me warned. "It'll drag you into it! Run!" I uttered a quick prayer to the God who presided over all this and climbed out of that horrible scene.

The cop looked at me. "He was the father of twelve kids," he said matter-of-factly. "Had a heart attack at Jones Beach this evening. His wife and daughter are in the waiting room." He paused. "Would you go and speak with them?"

I am a fragile man, too sensitive for my own good. My heart sinks when I see groundhogs run over in the road. The thought of starving people makes my eyes water, and I'm a sucker for a panhandler's tale. I am a coward to show my own anger most of the time for fear that someone will not like me or even have cause to slug me for it. What can I say to someone who has just lost her husband, her father? Something that will make sense. It doesn't make sense, so why try? Why don't you do it, cop?

Through the steel door to the waiting room I could hear the women wailing in some strange language. Italian, I thought. They are so emotional. It burst in loud upon my ear drums like some sound always present in the world. The teenage daughter in shorts and a halter turned in my direction as she heard me enter and then turned away. She doesn't want me to see. They're crying for him and he can't come back.

"I'm Father Morrissey," I said as I approached them. They wailed even louder. All I could think to do in my helplessness was to put my arm around the wife's heaving shoulders. Shaking my head in disbelief with them, the tears welled up out of my own soul too.

This was before my mother died. It was still before I had discovered death as more than just a word. Since then I have gotten a little more used to meeting other people while they deal with this most unbelievable of human events. Not that I am any less shocked, less thrown into deep questions by someone dying. It is just that now I am more likely to be aware of my own losses as I get closer to another person's and to realize that we are in this together.

It is not a matter of giving others solace out of my fullness, but of reaching out to them with the awareness and the feelings born out of my own losses. With all of our differences in race and sex, class and religion, it seems that we can meet down in the subways of our hearts.

Somewhere down in the pain, God is. Maybe God is simply in our raging and longing and what we do with it. This I believe: God can make sense of suffering and death if we trust God with all our questions. We need to trust God with how we really are today, and God needs a little time to answer us too.

~

Every Wednesday morning from 9:00 to 11:00 a.m., the hospice team of the Visiting Nurse Service of New York City would gather in a small office on the fifth floor of the Empire State Building. A dozen of us would gather around two large tables pushed together in a room with a large window that looked out on Thirty-fourth Street and Fifth Avenue — shoppers, tourists, and executives scurrying in the street below us. It was a time of reconnecting after the individual "field work" everyone had been involved in during the previous week, a time of hard work in agreeing on and recording all the plans of care we made for the coming week.

Just as important, it was a time for bantering and support as well. We would make macabre jokes about our work, share crazy stories about our patients or the medical profession that could help us laugh, believe in ourselves and life, and prepare to go on for another week. If our patients ever heard us laughing about their pain and tragedies they would be horrified. This was our medicine though, and we knew it as we looked across the table at each other with love and concern in our eyes, the hurting we felt along with our patients even as we spoofed them.

When the crowd of us slid around the table, juggling our coffee and bagels along with patient records, pocketbooks, bereavement cards, thank-you notes from families, prescription blanks, and the other paraphernalia of our work, there was no room to feel disengaged or self-important. Simply by coming together we were reminded that we needed each other. This was no one-man or one-woman show. Our professions needed each other, and the enormity of death and the home hospice care in which we were involved challenged each of us out of our professional self-sufficiency. This didn't come easily. As professional nurses, doctors, therapists, nutritionists, and pastoral caregivers, we didn't immediately merge into a splendid synchronicity. It was our director, Kate, who nurtured this.

Recently married, Kate was a tall, willowy woman with a rather plain face that lit up like a Christmas tree when she engaged you in conversation. The dashing and colorful outfits she wore contrasted with her silver hair, cut very short on the sides and almost punked-out on the top like David Bowie's. A social worker by profession, Kate delighted in getting us to blend together as a team and not just do our own job, no matter how well.

The team had to work at this. Just picture the line-up each Wednesday and imagine the turf struggles that could develop. On one side of the table, nearest the patient record books, sat Kate along with the nursing clinical director, the volunteer coordinator, perhaps the nutritionist. This represented the administrative arm of the program. Across the table from them would usually congregate the doctor and the nurses, the latter being the indispensable grunts of the whole operation. Back and forth between these two groups ricocheted an astounding array of medical facts and questions, concerned mainly with physical pain and its control.

Perpendicular to this axis sat the "psychospiritual" component of the team — the social workers on one side of the table with the pastoral caregivers facing them on the other side. Only mildly interested in the discussion of physical illness, this group was champing at the bit to get to what they considered the real matters of importance — the inner psychological and spiritual dynamics of the patient and family. Members of this psychospiritual group could often be seen with our eyes drooping at the lengthy discussion of medicines, as though physical intactness were the key to a patient's well-being at this time!

The medical-administrative group, on the other hand, could often be seen drumming their fingers at the long-winded stories of psychological or spiritual "breakthroughs" going on with our patients or families. As one nurse remarked, "If the patient is conflicted with pain, these things are dessert!"

To add a little more zest to this mix, the psychospiritual contingent would sometimes clash among ourselves. Beverly, a married Jewish woman in her early forties who supervised the social workers, saw religion as a way that patients and families often avoided dealing with the hard realities of a wounded ego or dysfunctional family system. At first she and I would spar whenever these issues came up. Beverly delighted in pushing "Father," which she called me in an affectionate, mocking way, to recognize the basic spirituality of all persons whether they believed in God or not. And I would challenge her and the rest of the team not to see pastoral care as something you call upon only when all else has failed.

The team was composed almost entirely of women. Only the doctor and myself interrupted this woman-space. Because of this, the dynamics were more person-oriented than most male-dominated organizations are. A stress was put on process, and feelings as well as facts had to be considered in decision-making. This usually served the particularly sensitive needs of the terminally ill very well. A fine line had to be walked between respecting people's feelings and speaking the truth.

~

A few weeks later I was scheduled to meet Isha's daughter, Lilianne, in my office. She worked downtown near us, and it was easier to meet at our office to talk about how funeral plans for her mother were going to be arranged. Lilianne had skipped the past few meetings with our social worker about this. Beverly wanted to convey to her that the state requires an application *before* a person dies if the family claims to be too poor to pay the funeral costs. Otherwise the money isn't made available. Lilianne was having great difficulty making any preparations that would acknowledge the true gravity of her mother's illness. The hospice team was concerned that this would leave her — and us — in some chaos when Isha died. Though I had spoken to Lilianne only a few times on the phone so far, because of my relationship with Isha I had been asked by the team to see if I could make some progress with her on this.

I phoned Lilianne at her place of employment around 10:00 a.m. to remind her of the appointment we had arranged for that afternoon.

"Father Paul, I forgot!" she said cheerfully. "But I can still come over to see you on my lunch break, okay?"

"Fine." Nervous how I would handle a potential emotional blow-up by this young girl, I bit my nails as I hung up.

It's important for her, I assured myself. We've got to help her realize that any way she can prepare now will make it that much easier for her when her mother actually dies.

A little later my secretary showed Lilianne into my office. With her sprightly elfin figure Lilianne barely reached my shoulder, and as she curled into one side of the easy chair I could see the resemblance to her mother: the wide-set almond eyes, the petite nose and mouth, the texture of her hair that stood out in a sunburst look. Twisting one leg around the other protectively she quickly scanned the room and then looked at me apprehensively.

We made some small talk about the subway and the elevator, whether she had had any problem finding the office. Then I got to the point. "Lilianne, how serious do you understand your mother's illness to be?" She fidgeted with her hands.

"I know my mom is very sick, but she was so strong a year ago that I find it hard to accept that she is dying." I was relieved. Lilianne had mentioned "dying" first.

"Do you want to hear about information we have on financial help with a funeral whenever your mother dies?"

She looked toward the far wall. "I don't want to talk about funeral plans."

"I know it is hard, but it would be good to have some options in place when that time comes."

"I don't want to do anything that would mean I want my mother to die. Talking about funeral plans now would feel like that. I enjoy each day with her and don't want to give up hope." She brushed away a tear.

I said that I understood, but that if certain steps of investigation on her part were not taken now, the funeral would cost twice as much. Lilianne said she didn't care. "I would rather work overtime to pay for it than to give up hope now."

I was struck by the determination of this attractive young woman, so vulnerable and yet strong in her own way. "Okay," I gave in. "You give us the word when you want to talk about any of that. We want to respect your wishes."

The mood shifted. We talked about how her mother was doing and my recent visits. Lilianne said that Isha enjoys Ruby because the nurse makes her laugh. "Would you believe she had my mom up dancing to some reggae music last week?" she said with a grin.

"It's all part of the medicine."

Before she left a few minutes later, I gave her my home phone number as well as my office number. "In case you want to talk sometime...or an emergency comes up and you can't get me at work." I wanted to pull her toward me in an embrace, but the soft lights and closed door made me shy.

"Okay, Father Paul." She was back in her cheerful public mood. Promising to see Isha again the following week, I walked her to the elevators and there I hugged her goodbye.

Later as I rode the subway home to the Bronx, I thought about Lilianne and Isha. A child's relationship with a parent — especially the mother — is an incredible mix of attraction and resistance. Bound together not by bands of steel but of flesh and blood, which eventually need to break. But how? I knew something about this. Years before I had learned the hard way about breaking this connection with my own mother....

~

I was living in a Quaker commune in Philadelphia to learn nonviolence. It was 1973 and I had been ordained for seven years. One night while I was sitting in the living room of Rainbow House, where I lived, watching a three-year-old child play on the living room floor after supper, some thoughts about his mother and her mortality crept up into my consciousness. It made me think of my own mother. I remember being paralyzed by what I was feeling and how desperately I needed someone to share it with, wishing someone would come and find me because I did not have the power to get up and move, praying to God for that to happen.

At that point Jeanne O'Hara, a stout, middle-aged ex-nun whom I had become close to over the past few years, came home. She took one look at me sitting there and said, "Paul, something's the matter, isn't it?" Nodding blankly, I went to my room with her.

We sat on my bed. Her matronly breasts supported me as she drew my head against her and I began to weep. "It's my mother!" I wailed. "Oh, Jeanne, I feel as though she died tonight and I'm all alone." Great billowing sounds came out of me as Jeanne rocked back and forth, letting me cry. It seemed as if I wept for over an hour in her arms, soaking Jeanne's blouse and a few handkerchiefs, puffing my face out like a red balloon and clearing my sinuses at least for a year. Finally my heaving body found a place of peace.

Quietly, softly my breathing returned. I could almost have gone to sleep, by this time lying flat on my back with my head resting in Jeanne's lap. Looking up at her, a grin of acceptance spread out on my face. "Want to go out for a couple of beers?" I asked.

"Are you sure you are done crying?" I wasn't sure, but answered yes by standing up and blowing my nose.

It was midnight. We strolled the four blocks to the Shamrock Tavern on Forty-fifth Street, mostly in silence. It has little dark booths in the back where you can talk without the sound of the jukebox drowning you out. I didn't want to think about what had happened. I was having a premonition of my mother's death. She was then sixty-two years old, very much alive, and the heart and anchor of the huge Morrissey clan.

Jeanne and I played darts. Flinging them hilariously against the wall, Jeanne would shriek whenever she missed the board. It helped to have her acting the fool, making me choke and sputter in my beer. I intended to get numb. Gradually the traumatic feelings of the evening subsided, disappearing into my soul like the foam at the top of my glass. The boisterous crowd of working-class men around the bar and the bowling machine trickled out toward home. A few stray women still perched on the well-worn stools, occasionally glancing into the mirror behind the bar. Jeanne and I helped each other out the door.

On the way home, we playfully pushed each other into hedges, laughing that we hadn't done such wicked things since childhood. Jeanne tried to whistle. I complained of a pain in my stomach.

"Well, you had four beers. What do you want?" she chided.

"But it's weird! It's a band of pain across my stomach!"

"Hell, a good long fart'll probably cure you." She shoved me into another hedge.

On the corner of Forty-sixth Street where the trolley stops, we hugged goodnight long and deeply before separating. Unlike my usual independent self, I didn't push away, but kissed her swiftly on her cracked lips.

"Hey, Jeanne, thanks so much."

"Anytime."

Crossing the tracks, I turned and watched her walk up the darkened street alone. Except for my belly, my body felt loose, like I had been shaken on the clothesline for the afternoon. When I got home, I tiptoed up the stairs so that I wouldn't awaken the others, stripped in the dark, and collapsed on my bed, a convertible futon. The streetlight out back glowed eerily, hardly doing more than highlight the shadows where you could hear the rats searching for garbage if you listened. A light was on in an apartment across the way, but the shade was down. Before falling asleep, my hand searched my stomach for the band of pain. It was still there.

Toward dawn I awoke to relieve myself and felt for it again. Gone, thank God. No, wait! A single concentrated spot of it remained. My navel felt like it was on fire. Dreaming again, I thought. Or else drunk. Gingerly I touched again. *Oooowwww!* Then it dawned on me. My umbilical cord was severed last night, at least psychologically, and I'm feeling the pain. My body is just going along with my brain. My mother "died" last night, or maybe I just relived my birth. As I rolled over and pulled up my covers, my mind slid back into unconsciousness.

Late that morning my eyes opened slowly to see the sunlight dancing off the little particles of dust that normally are invisible. I reached carefully below the sheet. No band of pain. Then my navel. Touching it carefully with my middle finger, I then pressed deeper to search for the fire of the night before. Vanished! Bolting up quickly, I threw off the covers to have a look.

A slight hangover slowed down the investigation, but truly I was amazed at what was going on. My insides shouted happily that I had witnessed a unique adventure, some kind of separation experience from my mother. Telling her about this was another story.

One evening a few weeks later when I was home for a visit, I cautiously broached the subject to Mama in the kitchen during a pause in the dinner preparations. We were alone, which was difficult to manage in our house, especially during the tumultuous period before a family meal. Ten kids were still at home; Daddy was upstairs resting after work; the kitchen was cramped. Almost casually I began, "Mama, something really scary happened to me the other night."

"Oh," she said, looking up with interest from the sink where she was rinsing something, "what was that?" How does a grown man tell anyone, let alone his mother, that he's been frightened, that he feels small and weak?

"Mama, I felt like you were dying and how lonely I'd be without you." With watery eyes and quivering voice I let the words tumble out of the little boy in me.

"Oh, Paul," she said, giving me a little sad upward glance from her work, "you'll be all right. I'll be watching over you with God from heaven." She gave me a consoling hug, her hands wet from the vegetables.

"Mama," I went on, "I cried for a couple of hours and I even had a pain in my belly-button!" She smiled, interested as usual in the great adventures of her children. But the brood were waiting for dinner.

"Let's talk about it again sometime," she said.

My mother was always interested in whatever happened to me — which drove me mad sometimes. The smallest, most insignificant things in my life were always important to Mama, almost as though they were happening to her. It was something I could count on. Most of the time I felt blessed by this and wanted to give something in return. But who could respond to such an unconditional gift, even with one's whole life? I was a rich man. Here I was telling her about her death and she was worrying about me....

~

The subway rumbled to a stop at Fordham Road. Snapping out of my daydream, I was swept to the doorway with the throng of black and Hispanic people who lived in this part of town. The constant subway travel in the bowels of the city is hidden from view, as death is most of the time. You get closer to death and life when you go down into those subways, crammed with a multi-colored humanity, their erotic life spilling out of their sweaters and jeans. Legless ones in wheelchairs push their way through the crowds, telling only half-believable tales to squeeze a quarter out of you if you weaken. It's the Good News that a priest is sent to proclaim to the people, but most of the time it's Bad News that you've got to break to them. They don't tell you about that when you get ordained.

~ Candida ~

MANY OF OUR PATIENTS, struggling with the terrible paradox of how a supposedly loving Creator can allow suffering to afflict innocent people, wound up putting their faith in *either* God *or* medicine. In ancient times, religion and medicine were inextricably linked. Priests of various religions were often the most educated among the people and used their knowledge to cure people. Sickness was seen as connected to morality. Health was a blessing for goodness, its absence a result of sin or even a direct punishment from God. Since the advent of modern science, professional medical care has been effectively split off from the realm of religion, often for good reasons. Some of our patients who were religious would even look upon the taking of medicine as a lack of faith, a giving up on God who has the real power to cure. Others who were more "worldly" would give a token nod to prayer as a kind of insurance policy if all else failed, while really basing most of their hope in the miracle of medicine. One of our patients, Candida Perez, profoundly demonstrated this struggle between God and medicine.

As usual, the nurse would see the patient first to assess the appropriateness of being in our program. Those chronically ill with a serious disease, but expected to live longer than six months, were not appropriate candidates for the program. They might be referred to a nursing home or our Acute Care Department. Without wanting to play God, the doctor would have to make a judgment whether any more aggressive care (such as chemotherapy or radiation) would help the patient and whether he or she had less than approximately six months left to live.

Before we began treating the person the nurse also had to obtain a "Do Not Resuscitate" statement. The patient or a proxy had to sign this legal document that allowed the hospice not to provide emergency cardiopulmonary resuscitation (CPR) if the patient's heart or breathing stopped in the course of the illness. In other words, the quality of life was such that if the patient's heart stopped, he or she would not wish to be revived and placed on respirators or other life-prolonging equipment.

All of these decisions, of course, usually confronted the patient and the caregivers with the true nature of their situation. "I am dying" had to be recognized in some fashion. Yet how the patients and families reacted emotionally to this information varied from flat-out denial on the one hand to patient or family hopes and prayers for a miracle on the other. "I want to live" — at least a day at a time — coexisted with the incontrovertible fact of dying. In our use of medicine and prayer, the hospice staff tried to walk this fine line between hope and acceptance with each patient and family. As best we could, we tailored our intervention to their specific needs.

Matilda gave the initial report on Candida Perez at the team meeting. Of West Indian origin, Matilda was the epitome of the professional nurse and was cherished deeply by her patients. Admired as well by her nurse colleagues, she had been voted by them the Hospice Nurse of the Year for the annual company awards dinner the previous year. With ten years of service, she had been on the team longer than any of us.

As she described Candida in her mellow voice, you could feel our antennae go up. This was one of those patients who immediately engaged the entire team's interest. Something about the combination of her ethnicity, her religion, her family dynamics, her specific illness, and most of all her approach to medicine and pain stirred our juices. Unlike some cases, it looked as if every profession on the team would have to be involved.

"Candida is a forty-eight-year-old Venezuelan woman who came to the United States twenty-two years ago. Married to a Colombian man she met here shortly thereafter, she has one son who is fifteen. Twelve years ago she was diagnosed with breast cancer and had a radical mastectomy. The cancer continued to spread, however, to her other breast and to her jaws. She has had many bouts with chemotherapy and at least one radiation treatment five years ago. In and out of the hospital eleven times during these years, this lady obviously suffered very much.

Her present diagnosis: inoperable cancer of the right breast with metastasis to the bones and lungs.

"Economically speaking, the family is moderately well-off; they live in a lovely apartment in a middle-class neighborhood in Queens. Candida's fifty-two-year-old husband, Juan, is employed as a clerk in a midtown hotel. Candida has never worked outside the home since they married twenty-one years ago."

Matilda described Candida as a very religious Roman Catholic who took only the barest amount of medicine to withstand the worst pain. She did all the cleaning and dressing of her large bleeding tumor by herself and was still ambulatory in her apartment, doing the cooking and cleaning. The patient's chief complaint: she was worried about her son, Angel, who had been absenting himself from school the past few months and hanging around with bad companions. Other measurements included: appetite, bowel regimen, mental state — all surprisingly good for this stage of the illness.

Matilda would see Candida twice a week to check her pulse, heart, and pain, to observe the tumor's growth, and to monitor the pain medication. The family asked if Dr. Cohen, the team physician, would make a home visit. They were open to a social worker's coming and would welcome pastoral care, but did not wish a Home Health Aid or a volunteer.

"Candida looks and sounds like a woman who is not sick," said Matilda, her eyebrows raised, "yet she has a tumor the size of a grapefruit on her right side. She wants to take as little medicine as possible...it has something to do with her faith." Our curiosity piqued, we discussed this family energetically for twenty minutes before Beverly, our staff social worker, interrupted: "Which of our own personal issues are being touched by this lady?" There were many.

Dr. Cohen, whom we had nicknamed "Doc," said he could make a visit early the following week. Beverly would follow that with a social work visit, and our nutritionist would phone them for a consultation. So that we wouldn't overwhelm them at the start, pastoral care would wait until the following week. In the meantime we would receive further reports from the doctor and social worker.

"If the husband or son are not present, a translator will be needed and must be arranged ahead of time," Matilda concluded. "The patient only speaks Spanish." So began our odyssey with the Perez family.

When I phoned to set up a visit, Juan Perez answered in a muffled, guarded sort of way, but warmed up immediately when I introduced myself as Father Paul. Speaking of his wife with great admiration, he asked if I could bring her Holy Communion. I promised I would and we agreed to a 10:30 a.m. visit the next morning before he left for work.

At home the next morning I said a prayer before leaving to see Mrs. Perez, wanting to be open to whatever I would encounter. Doc, a single Jewish man who attended synagogue regularly, had visited them already and had words of praise about Candida's deep faith, though I had a curious cynical streak in me toward deeply religious people. They reminded me of my mother. It also had something to do with my own deep religiosity and a need to be vigilant against its tendency to overwhelm me.

Doc said that he thought it would be good to talk with the fifteen-year-old son. "He's a lovely young man who needs help. He's having a lot of difficulty with his mother's illness."

Intrigued at the possibility of getting to know this family, I arrived ten minutes early at their apartment house near Roosevelt Boulevard in the Elmhurst section of Queens. In a small gold pyx in my pocket I carried the consecrated wafer of bread that to Roman Catholics is the Body of Jesus Christ.

I searched for the Perez name on the directory and pressed the button for apartment 13C. "Yes?" an accented voice spoke. "It's Father Paul," I said in my friendliest tone. The door buzzer rang. A middle-aged white man in a wheelchair nodded to me as I entered the spacious, well-appointed lobby. I nodded back and then pressed the button and waited for the elevator. The elevator was equipped with floor number panels, which included braille, and a low handrail for those in wheelchairs. It crept so slowly you hardly knew it was moving until it got to your floor. The doors hummed open and I looked around for their apartment.

When I ring the bell at the home of a new patient and wait for someone to open the door, it never fails to strike me that they are about to admit me into their private world — their world at its most vulnerable, especially when someone in the house is dying. What lies beyond the door is always a mystery, how people face this most difficult of moments in varied ways. Some wear their hearts on their sleeves: you can read unmistakably on the faces of some caregivers — if not the patient — the trial they are going through. Sometimes the physical status of the house itself is in disarray, either because this is how they have always lived or because they cannot be bothered to make everything tidy when their world is tumbling down around them.

Others appear at the door freshly groomed and smiling, as if greeting someone for a dinner party. Their rooms may be gracious and clean, again because they are normally so inclined, because the chaos of the illness drives them to grab some shred of control wherever it is possible, or possibly just because a guest is coming.

There are all sorts of combinations of this self-presentation, and the patient, of course, is the one in whom these dynamics are most important to notice. Some get exhausted being nice for their visitors, and it is important to provide some boundaries for them. Some are cranky and demanding, either unable to concern themselves about others because of their pain and loss or inclined to take it out on whoever's around, even those they love the most. It is helpful not to take such swipes too personally and to be as direct and honest as one can be. Sometimes it can be helpful to risk a comeback to such testing behavior in order to check their response.

Gradually I was becoming aware of my own proclivities in this regard. At least on days when I got a good night's sleep I would present myself as a friendly, easygoing person without any big agenda. As a religious and spiritual person, yes, but not one who had come to check up on the family's religious scorecard or to proselytize.

On the other hand, I was not just popping in for a friendly visit, content to chat about the weather. I did want to be part of whatever the patient and family permitted me, and to help them see some things they may not want to see at first — their relationship with God for instance — whenever they were ready for it. This called for tremendous tact and delicacy. There was a need to strike a balance between complete nonjudgmental disinterest and the thirsty desire of God to meet them as they truly are. When they died they would have no choice about such an honest encounter.

I had at least two goals in mind for the Perez family. These were not to be accomplished on the first visit, of course, but to be initiated if possible. The first was to assess Candida's spiritual dynamics, her way of relating to God and how that played itself out in her approach to her sickness, especially her use of medicine. The second was to get a handle on Angel's place in the family, how he was dealing with his mother's illness and impending death. Pondering these things, I straightened my collar and tapped on the Perez's door.

A short, balding man with a swarthy complexion cracked the door slightly and then swung it wide open when he saw me. Smiling tightly, he stepped back onto the inlaid wooden floor.

"Father Paul?"

"Yes." I shook his outstretched hand.

"Juan Perez, . . . did you have trouble finding the place?"

"No, and I even found a parking spot!" Chuckling, he offered to take my coat and briefcase.

"I'm a little early, aren't I?"

"That's all right. Candida has just finished dressing her tumor." He whispered this as though it were a secret. "You can go right into the bedroom to see her." I followed him through a dining alcove into a white, sunlit room where the patient, a petite lady with prominent cheekbones, a heart-shaped face, and dark wavy hair, lay in a half-raised hospital bed close to the door.

"Candida . . . Father Paul." Juan introduced us. Her face, which had been impassive, lit up with a sweet smile, her hands reaching out from under the fresh bed linens to grasp mine.

"Ahhh, Father!" she exclaimed, holding my hands tightly as she looked up at me; her brown eyes carried pain despite her cheerfulness. Speaking in Spanish to her husband, she indicated that he should draw up a chair for me next to her. He did so and then sat down on the double bed on the other side of her. I noticed the statues of Jesus and Mary looking down at her from the dresser, and a huge wooden rosary draped behind their bed. A framed photo of the two of them when they were much younger, a young boy with a pixie haircut between them, was hung prominently on the wall. An oxygen tank stood by the door.

"I no speak much English," Candida apologized.

"And me no comprehendo mucho Espanol." We laughed together and I felt more at ease.

"Juan, will you help me translate?"

"Sure." Candida said something to him. "She wants to know if you brought Communion."

Glancing down at her, so feminine in her pink nightgown, I reached without a word into my pocket and took out the gold container with the engraved picture of the Sacred Heart of Jesus on the front. Carefully I opened the latch and placed it on the small table next to us. I had something tangible to give her now, a ritual we both knew; that felt good.

Candida whispered something to her husband and he went and got a candle. He lit it and placed it next to the pyx. Blessing herself three times with a green scapular she wore around her neck, she kissed it and then folded her hands reverently in her lap. In this posture for some minutes, Candida moved her lips silently in prayer while Juan and I watched. When she opened her eyes she gave a little smile to indicate that she was ready.

Taking the pyx in my hands, I looked up. "O God, we know you are here in this house," I said, "with Candida and Juan and Angel as they bear with Candida's illness, but you come in a special way in this Holy Eucharist, your Body given as food for Candida, to enter into her sickness with her and give her strength. Show her your love for her, Lord, which is stronger than any sickness. Help her know your healing peace."

Then taking the small round wafer in my right hand, I made the sign of the cross with it in front of her as she opened her mouth. "Candida, the Body of Christ."

"Amen." I placed it on her tongue. After she had swallowed it I noticed her take some saliva with her index finger and touch her eyelids with it.

I had another communion host too, but Juan showed no interest in receiving so I closed up the pyx and replaced it in my pocket. Again we sat in silence for a few minutes while Candida moved her lips in prayer. I heard a shower in the next room. Angel? When her eyelids fluttered, Juan came over and blew out the candle.

With Juan translating but mostly offering observations himself, he told me that his wife has been plagued with breast cancer for over eleven years. "Since Angel was four years old he has seen his mother in this pain. Her faith and her strong will have enabled her to stay well despite this terrible sickness all these years, and even to go without pain medicine." Juan said this with awe, searching my face for a response. All the while Candida lay there rubbing her scapular, occasionally looking over at me with deep love in her eyes. I just nodded noncommittally.

Juan then asked if we had a counselor who could speak to his son. "He hardly goes to school anymore," he said with concern.

"What have you done about it?"

"When I am gone at work, he doesn't get up, says he's sick. And when he does go, he often just hangs in the streets with other kids." He paused as though weighing how I would hear it and added, "And they are no good."

I shook my head in sympathy. When Candida heard her son's name mentioned, she added that he does not go to church anymore either. This worries her very much; she prays for him constantly and offers her pain for him.

Slowly I began to grasp the situation, the battle being waged in this house, the religious pressure cooker it could be. "I am a counselor and I'd be glad to talk with him if he wants to."

"He's in his room now," Juan said. "Let me see if he will talk with you." He jumped up enthusiastically and left the room.

"Yes," he announced on his return. "Come into the living room and the two of you can speak alone." I bid a quick goodbye to Candida and said I would try to see her again in two weeks.

"Ahhh, Father Paul...God is too good to me." Too good? What could that mean? This little lady was so brave, so sweet, as she smiled goodbye. Yet something in me did not want to embrace her. I clasped her hand and left the room.

A skinny kid in faded jeans and an oversized polo shirt stood looking out the big picture window that faced a spectacular view of the Manhattan skyline across the East River. His hands were jammed into his back pockets.

"Angel!" Juan called. A young kid about five-foot-five with a narrow, pale, expressionless face turned toward me. His sandy hair was brushed up punk-style.

"This is Father Paul," said Juan, leading me over toward him between the easy chairs. "He is a counselor with the hospice program and he wants to talk with you."

"Hi," said Angel. With a shy smile he grasped my outstretched hand weakly.

"How're ya doin' Angel? . . . that's quite a view!" I pointed toward the window, wanting to get our attention off ourselves.

"Yeah, it's even nicer at night." We stood awkwardly while Juan made some small talk about how you pay for this view whether you like it or not. Angel shot him a glance of — condescension? boredom? — I wasn't sure. Then Juan turned and left us by ourselves.

The boy sat on a big overstuffed chair with his back to the window while I sat near him on the sofa. "What do you want to talk about?" he asked.

"Well, your mom for one," I began carefully, "I'm wondering how you're doing with her being so sick?"

"I don't have any feelings." Scratching his head, he looked straight ahead toward the far wall. I waited. Soon Angel glanced over at me and continued. "One day a few months ago when I was with my friends, I felt tears on my face." He checked me for a reaction. A little affirming grunt came from my throat. "And sometimes at night . . . I get angry."

"Angry," I repeated, "at what? . . . do you know?"

"At God." Angel, obviously very bright and articulate, then launched into a description of how he views God. "I don't believe in God anymore," he stated categorically. When he saw I wasn't shocked or about to try to convince him to abandon his teenage atheism, he elaborated. "We are taught to be free to choose and yet God intervenes . . . it doesn't make sense."

"What do you mean, 'God intervenes'?" I was trying not to throw my ideas in.

"Take earthquakes for instance . . ." He was warming up. "Why does God cause earthquakes? . . . and even if you say he doesn't, why do we pray for miracles? How are we really free if God can intervene and change what is happening, either for good . . . or bad?" Angel turned toward me now with a challenge in his dark eyes, but still with the soft, pliant voice.

At first I bit, hooked into trying to explain to him how we are free but might still need God to intervene, until I remembered the kid's feelings that brought these ideas on. I decided to be more direct. "So, do you tell God how you feel?"

"What do you mean?"

"Look, your mother's been seriously ill almost your whole

life. Do you think God gives a damn about her, that he can intervene and doesn't?"

Angel pondered this a moment. "I don't see him doing anything about it." His hands were gripping the chair intensely.

"So how do you feel about that?"

"Angry."

"Does God know that?"

"He's supposed to know everything."

"Yes, but maybe he needs to hear it from you before he can act."

I could see Angel's mind working. "I tell God I'm angry, but there's no response." And then, as though to ram this point home, he added, "...if there was, I'd believe in him!"

Damn! This kid had such real questions. *My* questions. I couldn't just give him any old bull; I would have to be as real as I could with him and try not to intellectualize. But what a contrast with his mother's view of God! Even if they both see God causing her sickness some way, they seem miles apart in how they relate to God about it. Candida feels God is blessing her by allowing her to suffer: she thanks him for it and doesn't take her medicine. Angel feels God is cruel or impotent to let his mother suffer so long, and he hates him for it. Could God suffer when we do? I wondered. God might have tears on his face for this poor kid. But this kind of thinking tries to "answer" Angel too much. I concluded I had better just stay with Angel's questions, but on another day.

Our discussion tapered off. I felt we had made a good connection. Among other things, Angel said, "I used to want to be a priest, but now I want to be able to help people more, so I'm going to go to medical school, be a doctor."

Oh, you mean doctors can really "intervene"! I grinned at the not-too-subtle put-down, thinking Doc would enjoy that one. "Maybe Dr. Cohen and I can come over together sometime?"

"Yeah, that'd be okay."

A few moments of silence passed while we stood. I reached to shake his hand and then went back toward the bedroom to say goodbye to his parents.

After dinner that night I went to my room. I didn't want to watch the evening news and *Wheel of Fortune* with the other priests, a daily ritual to cleanse our brains of the pastoral problems we dealt with all day long. Instead I planned to make a few phone calls to friends. But I felt too full of the day's events and needed to let them go somehow. I turned on a tape of flute music, lit a candle, took off my shoes, and lay on the floor of my sitting room, letting the day's events wash through me.

First there were many thoughts — images and words from the hodgepodge of the day — each calling for attention. My body was tense and the Mexican dinner rumbled in my stomach. Street sounds pierced through the soot-stained windows: buses were revving up at the corner light; somebody was honking a car horn with impatience; salsa music pounded out of huge speakers mounted in the trunk of a car; a far-off ambulance siren was coming closer; and what sounded like two car alarms rang out their cry of help to whoever might listen. My mind came back to the sound of the flutes and my clenched hands opened.

Gradually, imperceptibly, the muscles in my legs and back relaxed. The hard floor helped. The dinner calmed down. Even the insistent thoughts of the day — Angel's questions, for instance — came and went like birds soaring over a meadow. No need to hold onto them, to understand. My mind began to vibrate with the breath of the flutist. Soon I was simply lying there, breathing in and out deeply, my mind blank. Wonderful!

It was a way of praying I had discovered almost out of desperation from the intense work at the hospice. Don't concentrate on God or any specific intention. Just let each day's events come and go, and in so doing hold them up to God as a prayer for whatever God sees as the need. Like Isha does. This way I would let go of the overresponsibility it would be easy to develop in this ministry. It enabled me to enter into the next day refreshed; it kept me from burning out.

Twenty minutes later the tape finished. I lay there for some moments in soothing silence. Even the incessant street sounds had become just a background hum. Slowly my eyes opened. The candlelight played with its shadow on the walls and ceiling. I got up and called a friend and made plans to go out that weekend.

~

I have begun to notice a connection between how people encounter "the other world," the invisible, unknown world beyond death, and how they relate to the world of the spirit while they are alive. In other words, how people "pray," or notice the spirit world around them now, prepares them for the moment it is finally inescapable, at death. This world of the spirit is in such contrast to the world of New York City, which acts as though only the material, visible world exists.

In interacting with patients, I have begun to see myself as a sort of "marriage counselor" between them and this world of the spirit. Helping them to pray whatever they felt in the way that was most natural for them became my goal. I seemed to stumble into this approach. In any case, convinced that it would make their moment of death more peaceful, I wanted to facilitate this encounter with the Spirit (or their spirit, whichever way they looked at it) before they "breathed their last."

One of the patients who showed me this world of the spirit was Gertie. A seventy-one-year-old black woman who had never married, she lived in Harlem and suffered from end-stage lung cancer. Gertie had been in the hospice program for two-and-a-half months. When asked by her nurse, Ruby, whether she wanted pastoral care, she had always declined. Ruby told me that if I just came along with her on a nursing visit, Gertie, a Southern Baptist, would talk with me.

Ruby, a black Southern Baptist herself, had moved up North from South Carolina to go to nursing school and had stayed in New York and married. Now with three teenage daughters, she took delight in saying racy things at team meetings and especially liked to make "the pastor" blush. This brash style seemed to hide another, more private side that was shyer. Ruby used this saucy, aggressive public style to warm up and push through to the most difficult patients. I was beginning to trust her instincts.

As we threaded our way through the pedestrians on Thirty-fourth Street toward the subway to Gertie's house, I indicated that I was not sure how to relate to Gertie, whom Ruby had described as having a "Pentecostal" style of prayer.

"Paul," said Ruby in her sing-song way, rolling her eyes and rocking her body, "don't worry about being a priest. Just be Paul! Let Paul come out rather than the priest, and more of what is spiritual about you will be there for people."

Amazed and challenged by the street wisdom of this nurse who addressed me as her spiritual equal, I resolved to try to speak to Gertie from my heart that afternoon. From Paul, wherever he was.

When we knocked on the door of the apartment a short time later, a small middle-aged woman in a house dress and slippers let us in, introducing herself as "Jessica, a friend of Gertie's." She had been sitting in the semi-dark bedroom with Gertie, who was all hunched up in her bed, covers pulled all around her except for a little slit for her eyes, which were closed. The patient could have been asleep or drugged, but Ruby introduced me as "our pastoral care director."

Gertie's eyes remained closed. "Talk to her, Paul," said Ruby. "She can hear you." With a nervous smile, I took a seat on the edge of the big double bed. After a few moments, Ruby and Jessica went into the kitchen to prepare some creamed wheat to feed Gertie. I looked around the room at the drawn blinds, the diapers, and the commode. Not much time left, Gertie, I thought. A worn Bible lay open on her friend's chair.

As I reached for the bony hand of this woman and felt the cold lifelessness there, I couldn't imagine her being able to have the strength to talk, let alone sit up and eat. Yet stroking her hand, I thought of Ruby's admonition and began to speak in more explicit ways about death than I ordinarily did with patients.

"Gertie? . . . Gertie, can you hear me? I am Father Paul, a friend of Ruby's. . . . I'd like to pray with you if it's okay." She didn't stir.

I remembered her Pentecostal roots. "Gertie? . . . I think you are getting ready to meet the Lord Jesus. Don't be afraid . . . he is waiting for you with his great love whenever you are ready." I couldn't believe I was speaking like this. Her eyelids fluttered.

Peering at me out of the darkness of the little cocoon she had around her, Gertie opened her eyes in a squint. She squeezed my hand lightly. Some moments passed, and then she moaned softly, "Glory . . . glory! . . . thank you, Jesus . . . thank you!"

Soon she began to sit up. At that point her friend came back into the room, but she didn't seem disturbed by Gertie's actions.

"Would you like some Scripture read?" I asked. When she nodded yes, Jessica picked up the worn Bible and read a psalm with rhythmic feeling.

I trust in the Lord;
  my soul trusts in his word.
My soul waits for the Lord
  more than sentinels wait for the dawn.
More than sentinels wait for the dawn,
  let Israel wait on the Lord,
For with the Lord is kindness
  and with him is plenteous redemption;
And he will redeem Israel
  from all their iniquities.

—Ps. 130:5 8

"Thank you, Jesus!" Gertie murmured and then began exclaiming "Ohhhh, ohhhh!" while she gestured with her hand at some invisible images as though to chase them away. Her hand gripped mine firmly.

Ruby appeared with the cereal and was able to feed Gertie several spoonfuls. Then she reclined on the bed again, and I read her the passage from John's Gospel where Jesus speaks of the pains of death being like a woman's labor pains. "It seems like this to me too," I murmured, "that we are being born into another world."

At this point tears came from the corners of the old woman's closed eyes. "I'm going home... I'm going home to the King," she said with deep emotion. "Thank you, Jesus!" It truly felt like she was and that the tears were for the letting go of all she knew in this world as well as for joy to be finally going to meet her "King." I glanced over at the others in the room, Ruby with her impassive but knowing look, still holding the bowl of creamed wheat, and Jessica now standing to come over and join me in laying hands on this fellow believer.

Finally — unbelievably — before we left Gertie wanted to get up and walk! Ruby stood behind her, supporting her underneath her arms as she stepped shakily across the room, all the while gesturing with her hand at whatever she was seeing and saying with more and more gusto, "Ohhh, I'm going home! Going home to the King! *Glory!*" All I could do in my awkwardness was say "Amen!"

When we finally put her back under the covers, she looked spent but peaceful. We said goodbye. Ruby gave Gertie a little hug like some mother tucking her baby into a crib. We descended the stairs in silence, and only when we got outside did Ruby say to me, "See what I mean?"

"Ruby, that was incredible!" My heart was racing with excitement.

"Gertie could express her faith because you got down in there with her where she was at, Paul. You went halfway over to the other side with her, so she wasn't afraid to be there herself."

I shook my head in awe, not sure what I believed about all of this, wondering just what is waiting for us "on the other side" beyond death. Now I knew why I was in this hospice ministry. I needed help with "the other side" too.

~ Pedro ~

I VISITED ISHA AGAIN on an unseasonably sweltering day after arranging the visit by phone the day before. When I arrived I was greeted by a Home Health Aid (HHA) and then by a young Ethiopian friend of Lilianne's, Bambi, who was staying with them. Lilianne was at work. Isha, who had been reclining, sat up with a smile, looking thinner and sounding weaker to me, but still apparently in good spirits. When I asked, she indicated that she felt pain in her abdomen. I had learned to inquire about pain when I first met a patient so I could moderate my visit accordingly, and so I could report to the team back at the office.

It was helpful having an interpreter. Isha and Bambi spoke about Lilianne's difficult situation in ways that were not out in the open before.

"What do you think of all day?" I asked Isha, turning to Bambi while she repeated this in their language.

"She says she used to think about dying and worry about leaving Lilianne, but now she doesn't. She just lives each day."

Isha was quite talkative, describing the Oprah Winfrey show that they were watching. A very fat woman who kept eating voraciously despite the consequences was being interviewed. For her part, Isha eats bananas, bread, rice, and yogurt. She is sleeping well enough but because of the extreme heat hasn't gone out much this past week. Lilianne, she said, only eats a little food.

A fuse blew, wiping out the power for the TV, refrigerator, and air conditioner. It was so abominably hot in the tiny room that I got brave and volunteered to see what could be done. Amazingly, I was able to fix it. The ancient refrigerator began purring. Isha clapped and thanked God.

Before leaving, I read Psalm 150, which speaks of everything that has breath praising God. Isha looked up toward the ceiling with her hands open in a trusting gesture. After a few moments she placed the Bible against her head twice and kissed it. She was teaching me something about prayer.

Some weeks later I found a note on my desk that said Isha had called the office and wanted to see me. Because of a number of emergency cases and vacations of other staff, I hadn't seen her for three weeks. Lilianne answered when I called. She was on vacation too. We talked more familiarly than in the past, Lilianne joking about staying at home because the beach was too dirty. She put Isha on and I heard her thin voice ask, "You come see me?"

"Is Friday all right?"

"Not today?"

I felt guilty. "Maybe on my way home, okay? How about five o'clock?"

"Five o'clock good."

When I arrived, Lilianne opened the door; she was dressed in jeans and a light cotton blouse. I was surprised to see Isha sitting up in her bed, clothed in a salmon-colored chiffon gown and a green silk jacket. It even looked as if her hair had been done. "Wow," I said, "you look dynamite!"

Her coquettish eyes peered up at me, and she smiled shyly as I took her hands, pointing at a ring with a large green stone on her finger. It was so loose on her bony hand that she had to keep it pressed against her palm so it wouldn't fall off.

"What is this?" I asked. She looked over at her daughter.

"Mom went out and bought the ring for herself. She bought it to match her jacket." I grinned while I held out my hand to admire it. The juices keep flowing until you drop, they say. Whatever works.

Lilianne described how Isha had been going out again, taking walks around the block with the HHA, looking in store windows. It was hard to believe. Ten months after she had been given six months to live Isha was out window shopping in the afternoon.

"You seem weaker," I offered.

"Me feel better," she insisted.

"What are you hoping for?" I was thinking of the various stages of hope we had learned about at our orientation: from the initial hope for a cure to the hope for a peaceful death. I was wondering where Isha fit, what the mother and daughter communicated about this.

"She wants to get better and go back to work," Lilianne translated, but I couldn't glimpse what the daughter's feelings were about this statement.

When Lilianne went to the kitchen to get her medicine, Isha held her hands up in prayer. I placed mine under hers. She twitched her right arm and hand in a nervous reaction. Looking down, I noticed that her ankles were very swollen. They hardly fit in her slippers. After the prayer, Isha took the pain-killing pills and then lay down to rest. Lilianne said she lies only on the right side now because she's afraid the tumor will break off.

All these conflicting signs left me confused: Isha wants to get well and go back to work, but we know she's not going to. She's in pain and afraid her tumor will break off, but she dresses up and gets her hair done as if she's going out on a date. Her ankles are swollen, but she walks around the block to buy herself a new ring. Is she doing this for Lilianne's sake, and if so, is it helpful or not?

I brought up the idea of anointing. Lilianne explained this to her mother and Isha said she would like it. We agreed that I'd come over for this ceremony some weekend or evening when Lilianne was free.

Over the course of the following month, I noticed some new indicators of Isha's and Lilianne's awareness of the gravity of Isha's situation. As usual, Isha was pleased to see me when I arrived. It was a Saturday morning and Lilianne planned to be home, but she was out shopping for groceries during the first part of my visit. Isha was reclining but got up and sat on the edge of the bed, placing a shawl over her head. Eloise, the Home Health Aid whom I was getting to know by now, sat quietly nearby.

Isha looked tired and weak. When I inquired how she was feeling, she jiggled her hand back and forth. "So-so." The way she used idioms was charming.

From underneath her pillow she fished a copybook and then from a side table took a pair of designer glasses, adjusting them meticulously before looking up at me with a grin. Before I could speak a word, she opened the book and showed me a page of scrawled letter *A*'s, done in columns as first graders do.

"What's this?" I marvelled at her yen for education in the midst of a serious illness.

"Ruby teach me," Isha said proudly. "Me do homework." Flipping the pages, she indicated five or six letters she had practiced in this manner. "Me get new glasses."

"Well," I joked, "maybe I'm going to have to learn some of your language then."

"Yes." The Home Health Aid giggled at our interchange.

The visit became more cozy, at one point Isha asking me to get an album for her that was on a cluttered bookshelf. As we turned the pages together, I saw her life before she got sick. Except for her swollen belly, Isha was a bag of bones now. But in the photographs, most taken at her house in Mount Vernon where she had lived while working for the diplomat, a cheerful, buxom woman with strong arms smiled out from the midst of other black people, some in native dress. In one she was dancing with a bandana on her head.

"Where are these people now?" I asked, but Isha did not understand me. "You were fat!" I kidded, making gestures to show what I meant.

"Yes, me nice." What must it feel like to have your body change so rapidly? She pointed out some pictures of a younger Lilianne, maybe ten or eleven years of age. What a contrast between these happy times and now.

It is especially poignant when a terminally ill patient shares significant memories. We call it a life review, which is important to do before one dies. Recalling that I had a picture of my family in my wallet and wanting to reveal more of myself to her, I took it out to show her. "My family," I explained.

"Ohhh!" She studied it carefully.

"My mother and father, my brothers and sisters."

"No!"

"Yes, my mother died years ago, but my father is alive and married again."

Wide-eyed now, she peered even closer. "Your sisters and brothers alive?"

"Yes, they're all alive . . . nine sisters and four brothers."

Isha told me then that she had given birth to six children. All had died as infants before Lilianne was born. She had written to her husband and told him he has permission to marry again.

"Why?" I wanted to know.

"Cause I no go back again."

The TV had been on all this time. At intervals we began looking at it, now and again one of us saying something that the other only partially understood, but it didn't matter. Once I looked over at her and saw a blankness in her face, almost as though she were staring into space. I imagined it was what she was really like when she wasn't trying to be "on" for me.

Soon Lilianne returned with the groceries and joined us in the living room. "Hi, Father Paul! Hi, Mommy!...I got the crackers you wanted." I reminded them about the anointing ceremony and explained to them what we would be doing. Lilianne brought olive oil from the kitchen. I asked her to pour a few drops into my palm, which I held up and blessed. Meanwhile, Eloise read from a Bible:

> The Lord is my shepherd; I shall not want.
> In verdant pastures he gives me repose:
> Beside restful waters he leads me;
> he refreshes my soul.
> He guides me in right paths
> for his name's sake.
> Even though I walk in the dark valley
> I fear no evil; for you are at my side
> With your rod and your staff
> that give me courage.
> You spread the table before me
> in the sight of my foes;
> You anoint my head with oil;
> my cup overflows.
> Only goodness and kindness follow me
> all the days of my life;
> And I shall dwell in the house of the Lord
> for years to come.
>
> —Ps. 23

When I made the sign of the cross on Isha's forehead with the oil, she wanted it on her knees too. I rubbed them as she wished. Lilianne did the same while Isha looked upward. We waited some minutes until she looked back to us with a sigh, Lilianne blinking back tears.

"I better go now," I announced. "Gotta see some other patients." Isha pointed at the small wooden crucifix around my neck and touched her finger to her mouth.

"You want to see my cross?" I leaned down over her so she could see it. She reached and took it in her hand and then kissed it with great reverence.

"Thank you, God. You come nice."

"Thank you, Isha." I felt as if I had been blessed and kissed her gratefully on the cheek.

When Lilianne walked me to the vestibule, she told me in a hushed tone that she had asked Ruby to make some inquiries about the funeral preparations. So it's finally being accepted, I thought. Through the half-open door I saw Isha giving me a little wave, and I returned it.

Later while I waited on the subway platform it occurred to me that I actually felt good about these visits, as though something extremely difficult but natural was happening, and that we in the hospice ministry were privileged to be close to it. It was different from the way I had felt as the chaplain in the hospital. There the unnaturalness of sickness and death is emphasized. The tiled walls and floors reject any yearning for warmth and closeness. The nurses and doctors appear more controlled by the professional boundaries that make these institutions operate with such efficiency. Maybe it's the sheer numbers, but something is lost in the hospitals. The essential humanness of the dying process is best experienced at home.

True, death is "normal" in that it happens to all of us. But an utterly unique and unrepeatable person is leaving this world. That is extraordinary! How to personalize this process while making the patient as pain-free as possible is the goal of the hospice movement.

A train crammed with home-bound riders hurtled by us without stopping. With the patience born from calling a city of seven million people home, the crowd glanced up in unison, shrugged, and then turned back to the world of our newspapers.

Each of us utterly unique and with a special reason for being in this world? Some days my faith felt pretty thin in this regard, but then my family's beliefs would come to mind. When we were growing up we would pray about this specialness each night around the dining room table. With all the dirty dishes piled in front of us after dinner and with our young blood anxious to get out and play with our friends, Mama would make us spend fifteen minutes reciting together an Our Father and ten Hail Marys along with numerous other prayers to the saints that we were named after. This family rosary would conclude with a prayer that each of us be given the grace to find our "true vocation" in life and that when we found it we'd have the courage to follow it.

The hospice ministry was beginning to feel like my true vocation. The home setting of our hospice program was what brought this out. What felt so good about this work was that in people's homes you got to share their world. You got to treat them not just as patients, clients, or social security numbers. Whether the ambience was pleasant or revolting, you met them in a context, as a member of a family or social network. In this way you had to encounter their uniqueness.

It boils down to this: in a person's home or apartment, that person can offer you — "the helping professional" — something, as well as vice versa. Surely it is important in the healing process that the sick or dying one can realize the dignity of being able to give as well as receive, especially in the midst of losing control of so much.

For the patient to place her illness in the context of her whole life is essential. How much more likely this is when her album or pet, her Bible or tea kettle are there to show you: *This* is my life! *This* has been my "vocation." Not just my pain and medicine, not just my body's decay. I want to share it all with you.

I've got to remind Isha of this, I thought, how much she is giving to me, how much her life is a whole and I am being blessed by it. Yes, thank you, God; you come nice.

~

One afternoon in the office toward the end of a particularly gruelling day devoted to paperwork, I was handed a message. "Please see Pedro Gonzalez as soon as possible." It was signed "Joanne." Excitement stirred in me. This was the young Dominican man who had AIDS. Up to this point he had refused any pastoral care. A Lutheran, he was not active in any church, but I had felt that if I could get to see him he would have a lot to work out about God and his illness before he died. Joanne, an Italian nurse who covered the Greenwich Village area for us, had told me she would keep trying to get an opening with him for me.

I grabbed the Number 1 subway and got off at Christopher Street. Joanne had told me that Pedro was gay and that he had contracted AIDS through sexual encounter. He was a twenty-four-year-old airline steward and, except for a sister who lived in the Bronx, without his family to support him. Ten days ago, however, Pedro's mother, Carmela, had flown up from the Dominican Republic to assist in his care. His lover, Charlie, shared the apartment with him too. As I dodged the traffic on Seventh Avenue, I wondered how all these people were coping with Pedro's condition. Not well, I presumed.

In contrast to many apartment houses in the Village, the one Pedro lived in was modern, evidently some former dwelling having been demolished to make way for it. A sterile vestibule was visible from the street, graced with large vases of artificial flowers that cast ominous shadows on the antique white walls. This wasn't one of those establishments we were told to be wary of, the ones with drug dealers and other dangerous folk lurking in the hallways. That possibility was one of the reasons I kept wearing my priest's collar in this ministry, thinking it might help me explain my purpose and give pause to a potential mugger.

The sleek elevator opened on the seventh floor. This was my first AIDS patient and a very young one. I felt nervous, so I "surrounded myself with blue light," as the nurses had taught us to do at orientation. "You can enter a home with peace," they said, "and let the troubles go when you leave." "Okay, Lord," I prayed at the doorway, "here goes."

"Yes? Can I help you?" The slim blond man who opened the door gazed at me with a stone face.

"I am Father Paul. Joanne, the nurse I work with, told me Pedro wished to see me."

"It's not Pedro's idea to see you; it's his mother's." The voice was strained, the gray eyes harsh.

"Oh..." He didn't move. I just stood there. "Well, look," I gambled, not wanting to waste a trip downtown if I could help it, "if he wants to throw me out after I see him, that's okay, but I would just like to say hello." He surveyed me from head to foot and then locked his eyes once more on mine.

"All right." The face finally softened a bit as he extended a hand. "His mother's in there with him now, but she can't speak any English. My name is Charlie."

"Thanks." Standing aside, he permitted me to enter.

A pleasant looking, heavy-set woman in a flowered house dress appeared in a doorway beyond the front room, her hair in braids. Her strong hands were evident as she placed a bed pan on a side counter.

"This is the priest...the Padre," said Charlie. The woman gave a little bow and I reached for her hand.

"Padre, Padre..." she began, but I could not follow the rest of her Spanish words. Obviously she was of the old school, very devout, the kind that treats a priest with great respect and in some way expects miracles from him. When she drew closer I noticed the weary look in her eyes, with dark circles underneath.

"No comprendo, señora," I apologized with a smile.

"Oh?..." Hesitating for a moment, Carmela then turned and brought me into her son's room.

My heart was pounding as we approached the bed in which an emaciated figure lay. Pedro was holding an oxygen mask up to his face. Carmela simply said "Padre" and then left. Not until I adjusted to the late afternoon sun streaming through the window did I notice Pedro's black and luminous eyes staring at me for a moment above the mask. Quickly they darted away as my gaze met his.

What could I do? Those eyes said everything: "Padre, I don't want to see you. What you represent — what that Roman collar says — is against everything I stand for. In fact I am suffering cruelly, about to die in my youth because your God must hate me." I plunged in anyway.

"Pedro, I understand it is not your idea that I am here, that it is your mother's." His face was still turned to the wall. "If you want to throw me out the window, I can understand...but I just wanted to say hello. In any way that I can I would like to be of help to you." Frigid silence, except for the sound of him breathing the oxygen.

"My name is Father Paul," I continued. "I work with Joanne,

your nurse. I try to see if there is any way your faith can help you deal with your suffering...maybe a prayer if you'd like." Still standing there like a buffoon, wishing I could evaporate, I noticed his legs, visible because of his short pajamas. The dark purple lesions of the Kaposi's sarcoma, one of the opportunistic infections that afflict AIDS patients, had sprouted on him like some grotesque camouflage. I got an idea.

"Pedro?" The quaver in my voice was noticeable even though I was feigning nonchalance. "As a priest I've worked with a lot of gay and lesbian people...and that's been good for me." All of a sudden the dark eyes turned back toward me, though still like a wary animal. "There are probably lots of feelings you have about your illness which would be good to talk about with someone ...and I..."

"What is John Three Sixteen?" Pedro pulled the oxygen mask back suddenly to ask.

"What?..."

Caught off guard, I listened while this twenty-four-year-old kid with shiny black hair who looked like he weighed about a hundred pounds repeated laboriously, "What is John Three Sixteen?...I keep thinking of this Bible passage and I can't remember what it says."

You've got to be kidding! I thought, but decided to try some humor. "Pedro, I'm a Catholic priest, so you probably know the Bible better than I do...Hey, wait a minute! That's the one on the billboards, isn't it?...'God so loved the world that he gave his only Son...that whoever believes in him may not die, but may have eternal life.'" I was amazed that this came out of me and even more that this young man had been wanting to hear this Word of God. The hostility in his eyes relaxed. I knew I could stay then and sat down on the edge of the big double bed.

I forget what we talked about. It had something to do with how God loves us, forgives us even when we sin, and that suffering is not so much God punishing us as a way for us to deepen our faith in this Creator of ours. "...like Jesus did," I suggested.

Soon Pedro gasped through the mask, "I'm getting tired now. I have to ask you to leave."

"May I say a blessing before I go?" The young man nodded.

Perhaps because they were the most ugly and visible aspects of his illness, I placed my hands on the dark lesions on his forehead. I prayed in my own words that Pedro might feel God's love for him deeply, that he would not feel too much pain or despair, and that he might experience God's healing touch in whatever way God gives it. As I did so, I gradually moved my hands down the side of his head to his shoulders, his arms, his legs, his feet, gently touching the purplish KS lesions as I did so. It almost seemed that by this action I was being healed more than he was: healed of my fear of the lesions and of my fear of what Pedro stood for.

"I'm glad you came," he said softly.

"I'll come again if you wish. I'll give you a phone call in a few weeks, okay?"

"Okay, Father Paul."

I went into the next room reeling from this interaction. There I found Carmela sitting with a young Hispanic woman who introduced herself as Pedro's sister, Marta. Attractive, with long, wavy dark hair, she sat on the arm of the sofa next to Carmela and stroked her mother's head. Charlie, with a polite comment, went past me into Pedro's room while I sat on the sofa next to Carmela.

Out of the blue Marta asked, "Does God hate homosexuals?"

Stunned, I raced through some ideas for a moment, some church ways of speaking about this that would respond to her question. Instead, the situation of the household provided the answer. "You know," I fumbled for some opening, "the shortest sentence in the Bible is my favorite one — "God is love" (1 John 4:16). Three words that say everything — "God is love... and wherever there is love, there is God." Have you heard of this?" The daughter nodded her head yes, while Carmela just stared straight ahead.

Addressing Marta, I asked, "What do you see in this house ... between you and your mother? Between Carmela and Pedro? Between Pedro and Charlie? Do you see love?"

"Yes." She stopped stroking her mother and leaned toward me.

"Then God must be here, don't you think?" Nodding, Marta's eyes widened. "No, I don't believe God hates homosexuals," I went on. "How could he if there is so much love here? No, I believe God loves homosexuals, and whenever Pedro is ready to meet him, Jesus will be waiting with open arms to receive him with this love."[1]

We sat gazing at each other for a moment from our different worlds; I hoped for God's help in this impossible situation. Just then Marta turned to her mother and said something in Spanish, flinging her hands toward me and then toward the room where Pedro and Charlie were. A little smile broke out on Carmela's face. A tear rolled down her cheek.

She opened her arms toward me and we hugged. Then I explained to Marta what I had told Pedro about further visits.

"Gracias...gracias, Padre," Carmela said as they let me out the door.

It had only been about fifty minutes, but I felt as if my world had been challenged to the roots by this family. It seemed that everything I had encountered in the priesthood so far had prepared me for this visit. Pulling off my collar, I headed down Christopher Street for the beer I had promised myself. Finding a barrel to sit on at Julius's, I slid off my shoes, disregarding the sawdust on the floor. With a strange sense of joy, I ordered one of their quarter-pound cheeseburgers and a mug of dark ale.

When I phoned Pedro again during the next few weeks, he wasn't interested in a visit. Finally, one Sunday — my day off — I decided to make a surprise visit. Carmela let me in with a warm welcome. Taking my jacket, she folded it carefully and hung it over the back of a chair. Pedro was in the living room now, in a hospital bed over against the far wall. Carmela walked me over to him and then sat in a chair in a far corner, knitting.

I hardly recognized him. Curled up in a fetal position, Pedro's body was even more emaciated than before. It was dark in many places now from the Kaposi's sarcoma. My belly tightened as I remembered from a lecture that you can get these black scab-like growths even on your insides — in your stomach, your throat, your intestines. I pulled up a chair and sat down beside him.

"Hi, Pedro!" He didn't stir.

"Father Paul..." he whispered after some moments. He seemed so like a baby that I reached out to stroke his forehead.

"Why are you touching me?"

Startled, I responded, "I thought it would be better than talking...maybe soothe you."

"I don't like it."

"Oh? . . . why not?"

"It feels sexual to me."

"What do you mean?"

"It feels sexual when people touch me."

"Oh, okay." I felt sad that this was so for him, that a touch for him could not be simply an expression of human caring.[2] He did not want to dwell on this topic and told me that Charlie had gone into the hospital because he had come down with pneumonia.

"My mother is doing better. She's getting used to New York," he said with a wry smile. Much of this visit was spent just sitting next to him. Because I had no other appointments and because he was having such difficulty talking, I felt it best just to "be" with him, not to try to communicate much unless he initiated it. Also, I kept thinking of his comment about touch.

About an hour went by and I was getting ready to leave. I told him about anointing, which I have also explained to other patients, even those who aren't Catholics.[3] Though blessing the sick with oil is a Catholic sacrament, it is also in the Bible, which this young man believed in as a Lutheran. It didn't need to be a sacrament for us to anoint Pedro with oil as the Jews and Christians did in the Scripture stories. I thought it would help him and his family own ritually what was happening.

"If you wish, sometime we might do this for you. Your mother and sister and friends might like to be here to pray over you this way." Pedro didn't respond, and I stood up to leave. Carmela rose and got my jacket. Then I heard him move.

Turning, I saw him roll over on his back with tremendous effort. He stretched his body out full length. With the sheet pulled up to his chin and his dark hair framing his gaunt face, he reminded me of Jesus. Pedro pressed a button on the bed and it raised him to a thirty degree angle from the floor. Then he spoke something in Spanish to his mother, and she disappeared into the other room. When Carmela emerged with a bottle of olive oil, I realized we were going to anoint him then.

"She says it's too cold," Pedro said in a weak voice.

"That's okay. We'll rub it in our hands until it gets warm." I held out my hands so Carmela could pour some. Rubbing my palms together until the friction heated the oil, I raised them upward over Pedro. "O God, please bless this oil and Pedro . . ."

"God seems very far away," I heard him say. His dark almond eyes were sunk in a painful stare. I stumbled on.

"God, wherever you are, you hear Pedro's words, you see his pain. We hold his life up to you now, all of it: his accomplishments, his failures, his feelings, his relationships, his questions. You see his mother's care, her feelings and questions. Please be here with us, be as close with your love for him as this oil in our hands. Touch Pedro, Lord. Heal him however you want to." And heal the rest of us too.

Then I rubbed the oil on the forehead of this young man who had told me only a short time before that he didn't like to be touched, that touch was only sexual to him. I made the sign of the cross on his forehead and beckoned for his mother to do the same. Carmela took some of the oil from my hand and began to make the sign of the cross on herself.

"No," I said, and motioned instead for her to bless him. She understood and blessed the body of her son as I had done.

Soon after this I began to leave. Glancing back at them I felt a power, a presence in that room in Greenwich Village. "Goodbye ...I'll see you in a week or so." I hugged Carmela; Pedro's eyes were closed. I would not see them again. Five days later Pedro died, and Carmela took him home to Santo Domingo for burial. Charlie had died two days before him — also from AIDS.

I cannot get the image of Pedro out of my mind. I thank God for meeting Pedro and Carmela, Charlie and Marta. There is something about mother love, sister love, gay love — yes, even priestly love — to learn from this. God's love is bigger than all of us. Bigger even than the church. The priesthood I had been ordained to twenty years before began to feel like it was for more than just Roman Catholics. When I visited patients from this point on, I stopped wearing my clerical collar.

~ Natalie ~

DURING A TEAM MEETING that spring, a case was brought up involving a forty-five-year-old Jewish woman with an inoperable brain tumor.

"Natalie is married to a thirty-seven-year-old Italian man," Joanne began. "The patient and Dominic were married two years ago, her second marriage, his first. She has one grown daughter. Natalie was a theatrical agent; Dominic runs a truck and limo rental agency..."

"Sounds like Mafia!" someone whispered.

Ignoring this, Joanne went on. "Dominic is having a very difficult time accepting his wife's condition. In fact he doesn't want us to mention the word 'hospice' around her."

"How do they expect us to treat her if we have to dance around the fact that she is terminal?" asked Beverly. "Doesn't the patient have to accept that before we go in?"

"Well," Joanne grimaced, "we'll just have to walk with them gradually until they can accept it. On one level they know. We take them where they are at." Beverly looked over at me and raised her eyebrows.

The director, Kate, broke in. "Look, the primary care person has to know that we're not going to lie. He needs to accept the fact that if Natalie asks any one of us what her condition is, we are not going to beat around the bush." She flipped her eyeglasses up on her head for emphasis. "We give the patient as much information as she wants to know."

"So..." Doc interjected as though he were a novice, "if Natalie asks us what is happening to her, we're not supposed to say 'You're going to die, Natalie.'" He exaggerated with a sheepish voice and laughter erupted.

49

Kate was chuckling with us, but made the point. "Rather, you can play it back to her. Say, 'What do you think is happening, Natalie?' As Joanne said, we help the two of them take it in their own time. But," the glasses came down again, "this is going to be a tough case."

Joanne agreed. "Natalie is alert, but not very communicative. A gorgeous, petite woman before she was diagnosed about eight months ago, she's bedbound now, completely dependent. Besides the tumor, she is suffering from anasarca."

"What's that?" I asked.

"It's a swelling of the body tissues," Joanne explained, "a side effect of the medicine she's taking for the cancer. Natalie has gained over sixty pounds, and her face is all bloated so she doesn't look like the same person anymore." I shook my head, trying to imagine.

"Dominic is like a big kid. He is distraught, even acting out," said Joanne, "and he weighs over two hundred pounds! But he's trying to lose weight," she added as though to defend him. "He's on a special diet and jogs each afternoon."

"Wait a minute!" Kate interrupted our laughter. "What do you mean 'acting out'?"

"He threw a pillow at me the other day," Joanne giggled.

"I hope you threw it back!" snapped Beverly.

"Hey, a good fight on the job never hurt anyone," said Doc.

"Yeah, Joanne, go get'm!" The meeting began to break down into private conversations and jokes.

"Okay, okay, let's get serious," said Kate, flashing her dramatic earrings. But she couldn't hide the fact that she enjoyed this mischief. When the meetings bogged down in dreary statistics or depressing descriptions of our patients' demises, it was often Kate who would make some wisecrack with a wicked New York twist that would have all of us laughing and involved again. "Who is going to visit them?" she asked.

"If he picks me up in one of his limos, I'll be glad to," I said.

"Hey, he might," suggested Joanne. "They do want pastoral care, though. She's Jewish, but he's Roman Catholic. I told them we have a good priest."

"A priest!" I had begun to question the way the nurses sometimes presented our pastoral care team to the patients; I wanted them to offer the more generic "pastoral care" instead of "priest" so that our ecumenical dimension could be maximized. "Who asked for the pastoral care? Maybe she wants a rabbi."

"No, they both said they would be happy to see a priest," said Joanne.

"Okay, I'll see her within two weeks."

"So, Beverly and Paul will be involved," noted Kate.

"Joanne, how often are you going in?"

"Three times a week for now."

"Carol?"

"I'll make a nutritional consult on the phone and then report back next week."

"Great. Dr. Cohen?"

"Joanne has it under control. We'll keep our eye on the Decadron."

"Okay, folks," Kate winked, back in her hard-driving mode. "We've gotta move on. We've got twenty-two patients to discuss this morning, not counting the four new admissions and the three who died since last week."

For the rest of the meeting I kept thinking about Natalie and Dominic. Delighted that they wanted pastoral care, I was intrigued by the thought of how the two religions would interact. A few days later as I entered the high-rise apartment building on the fashionable East Side of Manhattan near Eighty-fourth Street, I thought of Dominic's words to me during our phone conversation earlier in the week. I recalled his style of conversing, his Brooklyn-Italian inflection, even more than his words. "Yeah, Faddah, you can come over anytime," he said, and then the note of vulnerability in this tough guy's voice: "I gotta talk to someone." Charmed, I looked forward to meeting him but wasn't as sanguine about meeting his wife. I wasn't sure what we would talk about. Also, the brain tumor was too close to home; I had always thought that losing my mind would be the worst form of suffering.

I dread the day when it may be my turn to sit on the edge of a bed and stare out dumbly into space, half-drugged on pain-killers while people I don't even know patronize me, stick needles in me, feed me, and wipe my behind like a baby. I think sometimes that I do this work to bribe God beforehand so he'll have mercy on me if that happens. Secretly I can say: "I suffered when I was young, so I don't deserve it now." Foolish, I know.

It is even worse for me to consider my mind disintegrating. The mind — the seat of intelligence and understanding, of imagination and love. The place where if nothing else is interesting around me I can run to and find meaning. Search for it at least. Even if I were completely physically incapacitated and the whole world were ruined around me, I could at least stare out from some ancient seat of dignity at the ashes and ask, "Why?"

"Just a minute!" a man's voice yelled. The corridor was covered with a soft gray carpet that matched the color of the doorways. Indirect lighting accented pictures of nature scenes on the beige walls. The doorman had quickly surveyed me to judge if I belonged in this place; when I mentioned Natalie's name he motioned me toward the elevators with a knowing nod. The ride to the ninth floor had given me just enough time to compose myself, check my tie in the polished brass panel, and remember the team plan of care. Now as I waited for the door to open, I noticed it had a mezuzah attached.

"You must be Father Paul?" A tall, heavy-set, boyish-looking man announced with a beguiling smile as he swung the door open.

"And you must be Dominic." The two of us shook hands.

"I was just in with Nattie," he said as he welcomed me into a spacious apartment that looked out through enormous windows onto Second Avenue. "Here, put your jacket here." He indicated a wooden coat rack behind a brocaded room-divider.

"It's a nice day out; I hardly needed the coat."

"Yeah, I almost went running myself." Dominic patted his ample stomach ruefully. "Gotta do something about this. I've gained twenty pounds in the past six weeks."

The two of us stood unsurely in the alcove, as I waited for his lead. "You wanna see Nattie?"

"How about if you and I talk first?"

"Sure, make yourself comfortable." He motioned me into the main room, where a long white sofa stretched against one wall, set off on either side by an elegant pair of satin-covered armchairs. A low, polished bench completed the square around an antique coffee table on which rested a crystal bowl of fresh yellow roses. "I was making some coffee ... you want some?"

"No, it makes me nervous if I have more than one cup a day. I already had my jolt this morning." Dominic went over to the adjoining kitchen and dining area while I settled into one end of the comfortable sofa.

Dominic had the build of a football player or a wrestler gone to seed. He had a full head of dark hair, which was cut conservatively, and wore horn-rimmed glasses, a white dress shirt open at the neck with a T-shirt underneath, dark rumpled slacks, and a pair of loafers.

"You sure I can't get you anything? . . . some juice, a shot of bourbon?" he grinned.

"Okay, some juice would be great." I was beginning to like this guy. "Cranberry or grapefruit is what we got," he said out of the side of his mouth. "With me doing the shopping it's a wonder we got anything."

"Grapefruit will be fine."

"Nattie used to run this place with a flair you wouldn't believe," he said wistfully as he took a seat in one of the large chairs next to me. Along with his big, square head and olive complexion, Dominic had an expressive mouth that he curled downward like a sad little boy while he said this. No lines in his face, except some dark circles under his eyes that I noticed when he rubbed them wearily. His fingernails were ragged, but a gold ring set with diamonds adorned the ring finger of one big paw. Yes, someone had a flair. Someone had tamed this child-man.

"You're a Catholic priest?" He was surveying my tic. "I mean, you believe in the pope? . . . have Mass in a parish?" He smiled shyly.

Laughing at his litmus test of my orthodoxy, I assured him, "Yes, I say Mass sometimes at the parish where I live up in the Bronx, but I don't do it regularly because this is my main work. And I used to wear a collar, but it seems to put off the non-Catholics I visit, so . . . "

"Oh!" Dominic tilted his head. "But the pope? . . . Well, it would be even easier for me to believe in him if he were Italian!" We laughed together.

"Seriously, I was raised Catholic, was an altar boy and all that stuff. I don't go to church now except for Christmas, but I still consider myself Catholic."

"Does your faith help you deal with Natalie's illness?"

"Shhhh!" he whispered, "she doesn't know how sick she is."

But this had set him off. While I sipped my juice he launched into a religious diatribe.

"The way I figure it," Dominic said bitterly, "God must be playing a cruel joke." I looked over at the brown eyes, trying to imagine his worldview.

"Nattie is the greatest person in the world," he raved on. "She could do anything she set her mind to. Look at this place!" With a sweep of his hand he showed me. "She picked out the draperies, the furniture, the color scheme...Nattie knows how all this goes together."

He idolizes her, needs to impress me with her talent. On the window sill the confident face of a stunning blonde woman alongside another man beamed out at us from a beautifully framed picture.

"So what do you mean...'God's playing a cruel joke'?"

"God's like a kid who can do something to help, but he doesn't care...just sits there, if he sees at all, and doesn't lift a finger to get Nattie well. She was constantly thinking of other people, the one other people would call up for advice; she would give one of her friends the shirt off her back." I listened, beginning to get a glimpse of the extent of Dominic's loss.

"We were just married a little over two years ago. We met when she rented one of my limos for a party. Before I dropped her off I asked her for a date. She told me her name and said that her number's in the phone book. We were so happy you wouldn't believe it! Everything going right for once. Then Nattie gets hit with this. It's as though God can't stand to see us happy. What do you think? You probably think this is bullshit!...Sorry, I didn't mean to..." He finished his coffee.

"No," I hedged, shaking my head, "but I don't have an easy answer, Dominic." I fed back to him what I had heard. "I hear your pain and that you want God to do something about it." He searched my face, rubbed his stubble of a beard.

"You know, Father Paul," he confided, "I don't even know if I believe in God anymore."

I sensed the reality of his questions, but it felt somehow that this discussion was mainly intellectual, masking the anxiety I could hear underneath the words. As such it would go nowhere. I assured him that it's understandable how he felt, and then offered, "Maybe God feels as helpless as you feel."

He looked at me as if I were on drugs. "God is supposed to be able to do anything," said Dominic. "Isn't that what we were taught?" I shifted uncomfortably in my seat and stared at him, not knowing where to go with this. "C'mon!" he teased. "Isn't it a priest's job to save souls?"

"Dominic, I don't know what other priests do, but I'm not here to give my faith to anyone. I'll try to help you discover what yours is, even in this crisis." Then, to try to get down from the pedestal he had me on, I added, "I have some of the same questions you do."[4]

"If you've got my questions, how are you gonna help me?" he challenged.

"I don't know . . . maybe we can ask our questions of God together and help Nattie do so too. Could we look in on her now?" About an hour had passed. I felt at home with Dominic, but wanted to make sure to see the patient.

"Sure." His eyes filled up as we rose. We went around the corner to the room where his wife was. My heart began to race. "Baby? Baby?" Dominic called softly as he tapped on the closed door. "The priest is here . . . are you decent?"

He led me into the bedroom where in a huge four-poster double bed draped in quilts Natalie sat staring at the far wall. I could only see her profile. "Nattie, this is Father Paul." No response. "Honey, he and I had a good talk . . . ask him anything that's on your mind." A head that looked like a sumo wrestler's — round, full jowls, bald — turned slowly toward me. A questioning look was all that came forth.

"I'll leave you two for a little while," Dominic said as he left, the door clicking closed behind him. Natalie just kept looking at me.

"Natalie, I'm here to offer spiritual care . . . " I began the intro I had rehearsed. "Any way I can help or listen to what is in your heart . . . " I stood there not knowing what to do, the woman staring at me blankly. Above her head, a large framed picture on the wall caught my attention. It was Natalie and Dominic, she petite and vivacious in a white satin wedding gown with a train that swirled around their feet. Dominic looked bashful and handsome as he hulked over her in a black tux with tails, his arms twined around her waist from behind. My gaze dropped back to her, now bloated into another creature. "May I sit on the bed? . . . say a prayer?" I smiled, wanting to remember the beauty inside. Natalie nodded yes.

I felt a bit stupid, embarrassed at the intimacy as I pulled myself near her on the enormous bed and my feet left the floor. As I reached out my hand to take hers, Natalie grasped it fiercely. With a huge sapphire ring prominent on her finger, she dug her nails into my palm and it hurt. What could I pray for this Jewish woman, I wondered. About Abraham and Sarah? Moses? And how preserve the secrecy Dominic wants?

"Pray . . . I know," she said hoarsely. "Pray . . . I know . . . before I die."

"Know what?" I questioned, wondering what exactly Natalie knew. "Pray . . . I understand," she answered. I probed again to draw her out, but this was all she was able to communicate. After that she lapsed into strange comments I couldn't make sense of. All the while Natalie continued to grip my hand fiercely. Isaiah, I thought, tell her about God's promise to the prophet Isaiah.

"Okay, let's pray." Looking upward, I began, "Yahweh, you hear Natalie's desire. She wants to understand. What is the meaning of all this, Lord? . . . And Dominic, he feels that you are cruel. But you promised that you would never abandon us, Lord, never forget us. 'Can a mother forget her infant, be without tenderness for the child of her womb? Even should she forget, I will never forget you!' (Isa. 49:15–16)."

Natalie's eyes were closed when I finished with the words, "See, upon the palms of my hands I have written your name." I watched her heaving chest, the ring enfolded in her swollen finger. Gradually she relaxed her grip and leaned back on the pillows. Remaining with her for some moments, I noticed the purple bumps on her head. They brought back memories of years before when my mother first began to get sick . . .

~

One autumn evening in 1975, my twenty-two-year-old sister, Sally, phoned me at the house in Philadelphia where I lived with other priests.

"What's up, Sally?"

"Mama wants you to come home, Paul. I think she wants to talk with you about something." It was unusual to hear such a direct request since our Irish family didn't often speak with one another about our feelings. With a trace of worry in her voice, Sally indicated that Mama was acting strangely. The house was getting untidy, very unlike her. "Paul, I think she's been drinking."

Mama did have a problem with alcohol, though generally she kept it under control. I had never seen her drunk, but we had seen evidence of her drinking — puffy circles under her eyes and her speech a little slurred at dinner on occasion during those growing up years. When we were older she even told us she was an alcoholic. But that was later when alcoholism began to be seen as a disease. When we were younger we never talked about this flaw we saw in Mama.

Sally told me that she and another sister, Maura, had taken Mama down to the University of Pennsylvania Hospital for a check-up a few days before. Mama had been having persistent headaches for a few weeks and had been taking up to a dozen aspirin, a day which her doctor had recommended, but to no avail. The doctor at the U. of P. could find nothing wrong. But the family knew there was a change in her, so Maura, the youngest child at seventeen, had blurted out in disbelief, "But, doctor, did you check her head?"

"Oh, Maura!" Mama had reprimanded her as though this were an act of childish irreverence. The doctor, we later discovered, had not checked her head.

When I arrived home in Upper Darby the next evening, the family home on Copley Road was quiet. Dark too. Not normal, I thought. My father was always complaining that we singlehandedly supported the electric company the way we left lights on around the house. Pushing open the front porch door, which was never locked, I could see light coming from the kitchen where Sally and Maura were making snacks.

To me these two sisters seemed like the party dolls of the East Coast the way they socialized. Tonight though, they seemed more somber and communicative than usual as they flopped Indian-style on the living room floor and described Mama's condition in more detail. Clearly they were worried and seemed relieved that I was home. Just then Mama appeared on the stairway, her face shiny with Vaseline, in a quilted blue bathrobe tied with a bow at the neck. Her hair was in curlers. A smile wreathed her face. Dutifully I got up to kiss her.

In recent years I had reacted with a mixture of attraction and resistance to Mama's embrace and wondered if it was because her love was so strong that I feared it would smother me or because my need of her approval was so great. I was resisting the old closeness, though, with some sense of guilt. Promising her a long talk in the morning, I shunted her off to bed.

When Sally and Maura had gone to bed, I sat alone in the dim glow of the streetlight shining through the window, thinking of what the three of us had shared and wondering what the next day would bring. A door opened upstairs and Daddy appeared on the landing in his red ski pajamas. In a hushed tone he asked if I would get up and go to the supermarket with Mama in the morning. "I'm afraid she'll buy a bottle while she's out and hide it before I get home from work," he explained.

"Okay," I agreed, but resented the responsibility this put on me and swore at him inside. Never had I heard my father speak directly to her about the drinking. I never spoke to him about how I felt about it either.

The next morning I woke up late and was enjoying a pancake breakfast with Maura when I noticed our second-hand Chevrolet pull up out back. It was filled with groceries for us as well as an elderly lady across the alley whom Mama did the shopping for. Mama stepped out of the car spiffily in a dress and heels as usual, a bag of groceries in her hand. I was going to finish reading the newspaper until a gesture of hers caught my attention. Mama placed the bag down slowly onto a concrete wall, as though it were a bother or her mind were on something else — quite unusual for my mother.

"Mama's back with the groceries," I told Maura. The two of us ran out to help her. While we carried the bundles up the back steps, boldly I blurted out, "Mama, did you buy any liquor?"

Maura's ears perked up, and Mama said wearily as though for her benefit, "Oh, Paul, how can you ask such things?"

"Daddy's worried that you are drinking," I countered.

"I didn't buy any liquor," she insisted. Not knowing where to go beyond this, I didn't pursue.

Later over lunch after Maura had gone to work, I had a long

talk with Mama. At one point she held her hand to the side of her head and said, "I feel so guilty."

"About what, Mama?"

"About Richie and Maura, whether we raised them rightly." She was speaking in a halting way, expressing emotions about her two youngest in a way that seemed foreign to her. Generally she was so self-confident in her role as a mother.

I reached for her hand. "You did well, Mama. Richie and Maura have to live their own lives." We were searching for words, awkward in this shift of roles.

Noticing the dark circles under her eyes, I asked, "Have you been crying about this?"

"I can't cry, Paul," she answered in a thin voice. "I try to but I haven't been able to cry for years." This revelation crashed in upon me, touching something in my heart that took over against my will.

Standing up next to her, I drew her protectively into my arms. "Oh, Mama... I love you so much." Her little body cradled against mine while the napkins fell gracefully to the floor, my old fears overcome by pity and love.

I so much wanted her to let go with me. As I rocked her gently from side to side, a low humming sound arose from my throat. "Mama, doesn't anyone ever hold you like this?"

In a tired, little girl's voice, the strong one who had nurtured the whole Morrissey family sadly whispered, "No."

It seemed too much for me — and for Mama — to handle, her falling apart like this. Sensing there must be a connection between the drinking, the guilt, the little physical love she allowed herself, I asked if she ever talked these things over with anyone. "Maybe if you were able to share these things with a doctor, one who was specially trained to help people understand their emotions, a psychiatrist... it might help." There was fear in her eyes. "Maybe your own medical doctor could refer you to one who would be able to help you not to hurt so much." She was like a baby before me.

There was a lot of footwork over the next week. One of my mother's sisters called Mama's doctor and, pretending to be Mama, said, "Doctor, I need help now!" Mama finally agreed to be admitted to a hospital for psychiatric observation.

When Daddy was driving her down to Misericordia Hospital

in West Philadelphia, where she had given birth to their fourteen children, Mama leaned over on his shoulder and said wistfully, "Tom, I wish I was going in to have another baby." She was sixty-three then. . . .

~

The sound of Natalie's snoring pulled me back to the present. She and my mother were so different, yet similar in the way their minds had been affected first.

Dominic poked his head through the doorway. "Baby, you keeping Father Paul entertained?" He saw that she was sleeping. "Oh! . . ." A shadow of recognition crossed his face. "We better not disturb her," Dominic whispered. "Sometimes she drifts off like this." I followed him out into the parlor and said goodbye.

~ Elmo ~

THE FIRST TIME I met Elmo was a hot afternoon in June, the kind of day in New York when you start thinking of the beach or fantasizing about where you might get away on vacation. I was in fine spirits. The car radio was on. I hummed along with an old Beatles song... "Hey, Jude... take a sad song and make it better...." I was learning the ropes by now and understood many difficult aspects of hospice work. It felt terrific to be on top of my job and in good health, not yet fifty years old.

As I drove into the borough of Queens, the cabbies who cut into my lane in their mad driving style didn't get to me today. Even a traffic jam on the Grand Central Parkway due to an overturned tractor-trailer wasn't about to dampen my good humor. I just used the time to notice the seagulls soaring over Flushing Meadows. A flock of pigeons made continual playful circles over the line of stalled cars as though to remind us who is really free.

Since Elmo was my first child patient, I was especially looking forward to meeting him, though I was less sure how I'd actually relate to a teenager with cancer. What would I say? A queasiness stirred in my stomach. Elmo had been referred to me by a nurse in an adjoining office, the Maternal and Child Health Program, which handled all the pediatric cases for our agency. As with people with AIDS, young people with cancer normally were not in the hospice program because their parents usually wanted aggressive care up to the very end. You couldn't blame them. It is one thing to die, even from a terrible disease like cancer, when one is advanced in years. But for a child to die before he has even graduated high school, or dated, or made the choices we feel we were all born for is very hard and takes a heavy toll on parents and health care workers. Those caring for such a patient resist the inevitable even more, feel the wrongness, and grieve over it more intensely. When Bobbie, his nurse, asked me to visit Elmo, I could hear these emotions in her voice.

A fifteen-year-old albino black, Elmo was living in a foster home, one of many he had resided in since birth because his mother was a drug addict. Elmo had been born with a tumor on his spinal cord, what is technically called astrocytoma. Over the past few years it had begun spreading. Recently it had invaded his brain.

A paraplegic, Elmo was overweight and incontinent, Bobbie explained to me, and able to move about only in a wheelchair. When I explored further, she said his appetite and emotional health were fine, and he was very intelligent. I was surprised to hear that he was attending Bayard Rustin School and had just completed the eighth grade. According to the assessment sheet, the boy's chief concern was to be able to watch TV all the time.

"Elmo's a good kid," Bobbie said, "very knowledgeable about his disease. On one level he knows he's dying—the doctor told him so — but he needs to talk about it. I think you could help him because you are a pastor. His grandmother, who is very involved with him, is Protestant, but he especially needs a man in his life. His father split long ago, whether because of his illness or not I'm not sure. . . . Oh, and he loves cartoons!"

Elmo lived with his current foster family in a poor neighborhood in East New York, a dangerous neighborhood where drug deals were common and the crime rate was high, though you could see it had been nice at one time. I found a parking place for my little brown Honda, which looked so old I thought no one would steal it. Its windows had been smashed in three times in the past two years and the radio had been ripped out of the dashboard. As the only white person in the neighborhood I felt like a narcotics agent or a welfare inspector. An older lady sweeping her porch across the street looked up and seemed to return my nod of greeting. Searching a few unpainted doorways, I came up to what I guessed was the right address.

It took some time for the knocks on the windowless door to be answered. Eventually a middle-aged lady of Caribbean ancestry unbolted the latch and greeted me. In a house dress and apron, she was friendly enough when I introduced myself and showed me into a side room where the patient reclined in a bed. I was left alone with him. An obese young man with a moon face and wiry blond hair glanced up from some papers he was working on intently, and then focused down on them again.

"Hi, Elmo! I'm a friend of Bobbie's . . . Paul."

"Hi, Paul," he said in a childlike voice while still looking down.

The boy was in a bed against a wall. It was crammed in among other furniture: bookcases, a TV, chairs with piles of newspapers and clothes on them. A small table was pulled up near his bed, and this was the surface he was working on — drawing, I could now see.

"May I sit down?"

"Sure." When Elmo looked up, his pink-rimmed blue eyes squinted at me through thick glasses. I plunked myself down on the edge of a chair, and my education began.

It took me a while to engage this young man. I realized after some time that he was involved in his drawing for its own sake as well as to avoid talking to an adult. Yes, I would have to work at this.

"Whatcha drawing?"

"Superheroes."

"Hmmm . . . any in particular?"

"Yeah." He checked my authenticity, at least that is what I sense teenagers are always doing with adults, bored at how pretentious or out of it we are.

"Some I copy from the comics," he offered, indicating a pile of them sprawled on his bed, "but mostly I make them up myself."

Elmo went back to drawing, his legs twisted under his distended belly in what looked like an uncomfortable position. He was dressed in a hospital gown.

"Wow! You make them up yourself?" My voice sounded like a cartoon character's.

"Yeah, you wanna see them?"

Elmo turned a large drawing sheet up for me to see. I used the occasion to venture closer, turning sideways in the dimly lit corner so I could see. What I saw was an amazing array of cartoon figures drawn in pencil, all in action poses: jumping, diving, raising weapons, falling, kicking, punching. Spread out over the whole page, some were more detailed than others, but all had muscular physiques and were garbed in exotic costumes. I couldn't help smiling.

"All of that came out of you?"

"Uummhmm," he acknowledged, a faint sound of pride in his voice.

I pointed at one particularly ferocious figure who was flying through the air toward another with his fist clenched. "And who is this?"

"I drew that one when I was feeling mad," said Elmo with energy. Then in the child's voice he said, "Would you read me a comic?"

"Sure! . . . may I sit down?"

He nodded and I sat next to him on the rumpled bed while he searched for one of his favorites. He found an old Captain Marvel which he handed to me like a treasure. I settled down into his world. It turned out to be exhausting. I was not used to reading aloud, nor could I relate to the weird plot and the sound-packed words: BAM! KAPOW! BAZOOM! It occurred to me that Elmo not only had trouble seeing; perhaps he had difficulty reading as well.

As I flipped the pages I could see him playing out the action in his mind. For my part I was wondering how I might find out what this kid felt about his death, God, and prayer. This foray into the righteous good-smashes-evil world of the superheroes continued for about ten minutes until, blessedly, we came to the end.

"There!" I sat back, satisfied I had done my fatherly duty. My mind was like jelly from the endeavor.

"Would you read me another?"

"Oh, God, you've got to be kidding!"

"C'mon Paul!" He thrust another one at me.

I gave it my best and tried to maintain the same energy, but I was flagging fast. Halfway through I began to care very little whether he saw each picture. I was spinning those pages like they were hot to the touch. Finally I had had it. I gave up and told him I couldn't go on. "Elmo, we'll finish this the next time, okay?"

He stared at me with disappointment. "Aww, you started! It's just a little more!"

"I can't," I confessed. "My throat is too tired."

"You'll come back?" he inquired.

"Ummhmm...maybe next week."

Elmo seemed to accept this display of adult fatigue with a sigh of resignation. To salvage a little pride, I decided to get some serious assessment on him before I left and show him that I was there for reasons other than to read comics. Nonchalantly I inquired, "How long ago did you get sick, Elmo?"

"About five years ago."

"Do you know what it is, how serious it is?"

In a softer voice he responded, "I've got cancer. The doctor said it will spread to my brain."

Elmo sounded as though he weren't telling me anything more serious than the weather report. Chagrin registered on my face.

"I may die in a week," he added.

"The doctor said that?"

The boy nodded his head and his eyes expressed some veiled concern about this. Yet moments later he spoke of his desire to be a cartoonist when he grows up. I wasn't sure now whether he was in outright denial or just balancing his normal fear with other realities he might still have hope for, however slim.

"Elmo, do you have any religious beliefs?...I'm a priest and would like to help you in your faith at this time...if you want."

To my surprise he responded, "Now that I'm sick I don't think of girls in the same way anymore."

I kidded him, "Oh, really? How was that?"

Blushing, he grinned. "You know."

"And you think I'm here to check up on that, right?"

"Well, not really." He gave a crooked smile. When he turned to his cartoon figures again, I stood to go. "Do you pray?"

"Yeah, sometimes when I'm in trouble, when I need something. But I don't go to church on Sunday," he added in a whisper as though it were a confession.

"That's not as important as talking to God the way you do. I bet God likes that...hearing from Elmo." I imagined how this fifteen-year-old black kid, albino at that, must have felt so estranged all his life. He must have seemed so weird to his peers — if he ever got to mix with them. I wondered what God must feel for him, what he must feel about God. Elmo just stared at me with his big eyes.

"I'll call you next week to set up a time for another visit if you want . . . okay?" I moved toward the door.

"Will you bring me some comics?"

I laughed at this childhood refrain familiar to parents, especially when Elmo very seriously explained the right ones to get. "Get Marvel and DC, Paul. They're the best!"

"Okay."

When I called into the other room for her, the woman I had met earlier returned, wiping her hands on a towel. "I am Mrs. Faron, Elmo's foster mother. Did you have a good visit, Elmo?"

"Mmmhmm." Elmo was already absorbed in drawing another superhero.

"He's quite the artist," I said.

"Indeed!"

Mrs. Faron accepted my handshake politely and let me out. As she bolted the door behind me, I was relieved to see that my car was still there. At the very least, this new patient would force me to become an expert in comic books.

When I reported on my visit with Elmo at the team meeting later that week, I had a vague feeling in my gut that I didn't understand. As the meeting was breaking up, our social worker, Beverly, mentioned that I seemed angry.

"I guess I am, but I'm not sure why. Something to do with the fact that this kid, Elmo, has had such a messed up life, I suppose. Nothing, Beverly . . . he's had nothing! There is something basically unjust about that. But who can you blame? It just makes me feel angry."

"And guilty maybe?" She arched an eyebrow.

"What do you mean?"

"You've had everything compared to this kid, Paul. So his having nothing can make you feel guilty."

"I suppose . . . "

"Hey, Irish guilt, Jewish guilt, what's the difference?" Beverly raised her hands mockingly and headed into the ladies' room. Her head suddenly popped back out the door, " . . . as long as we do something with it, right?"

"Right!" I intended to.

Later that afternoon I phoned Elmo to set up a visit for the following week. His advice to me in terms of his request about comics: "Go crazy!" Oddly enough, I couldn't find any comics in the stores I searched in, only crossword puzzles and romance magazines. I had to settle for some I finally located at a newsstand in Flushing — the heroes mostly yellow-skinned, the baddies white. It amazed me that whole blocks of stores in that neighborhood were for Asians, complete with signs in their foreign script. There were numerous Chinese and Japanese restaurants, Korean groceries, Pakistani and Indian clothing stores, even travel agencies and hairdressers that catered to the special needs of New York's Asian population. On a railroad bridge over the main intersection a pair of huge white hands stretched out on a billboard. "Flushing, Jesus Christ loves you!"

The next time I visited Elmo, he was sitting up in bed listening to a Walkman. Proudly I held up the comics I had bought. He didn't thank me, but just reached for them greedily while surveying the covers.

"They're not Marvels!" he announced in dismay.

"No, I couldn't find them. But these are unusual; wait till you see."

As I flipped one open to show him, Elmo winced. "What's the matter?"

"Oh, I got bedsores."

"I'm sorry. Maybe you should turn on your side."

"Yeah, but I'm sitting up so I can fix my comics. Would you read me one?" He seemed crankier and bossier.

"You wouldn't believe how many places I had to go to find these," I confided as I sat next to him on the bed. Soon we were lost in the adventures of "The Secret Warriors of the House of Chang." At one point Elmo leaned closer to check the artwork, squinting his eyes up close to the page. Soon a familiar acrid smell floated up from his bedclothes — urine he had evidently been sitting in. At first I meant to ignore it, but finally it became so nauseating that I had to get a breath of fresh air.

"I'm getting tired," I said, closing the comic.

"Paul, you're only halfway!" "I know . . . I'm sorry." Elmo shot me a look of disgust.

"I'm in a hurry today," I lied. "I have to see a number of other patients."

"But you just got here!" Elmo protested.

I was backing across the room and stopped. "Elmo, who changes you, who bathes you?"

"My foster mother."

"Did she do so this morning?"

He looked sheepish. "She had to go to work so she asked my foster brother to."

"And? . . . "

"Whenever he's supposed to, he comes into my room and yells at me, 'Change yourself!' "

"What's your response?"

"I yell back at him, but it doesn't do any good."

"How old is he?"

"About thirty."

"Well . . . you shouldn't be sitting in your own waste. We've got to do something about this."

His moon face dropped.

"I'm sorry, Elmo. That's why I was leaving; I couldn't stand the smell." He kept his head down. The silence was excruciating. Gritting my teeth, I sucked in a deep breath by the window and went back to finish the story.

On my way out, I convinced the foster brother to change Elmo's soiled clothes, but I think he reacted more out of fear I would report this to the nurse. The next time, I vowed to myself, I would be more honest when I felt repelled by him.

A few weeks later, I phoned Elmo, asking him if I could visit him sometime later that week.

"Bring some comics!"

"I'll try."

I did try, but again no luck, not even the Chinese ones. When I arrived, Elmo was outside in his wheelchair underneath a big tree in the yard eating lunch. Mrs. Faron and he were discussing something intently. When I came closer, they looked up and greeted me. Then she volunteered that they were talking about his catheter. "The condom won't stay on," she said. Detaching the bag of urine, she took it inside. She came out later and reattached it; all the while Elmo talked with me casually.

I have felt uncomfortable being around patients in intimate situations, embarrassed for them that they have to be so vulnerable in public. Lately though, I was learning not to worry unduly about their feelings; perhaps I just don't want to be seen as pitying them for being broken. When I have been able to see the most degrading treatment as just another aspect of care, not very different from my hidden degrading moments, it seemed to go easier for all of us. Mrs. Faron's easy way of treating these difficult situations helped me. Judging from their interaction, she and Elmo seemed to have a good relationship.

When she left us, he and I sat together in the shade. Elmo devoured a large sandwich and commented on his increased weight. "I look like a blimp." He frowned even as he wolfed it down.

"Yeah," I joked, "pretty soon we can fly you right up there next to the Goodyear blimp."

"Paul!" But he took the teasing easily.

"Hey, who cares? You want to go for a ride around the block?"

"Okay," he said, adjusting his New York Mets baseball cap.

Most of the way around he pushed his wheelchair himself, needing a little help only when we came to big cracks in the sidewalk. The heat baked the street and buildings, and sweat rolled down my back and legs. A few people on the block had little flower gardens in front of their porches, which interrupted the anchor fence and concrete look that dominated the neighborhood. Abandoned cars, some with their windows smashed out and stripped of everything worth using or selling, were interspersed with other working models including my own. At the corner Elmo paused as though to turn back. "Let's go on," I encouraged.

A lady in her yard next to us warned of dangers. "They sell drugs down there and you can hear gunshots!" It looked safe enough to me. It had houses similar to the ones on Elmo's block; only an abandoned lot overgrown with weeds on the opposite side had a look of potential threat about it. I didn't move. Neither did Elmo. He looked up at me and then down the street. Grabbing hold of the wheel rims with gusto, he plowed on with me following as the lady clucked behind us.

"The guns only shoot at night," he confided when we were out of her hearing. We made it around without incident, and even did it a second time. After this adventure we had a bond with each other. Before leaving I told him I would not see him for a few weeks because I was going on vacation. Elmo was disappointed but added, "Come whenever you can, Paul."

When I got back from vacation, Elmo's nurse told me that he had been admitted to Queens General Hospital. She didn't think he was going to last very long. I went immediately to visit him there and walked through the children's wing, where tiny red-skinned babies with jet black hair lay in cribs or were rocked in their mothers' arms. I found Elmo in a private room with Mrs. Faron feeding him baby food. She looked up at me with a tired smile.

I could see that Elmo was not up for a visit, and I said I'd wait outside, but soon Mrs. Faron came out and said she would be back in a while. When I returned to the brightly lit room and tried to speak with Elmo, I discovered he was conversing only by occasional nods, a hand squeeze, or a smile. With his eyes half-open, he seemed either depressed and very withdrawn or the medication was affecting his speech.

"Elmo, what are you feeling like?" No response. "If you don't want to talk, do you mind if I do?" He nodded it was okay.

"It is good to see you again. I've been thinking about you." I continued more small talk that drew no response. I sat quietly for some moments. It scared me to think that this young man could be drifting away without any way for us to know what was happening to him. "Maybe you are feeling scared, or maybe you are angry that you are stuck in this place. I would be." The nurse had said he might not last long.

"I don't know, maybe you even feel that you might be dying, and you could be scared or angry about that. You know what? Whatever you are feeling, it might be good if you could talk about it, even with God if you want to." Glancing around the room, I noticed his box of toys on the floor crammed with robot figures, the ones that can be transformed from an exotic car or spaceship into a superhero, Elmo's dream! His creative mind and spirit must yearn for a body that could match his imagination. Oh, I felt for this kid. I turned toward him in the pale light, "Maybe you just might want to communicate through mental telepathy, without words . . ."

Elmo was looking directly at me now but with a blank stare. In the background was the sound of young babies crying hysterically. Taking his hand in mine, I closed my eyes and shut up. His hand squeezed back and with his other hand he stroked mine.

His foster mother returned and asked if she could speak with me. I went out and closed the door behind me. In the hallway in the presence of the hospital social worker, she told me that Elmo's mother, who had legal power over him, wanted all possible life-sustaining actions taken in his regard: resuscitation if his heart stopped, a respirator to help him keep breathing, a feeding tube. Mrs. Faron and the social worker both felt that this was wrong, that it would not help now. "It will only prolong his agony," said Mrs. Faron.

"The hospital needs to protect itself against lawsuits," explained the social worker, "and will have to abide by the mother's wishes even if they are not appropriate." The foster mother looked at me with pleading eyes.

"What are Elmo's wishes?" I asked. The social worker said that a meeting was planned between the hospital staff, Elmo's mother, and Mrs. Faron. I would be welcome to participate if I were available. I told them I would be glad to come. We would meet within the week.

Before leaving the hospital I returned to Elmo's room to tell him I was about to go. His eyes were closed. I placed one hand on his arm and my other hand on his head, stroking his nappy blond hair. Remembering his foster mother's gesture as she was leaving, I asked if I could rub his stomach (which was quite large, almost looking as if he were pregnant). With his eyes still closed, he nodded slightly. I then rubbed his stomach gently in a circling motion and thought I saw him smile as I did so. While I was thus engaged, a nurse poked her head in the door. "I'm a priest with the hospice program," I explained. "We've been caring for Elmo and I'll be leaving shortly."

"I didn't know who you were," she said and then turned and left. Kissing Elmo on the forehead, I told him I'd try to see him in a week or so. I felt good about this visit as I left, about the attempts at communication and Elmo's hand gestures in particular. But I wondered what would become of this child in the next few weeks as the hospital and the adults in his life wrangled over him. And how would I be involved? I had an awareness of the growing risks I was taking in my ministry, the freedom I felt to speak about difficult emotions with those who were dying and to touch them tenderly. Yet I saw how I could easily be misunderstood in these words and touches too.[5] God bless Elmo! God bless me!

That night I had a dream, a nightmare really, though I am not sure it was just a dream. In the middle of the night I awoke and sensed I was sleeping in my bed in exactly the same position that I remembered falling asleep in. I heard noises — a scratching sound that I had heard earlier when I had first lay down. I searched the shadows over in the corner by the bookcase. Two red eyes, slitted like a cat's, were glaring at me out of the pitch blackness. My hair stood on end. It looked — no, it felt! — like I was staring at the devil. An acrid smell filled my nostrils. I yelled mockingly at the figure, "Yaaah, yaaah!" The eyes grew more intense and evil. Closer and closer they came as though wanting to burn me up in their hatred. Then this fiendish demon grabbed me in its claws, mattress and all, and whirled me around the room at a terrific speed. My mouth flew open to scream but no sound would come. Finally in total desperation I yelled, "Jeshua! Jeshua!" a Hebrew name for Jesus I had learned. I kept shouting this at the top of my lungs until I was utterly exhausted. Miraculously, something happened to save me, because gradually the whirling stopped and everything was calm once again.

I was breathing heavily and had my eyes jammed shut because I couldn't bear to see those red eyes again. Something told me to check if I was dreaming or not. I peeked up from my bed. "It wasn't just a dream," I thought. "That overturned lamp proves it!" But there was a soft glow in the room now, and it felt like the devil was gone, so I fell back into a restless sleep. When I awoke the next morning, I remembered and looked at the lamp. It was upright after all, but it still felt like I had come through something terrible.

I saw Elmo once more before the group met to talk about his treatment plan. Again he was in the withdrawn state, so it was largely a one-way conversation. He did nod agreement that I could stay and talk, and he smiled once at my jokes, notably when I prayed aloud for some good food for him. "You know what he likes, Lord, . . . southern fried chicken, mashed potatoes smothered in giblet gravy, cranberry sauce, hot buttered corn on the cob. . . . "

Elmo slept through the second half-hour, awakening only when Mrs. Faron came in with a container of home-made chicken, soup which she fed him. "Wow! Can you believe it? God didn't get it quite right," I said, "but that sure was a quick answer to a prayer, don't you think?" Elmo agreed, slurping it up with gusto. "Keep on fighting," I told him as I left.

The meeting about Elmo with the hospital staff was held later that month. I had spoken with him on the phone that morning, and he had demanded, "Get me out of here, Paul!" — the first words I'd heard from him in a month. At the meeting in a conference room off Elmo's corridor, I met his grandmother, a lovely, soft-spoken woman, and his sister, Charisse. Both evidently visited him often but never while I was there. His mother wasn't there but had agreed that Elmo could go to a special children's hospital in Queens that had a palliative care unit; this would take place as soon as there was a vacant bed.

A week later I telephoned Queens General Hospital to see if Elmo was still there. "I'm Reverend Morrissey, Elmo's pastor."

"Yes, he is still here," a nurse on his floor responded. "He's been asking for you."

"Oh?" Heartened that he would be so explicit, I inquired, "Any particular reason?" She hesitated, and then said softly, "He's afraid he's dying."

"Well, is he?"

"Not imminently. He's been short of breath and this has him frightened."

"I'll be over to see him soon."

When I arrived, Elmo was not in his room, but down on a lower floor at the eye clinic. I took a seat in a side room, unnerved by what shape I'd find him in and scared for him. I took a magazine from the table and tried to concentrate, but couldn't. In about fifteen minutes there was a commotion in the hallway, people walking briskly, the sound of a person gasping and whining. I saw them wheel Elmo by with an oxygen mask on, making panicked sounds as he rolled his head to the left and the right, his eyes searching for help.

Quickly I followed them into a twin room where they lifted him onto a bed, making sure the oxygen mask and tubes were properly attached. He spotted me and reached out as they explained that he was all right and that it was important for him to stay calm. In the bed next to him another teenager, who had a bandage around his chest, watched this scene warily out of the corner of his eye.

It was not the time to show him the robot I had brought

him, but I did so anyway because I was nervous. Elmo wasn't interested. Still breathing in a spasmodic way, his eyes bulged over the top of the plastic mask he held up to his face. While I breathed deeply to calm myself, I stroked his arm, imagining the terror of being unable to breathe.

"Calm down," I said in my most soothing voice. "Breathe very slowly." Rhythmically I breathed and spoke, and gradually Elmo followed the pattern. Soon he was able to take the oxygen mask off. I decided not to beat around the bush.

"The nurse told me on the phone that you were asking for me... that you were scared. What are you scared of, Elmo?"

Without hesitation the boy responded, "Scared of dying."

"What makes you think you are dying?" I noticed the other kid listening to us intently.

"Because of all the bad things that are happening to me.... I have diabetes."

"This is something new?"

"Yes, but the doctors didn't tell me what it means!"

"It means you have high blood sugar," I explained, "that you'll have to watch certain kinds of food like the chocolate cakes and pizza you dream about.... You'll have to ask the doctor to tell you more." This didn't pacify him much.

He glanced around the room. Ignoring his buddy in the next bed, he went on, "Can I ask you something, Paul?"

"Sure."

"What is hell like? Is it black?"

"Hell?..."

"And the devil...?"

"The devil! What are you worrying about the devil for?"

"All these ways I'm getting sick, God must be punishing me."

"Get out! Why would God punish a kid like you?"

Elmo didn't respond at first, but then haltingly explained that he was probably being punished because he didn't take me seriously when I wanted to pray for him months before.

"But you were sick before I ever met you!" I protested.

"Maybe the times I didn't go to church..."

"Look, God doesn't punish people for not going to church by making them sick. People get sick because our bodies aren't perfect. Don't you think God, who is our Father, wants us to be happy?" My attempts to reassure him felt increasingly inadequate. What good would these words do? "You know that blackness you are afraid of? ... It can't hurt you." Elmo grasped my hand tightly. "And when you get ready to die ... " — his pale eyes were locked onto mine — "rather than blackness you will see light."

"Really?"

"And you know what? If the light scares you, just call out the name of Jesus. He loves you, Elmo, yeah, Jesus really loves you." The boy relaxed his grip.

"Paul, would you teach me to pray?" The small voice touched me.

"Tell him whatever's on your mind, like you would do with a friend."

When I began to elaborate, Elmo interrupted. "Is this all right?" In a halting way he recited the childhood prayer, "Now I lay me down to sleep ... I pray the Lord my soul to keep ... if I should die before I wake ... I pray the Lord my soul to take." "Perfect!" I tousled his hair. "I'm amazed that you know that. Do you say that at night?"

"Yeah."

"Well, try to do it every night, before you go to sleep, okay? It will help you not to be afraid because God will be with you, no matter what."

Within moments Elmo had shifted out of this deep talk and asked me to switch on the TV. We sat watching reruns of *Star Trek* for a while. When I left I gave him a long hug cheek to cheek, catching the curious gaze of the other kid over his shoulder as I did so. Maybe I'll try Elmo's prayer tonight, I thought as I got up to go.

~ Andy ~

URING THE NEXT FEW MONTHS I visited Candida every two weeks. Rarely did I see her son, Angel, and even when I did he would give a brief hello and make himself scarce. The hospice team had decided I had a better chance of connecting with him than the social worker did, since Beverly sensed she brought out all his feelings about his mother. But whenever I tried to find a time when he would be home, Angel always had an excuse. I concluded I wanted the visit more than he did and let it go.

Candida, for her part, seemed to get even better, now always up and seated in a chair in the living room when I arrived. I was able to have a meaningful conversation with her even without her husband, Juan, to translate. Though my mouth ached afterward from trying to pronounce the words, I attempted to read her passages from the Bible in Spanish, while Candida encouraged me. The words that Jesus spoke to his disciples at the Last Supper seemed to touch her deeply:

> I tell you truly:
>> you will weep and mourn while the world rejoices;
>> you will grieve for a time,
>> but your grief will be turned into joy.
>
> When a woman is in labor,
>> she is sad that her time has come.
>
> When she has borne her child,
>> she no longer remembers her pain
>> for joy that a man has been born into the world.
>
> In the same way, you are sad for a time,
>> but I shall see you again;

76

then your hearts will rejoice,
with a joy no one can take from you.

—John 16:20–22

On a whim one evening I called Angel around dinner time. He sounded friendly and asked me about my car. From what I had heard from Candida and Juan, he hadn't been to school in weeks. Without mentioning that, I simply said I'd like to see him the next morning, when I would be over in Queens. "We could meet at the Roy Rogers up on the avenue." I thought he might be more free to talk if he were out of the house. He hesitated. "I'll treat you to breakfast."

"What time?"

"How about nine?" I was thinking I could juggle another appointment I had made until later in the morning.

"Okay," he said breezily.

"See you then, Angel." He hung up. Well, whaddaya know, we had a date!

The next day, a gray and rainy Tuesday with big cumulus clouds scudding through the sky, I waited for Angel underneath the elevated subway at Forty-ninth and Roosevelt, having parked my car in a narrow spot I found three blocks away. He wasn't inside, and after fifteen minutes passed I decided to give him a call. Juan answered and said Angel was sleeping. I mentioned the appointment and said I would still like to see him. Juan went back to confer with him and returned to ask if I could come over an hour later. Miffed at what felt like Angel's control patterns but determined to stay on him this time, I agreed. I bought a *Daily News* at a vending machine and grabbed a breakfast of French toast, bacon, juice, and coffee at Roy Rogers.

When I arrived, Candida let me in; Juan had gone to work. The pressure from the tumor was bad, she told me as she undid her nightgown to point out the bandages she applied so meticulously. After going to get Angel, who was apparently still sleeping, she returned and led me into his semi-darkened room, explaining that he was sick.

Angel lay in his bed, which was against the far wall, a spread pulled up to his neck. His eyes were closed. A computer setup filled one side of the small room, and a poster with a rock group provided a backdrop for a desk from which Candida pulled a chair for me and motioned for me to have a seat. A pair of high-top sneakers were flopped in a corner, but the room was remarkably neat for a teenager. "Angel! Angel!" she called with her accent and then left us alone when he began to stir. This was quite awkward because of the bedroom circumstances and the ambivalent signals I kept getting from Angel about whether he really wanted to talk to me. With Candida and Juan pressing me to talk to him about his late hours, his school absence, and his friendships, I felt like I was getting caught in the middle of a battle this kid was waging with his parents. And it looked like I could be of no help because he identified me with the religion of his mother: the one he saw killing her, the one he was trying to flee from. Candida appeared with two glasses of orange juice.

"Angel! Angel!" She shook him. "The Padre." When he opened his eyes, she left and closed the door behind her. I empathized with him and wanted very much to help. Angel stretched and rolled onto his side facing me. He reminded me of myself as a kid. "Hi!"

"Hi, Angel . . . you stood me up." I said this with a smile while sipping the juice.

"I'm sorry, I was sick," he replied softly.

"You've been missing a lot of school."

"Yeah." A note of apology was in his voice.

"What's causing that, do you know?"

"It's boring. I'm going to take the High School Equivalency Exam instead."

"Oh? . . . when's that?"

"As soon as I take the training course for it. It starts in two weeks."

"And your being sick, is that physical or emotional?"

"Physical."

"Have you ever been to a doctor about it?"

"Yeah, about a year ago."

"It could be nerves. You don't want to get real sick, do you?"

"No."

This kid had an answer for everything. I didn't know whether he was genuinely overwhelmed by the crisis going on in his family or just conning everyone.

"Want some juice? Here, your mom brought this for you." He

sat up, drawing the covers around his legs. He was wearing an old rumpled sweatshirt with a skull on it.

"What do you think of devil worship?" he asked, gazing at me intently.

"Devil worship!"

"Yeah, you know, kids who kill their parents and say the devil made me do it."

I shifted uneasily. Studying his blank expression, I guessed he was putting me on. "Why? Are you thinking of doing that?"

"No." A slight smile lit his face. "But I read about it in the papers. Do you believe in the devil?"

"Mmmhmm!" I murmured affirmatively. "How 'bout you?" I was hoping he'd open up on a personal basis, but it was like talking to a computer. "Why do you think one of these kids might want to kill his parents?"

Angel sipped reflectively on his juice and looked around the room. "Maybe that's the only way he could be free."

"Free?"

"Maybe they want him to be too much like them."

"And God is on their side?" He saw where I was going and clammed up, but now we had an opening. We sat in silence for a few moments.

"Do you feel trapped in this house, Angel?"

"What do you mean?"

"Well, your dad and mom say you stay out late at night, coming in at 1:00 or 2:00 a.m. Then in the morning you say you're too sick to go to school."

With rising intensity Angel shot back, "I stay away because I can't stand seeing my mother sick all the time — on oxygen, cleaning her tumor and all! What would you do?"

"Have you told your parents how you feel?"

"I never speak to them about it."

So! This miserable disease pervades all their lives. It's surrounded him like the air for as long as he can remember. But he doesn't talk about it and can't scream about it. It just corrodes him from the inside like the cancer. And his mother's sweet, godlike way of dealing with it makes any of his feelings of rage seem like they're from the devil.

I tried to get him to express more of his feelings, but Angel wasn't up to talking anymore about Candida's illness. He only spoke of how different he was from her. "She believes everyone is good; I think people are bad." He went on to explain this by speaking with growing affect about his friends.

Angel described the neighborhood scene he was part of. He thinks his peers see him as different: "I'm richer than they are, and I don't smoke or drink like them either." He will hang out with this rough crowd, he says, until he gets into college. "Then I'll change my personality." Angel didn't have a girl friend.

He hangs out, he says, with a sixteen-year-old Pakistani kid, Sai, who drives an unlicensed car. This kid also carries a beeper. Angel sees no danger in this in terms of the cops. Something else bothered me, his bully-like way of relating to the local kids: "They're afraid of me because they know I'll get them if they cross me."

"You sound like a devious righter-of-wrongs in the neighborhood." Angel sneered at this pious concern for legality. When I pressed him for examples, he spoke of a kid who had crossed a friend of his, and Angel in his righteousness got a whole gang of kids to turn against this boy.

"He's as good as dead in the neighborhood." When this boy later made threats against Angel's house and family, Angel bragged, "I asked my father to get one of our relatives to retaliate."

"One of your relatives?"

"An uncle in Colombia who can do this," he said without batting an eye.

Then as though to seal the threat — and give me a message? — "I'll kill anyone who harms my mother." Angel has a list of people he wants to get.

Sitting in this darkened bedroom and listening to this skinny fifteen-year-old-kid reel off his grandiose plans, I couldn't decide whether it was a boyhood fantasy being played out to impress me or was an expression of his desperate need to feel some control in his life. Or perhaps it was a frightening need to get even, to provide some bizarre system of justice in a world that in his eyes was so unjust toward his family and himself.

"Angel, you sound like a vigilante. . . . I'm afraid of what could happen to you." Shrugging his shoulders, he finished the juice he was nursing.

"Don't worry," he reassured me like a young godfather. "I

won't do anything stupid." He smiled as though he were completely in charge.

Thinking of the kid he had ostracized, I asked, "Have you ever forgiven anyone?" Angel looked at me as though I were speaking Swahili. "You know, someone like the kid who crossed your friend."

"Not unless he begs for mercy in front of the whole group." A shiver ran up my spine. Glancing at my watch, I noticed that an hour had passed. There were deep problems here; I needed to take a breather to assess them.

"Angel, I need to go soon because I have some other appointments, but I'd like to speak with you about this again, okay?"

"Okay, Father Paul . . . and please call me Andy. I prefer it to Angel." It was the first time he had called me by name.

"Sure." I handed him a card with my home number on it. "Call me if you just want to talk some time, okay? Leave a message if I am not there." He got up to take the card, and then went over to a dresser and returned with a pad of paper on which he wrote something, his slender legs lost in a pair of gray cut-off sweat pants.

"Here," he thrust a slip of paper toward me. "This is Sai's beeper number. You can reach me here most of the time."

"Okay, Andy." We left his room and a few moments later I bid a hasty goodbye to him and Candida at the door.

Man, this seemed too big for me to handle, too many issues. No matter what the family said, we would need to get a social worker involved. And Doc and I ought to try to have a joint meeting with this family. Kicking the brown leaves, I hurried to my car.

Later that evening as I aimed my car across the Whitestone Bridge, a driver cut across in front of me too quickly. A flash of anger burst out and I yelled some obscenity after him. Like Andy's anger, I thought, just beneath the surface of his sweet young face.

As though drawn by a magnet, my head swiveled left. There spread out like some mad architect's dream stretched the Manhattan skyline with the bridges draped underneath like necklaces. The lights on the Chrysler and Citicorp buildings dominated the thousand smaller lights shimmering in the purple haze at their feet.

Further down I could see the Empire State Building, where our office is located. Thrust skyward from midtown, more than anything else this glistening granite and steel pillar symbolized the aggressive masculine spirit that made New Yorkers infamous. "Get outa my face!" it said, or something more graphic.

I used to hate this pushiness, the speed of the city, and vowed I'd never succumb to such an inhuman pace and style of relating. Yet here I was swearing out of my car window when some one cuts me off! I've got the New York state of mind; the joke's on me!

The male symbol of the Empire State Building made me think of Candida's illness, of all illnesses in fact, and how they show us something physically that may correspond to what we feel or think. Depending on what part of your body is deteriorating, it can mean different things to you. If your mind is going, you have certain feelings about it. If your face is being disfigured by cancer, another set. If your lungs are going and you're a smoker, it sets up certain issues. Your liver, another set.

AIDS certainly stirs up feelings of "being punished," if not in the patient, in many onlookers. Incapacitated legs means something different from blindness. If you cannot talk, it feels different from not being able to eat or have sex. These symbolic meanings of people's sicknesses aren't insignificant issues. They have to be dealt with if real healing is to take place.

When the part of your body that is failing has been an important part of your identity, your self-worth, there is an even greater sense of loss. The former fashion model in our program who had cancer eating away her face; the author paralyzed from Lou Gehrig's disease whose husband was attempting to finish her book for her before she died; the once muscular longshoreman who could no longer even lift himself out of bed — grief is intensified and focused in these situations: for the patient and for those who loved the special gift now slipping like sand through their fingers.

Candida had breast cancer. I couldn't help thinking that for a woman to be dying from cancer in a part of her body that symbolized the source of life would be especially agonizing in its contradiction. Maybe even more so to a mother. No matter how religious she was, Candida was also Hispanic. They are a very passionate people. For her breasts to be eaten away must feel like God is destroying her at her roots.

Some of these sicknesses even seem like a sign of the ultimate horror, that the life of our whole planet could turn against itself, the life-force become a death-force, the end of us all, as though a mother's breast could spew poison to her suckling babies, or a man's semen kill! What once gave life — your body — has now become the source of your death.

Surely we need to be saved from this. How can we help each other talk about these questions, heal our children if not ourselves by facing our deepest fears regarding illness and death? This is what I wanted to do in my ministry. As I paid the bridge toll, an Emergency Medical Service ambulance pulled ahead of me. The insignia on the back door, a serpent twined around a staff, gave me a clue.

The Bible describes how long ago God sent serpents to attack the people, to bite them because they complained about his care for them. These bites caused many of them to die in the wilderness. When they repented, Moses prayed for them and God told him, "Make a saraph and mount it on a pole, and if anyone who has been bitten looks at it, he will recover" (Num. 21:8). What God had first sent as a punishment on the people was later used to cure them.

Today, this serpent entwined on a staff has become the sign of the medical profession. Like their forerunners Asclepius and Hippocrates in the ancient world, physicians use doses of the very poisons that afflict us as medicines for our healing.

As a priest and pastoral counselor I was discovering that I could help people similarly. We could hold their physical ailments up to God and at the same time lift up the long-buried "demons" within them. When we can look at what has "bitten" us — even our death and our dying — it no longer has the power to destroy us.

~

At the team meeting a couple of weeks later, Matilda described how Juan Perez had phoned to say that Candida was getting weaker. "She's down to eighty-eight pounds!" I reported that when I had seen her recently, she was bright and perky, sitting in the living room and conversing freely while her husband translated.

"She did complain of increasing pain in her right jaw and her eyes, also her feet," said Matilda. "But what can you do? The lady will not take her pain medicine."

"If I understand correctly," said Beverly, "Juan claims that Candida was blind for some months at one point in her sickness a few years back. They consider it a miracle that she has recovered her sight." She wondered whether it wasn't some psychological hysteria, a bodily playing out of her illness and her faith. After discussing Candida's pain situation from many angles, the team concluded it was time that Doc and I made a joint visit.

He and I huddled after the team meeting broke up and decided that our plan was simply to try to help the Perez family to communicate. We especially wanted them to talk about Candida's worries about Andy in his presence; her preoccupation about him was connected to her avoidance of the prescribed pain medicine. We would meet at the Perez's around 10:00 a.m. It was Juan's day off, and since Andy was still not enrolled in the high school equivalency program, he said he would be there too.

"Don't bet on it," I said.

I arrived first; Juan welcomed me. He went to the back rooms while I sat with Candida and gave her Communion. When I inquired, she said her appetite was all right but that her sleeping was bad. "I worry...Angel stay out all night."

When Doc arrived, he was greeted effusively; Andy and Juan had joined us by this time. We all sat down, and somewhat awkwardly I repeated what Candida had just mentioned to me: "Candida doesn't sleep because Andy stays out all night. We are here to see if there is anything we can do about this, whether there is some agreement that can be worked out." I looked over at Andy, hoping to show him that we were with him in this. He looked armored, as if he had on his vigilante mask.

A discussion ensued, heated at times on Andy's part. He minimized any disturbing behavior while Candida spoke quite strongly about her concerns and fears that he would do something that would have the police after him. They went back and forth in Spanish, with Andy doing the translating for us.

"What am I doing wrong?" he protested.

"If the police come for him," Candida insisted, "I am going to have a stroke."

I noticed that when Andy spoke in Spanish, his voice had a fire and command to it, almost like he was the master of this house. When he translated for us into English, his voice took on an innocent boy quality. Juan watched this ping-pong match from the middle, wanting to keep the two of them from an outright break with one another.

The pivotal point of the discussion occurred near the end of the hour. Candida looked upward and said in a pious tone, "I offer up my suffering for Angelito, that God will keep him safe and good."

Furious at this — we didn't understand yet what had been said — he yelled back at her in Spanish with bared teeth, "Mamita, take your medicine! Don't suffer for me!"

Candida appeared stricken. It was clear to Andy now: his mother wanted to suffer. It was her bargaining chip with God for the future of her son. Andy stared over at her with disgust.

Moments later Juan interjected, "All I care about is them, anything I can do to help both of them I will do."

"*You always say that!*" Andy screamed like a wild man and stormed out of the room, slamming the door behind him. Doc and I held our breath. Each of them was a martyr suffering for the others. In his anger, I thought, Andy may be the healthiest of them all.

In a while I went to his room and tapped on the door. Andy was plopped in front of a computer, pounding the keys to some game. Eventually I was able to urge him to return to the living room with the promise to keep a curfew of 11:30 p.m. For her part, Candida had agreed with Doc to take her pain medication, but only the Tylenol; she claimed the others made her nauseous. This trade-off would be tried for the next two weeks; then we would reconvene. When Candida got up and went to the kitchen, Andy excused himself and returned to his room.

"Juan," Doc inquired in his gentle way, "could you say more about Candida's understanding of pain? I mean, doesn't she want to overcome it?"

Juan spoke of a "Madre de Dolores, Our Lady of Pain." "This is a great devotion of Candida's . . . and she is really a saint," he purred, cataloguing her history of suffering endured cheerfully over the years.

"But Juan," I interrupted, "is *dolores* physical or emotional pain? Thinking that in translation *dolores* would mean "sorrows" — Our Lady of Sorrows — I was trying to suggest that the sorrow one experiences is one thing to "offer up," but to want physical pain to offer to God would make God a sadist.

"The Spanish word for sorrow is *tristeza*," Juan explained, "what Candida feels for Angel. But the devotion is to the Madre de Dolores, Our Lady of Pain." The Jewish doctor and the Catholic priest shook our heads at this belief and what it was doing to this family.

I was not sure the "bargain" between Candida and Andy would hold up. Deeper issues were at stake than curfews and even Candida's pain. It was a start though, and I suggested to Juan that the struggle that Andy and Candida were going through was normal. "He needs to grow up and make his own life, and he is trying to break away."

"Yes," Juan responded, "but I am caught in the middle trying to keep things from getting too explosive."

"Maybe you need to risk letting them get explosive," said Doc. "Your son needs you to draw some boundaries for him, and Candida can't do it."

Juan volunteered to try, but he seemed helpless. "I would beat him, but in your country it is not allowed." He shrugged. In the end he agreed it was his right as a father to make the curfew work, to lock the door if it came down to that so that his son would see he wasn't just a bystander.

We left, thanking Juan and Candida for welcoming us and wondering what would happen over the next few weeks. It almost seemed that one solution would be if Candida died. But then how would Juan and Andy get along? Maybe they would finally deal with each other directly and not just through Candida.

"Whew!" said Doc with a grin as we parted on the corner, "Good luck with Our Lady of Pain!"

~ Uncle Sparky ~

WORKING SO INTIMATELY with death has created the surprising, and at first embarrassing, reaction in my body of great surges of sexual energy. Ruby helped me to understand and not be afraid of such feelings. Chuckling and rolling her eyes saucily, she said: "Why naturally, honey, you're a priest and you ought to know this better than I. It's the life force, love-energy, rising up inside you to counteract all that death we're working around. Relax and enjoy it; that's what I do. Now give me a nice hug. That'll help you spread it around!" With that she laughed uproariously.

It is as though this life force — what the Greeks called *eros* — is responding with equal force to the power of death, *thanatos*, which is always so close in this ministry. Something primal surges up and shouts *"not yet!"* to the figure of death, which stalks closer and closer. The urgent message of this force is: "Live! Love! Hold and be held onto by flesh and blood now!"

It wasn't so much a drive toward anyone in particular I noticed, but a generally heightened sense of sexual energy. Ironically, instead of making me want to flee from my patients' disfigurement as though it were its polar opposite, this energy helped me overcome my fear of ugliness and death. And of love too.

On the Monday before Halloween I got a phone message from Isha. "Please come and see me this week." Even though I had other more pressing cases and in fact had begun to see my visits to Isha as a sort of personal luxury for both of us, I kept trying to see her every two weeks. But I had missed our regular rhythm the week before and had not phoned to say why, ignoring the fact that she may have expectations too. Strangely, I didn't know how to place this relationship in context with the other patients; somehow I did not want to acknowledge her special-ness. I called and said I'd be over the next day if that would be okay. She seemed somewhat distant.

It was a brisk day, and even the brilliant sun had not warmed up the concrete canyons of Manhattan by mid-afternoon. I was glad to get out of the office, tired of the paperwork the state de-manded. I needed some hands-on encounters with patients to remind me of what the purpose of all this was — and to remind myself that I was not just a businessman.

Men and women with briefcases and get-outa-my-way looks zinged through the revolving doors so quickly you had to pause, take a deep breath, and jump. Pray to God you wouldn't catch your leg or arm and have it broken off as someone swirled the door behind you. Yes, I had learned the pace of the Big City, but I was determined not to be completely sucked into it.

Ha! You either adapted to its aggressive timetable or were gazed at with a mixture of pity and disgust for breaking some-one's stride by a half-second. I made it through the door, passed a homeless man with a sign that said he had AIDS and didn't do drugs, and headed up the windy street whistling, "What a day for a daydream, what a day for a daydreaming boy...."

Eloise, the Home Health Aid, let me in. Isha was lying in her bed all covered up with sheets and blankets. She gave me a weak hello when I leaned down to hug her. "Don't get up. I'll sit right here beside you." But she was determined to sit up, and with great difficulty we helped her sit on the side of the bed, draping the covers over her head like a Madonna.

"I no feel good two, three days," she said with a sigh. Indeed she was more emaciated, looking even blacker with her white eyes and teeth piercing out of this darkness. I had on my mind the team's desire to respect this family's own way of accepting death. With her pain increasing, she had begun liquid morphine the week before.

"I'm sorry, Isha. I wish you felt better."

"Tea!" she said in a commanding way to the HHA. "You like tea?" she asked me.

"Oh, no thanks." I didn't want to be a bother, but her look made me reconsider. "Okay, that'd be nice."

"Eloise, two tea... and honey." She indicated the number

with her fingers. We sat holding hands, Isha trying to get comfortable. I noticed the large tumor in her belly and the very swollen feet and legs. Yet her toenails were painted red! I couldn't help smiling.

When the tea was prepared, Eloise brought a metal chair over and placed it next to us, balancing two large cups of tea on it while Isha produced a box of crackers from beside her bed. The fragrant steam rose in our faces. I needed to get away for a minute to sort out some of the feelings inside me that I didn't understand. "May I use your bathroom?"

"Sure." She motioned toward the back.

Fumbling in the dark, I found the light switch and entered the tiny room off the kitchen. It was in need of repair, with the toilet seat broken and the faded pink paint peeling off the ceiling. It hurt to see Isha suffering so much. Yet in the midst of this she had offered me something to eat, the first time. Isha really cared about me; I realized that I better be careful or I'd get hooked on her. I didn't want to be devastated when she died. When I returned, she had a photograph of herself for me.

"Isha, I love it! Thank you!" Her eyes brightened and danced for a second while I studied it. It was a picture of her gazing upward in prayer that I had asked her for. She explained that a friend of hers had taken the photograph of her, but I didn't realize what she was actually doing in the picture until moments later she reenacted it in front of me.

When we had almost finished the tea and crackers, Eloise brought Isha her medicine, a bottle of morphine. With a syringe Eloise carefully transferred it to a glass until it measured about an inch in depth. Then she gave Isha a glass of water to take as a chaser. That is when I realized what she was doing in the picture. The HHA explained to me: "Isha prays before she does anything—before she eats, before she sleeps or takes medicine. She prays to God before she takes the medicine so that it will work. She doesn't believe it'll work unless God wants it to."

I watched Isha hold these two glasses up as though offering a sacrifice. Her eyes were looking at something or for something for a couple of minutes, a poignant image I took for begging or maybe just presenting to God what she was holding.

It seemed to me that Isha was also holding up her cancer, her pain, her plight, and that of her daughter and her people — for

God to see and respond however he saw fit. "Look if you want to, God," she seemed to say without a single word. "Look what is happening to this daughter of yours, this daughter of Africa, Isha. If you want to, you can heal me." I couldn't believe that God would not be moved.

I experienced something else during this visit. Our roles changed. The tea she offered me, the photograph and view of her praying, and the silence between our words made our interaction more mutual.

A little later when I said I was about to go, Isha initiated the prayer we had become accustomed to. With her hands outstretched and palms up, this time I placed mine on top of hers facing down. We stayed in this stance for about five minutes in complete silence. I looked up after a while like Isha and tried to let God just look at me. "Yes, God, if you want to you can heal me." All of this felt very peaceful.

"Your hands hot!" Isha said. Electricity seemed to pass between our palms. I felt it too, and we embraced before I stood to leave.

"Isha, I'm sorry I didn't call you last week."

"You come next week?"

"The week after," I promised.

She gave me a mysterious look as Eloise unlatched the door. After waving goodbye from the hallway, I hurried out to get to my next appointment on time.

At a team meeting later that week, Joanne presented a new case that called for pastoral care. "Frederick is a thirty-nine-year-old black man who has a malignant tumor on his abdomen. He lives with his mother, Doris, in Brooklyn now, but has moved back there only recently from his girlfriend's, where he has lived off and on for about twelve years." Joanne paused so we could get the picture.

"There are lots of problems," she continued, "alcohol abuse by the patient and family as well as his girl friend, Tina. They'll need a social worker for sure and pastoral care — they're Protestant. Oh, and yes," she added almost as an afterthought, "they want the doctor to visit."

Doc, who was engrossed in signing a pile of prescription requests, glanced up. Doc did make home visits, but the sheer number of patients made him farm out all but the most crucial cases to the nurses. "He complains of a weakness, a knot in his chest," Joanne explained.

The two of them discussed the medical points briefly until I broke in, "Who requested the pastoral care?"

"The patient's mother. She'll be home most of the day; just call ahead."

Doc began to look at a map. "That's a high crime area," he announced. "I wouldn't go in there without an armed guard." I thought he was kidding at first, but his face told me otherwise. Occasionally we did send a team member out to a particularly dangerous place with a guard for protection, but it seemed that Doc was being overly cautious. I enjoyed this chance for pastoral care to look more macho than medicine and looked over at Joanne for a lead.

"I could see him later this week," I offered.

"If you go in the morning, you'll be all right; the streets will be empty then." I couldn't tell what Doc was thinking; he just nodded.

Though it was barely 10:00 a.m., I felt apprehensive as I parked across the street from what seemed like the address. No identifying numbers were on the curb or doorway; I had just counted down from a building back on the corner. The rubble-strewn streets were deserted except for a man sitting on the steps of one of the few buildings where people could still be living. I had bought a new car recently and set the alarm system, which caused the man to look up. I crossed the deserted street as though I knew just where I was going.

The door was ajar. Some women and men were lounging on the inner stairway, appearing as though they had been drinking all night. I greeted them perfunctorily and squeezed by, but didn't feel secure. For all they knew my briefcase could be filled with needles and drugs.

At the top of a rickety staircase on the fourth floor, I rapped on the door and was greeted by a chunky, gray-haired woman. She eyed me suspiciously at first, and only after I had stated my business did she volunteer in a gravelly voice, "I'm Doris, Frederick's mother." In an overly polite manner she showed me into a darkened apartment where we stood aimlessly until I finally seated myself on a plastic-covered sofa. Doris sat across the room from me.

"Reverend, Frederick recently moved back home from his girl-friend Tina's. They've gone together for many years." She said this as though to reassure me. "But she can't care for him the way he needs now." I remembered from the nurse's comments that the family had a history of alcohol abuse and wondered what role this played in these decisions. As I removed my jacket and loosened my tie, Doris spoke with gradually increasing comfort about her Baptist religion and how it gives her strength. "Oh, yes, Reverend, if I didn't have my faith I couldn't go on the way things are."

From below us in the street came the sound of arguing voices. Suddenly I thought of my car out there, ripe for the picking. Glancing behind me to the window in the front room, I asked, "Doris, would you mind if I check to see if my car is still there?" She seemed helped by the fact that this need of mine was out in the open and warned, "Yes, the drug-dealing and prostitution that go on in this neighborhood, especially after dark...oh, they make it a bad place to live in." She searched my face to see whether I grouped her with this riff-raff and pulled back the tattered curtains.

"Oh, good, it's still there!" Immediately I felt embarrassed at my worldliness. This lady was baring her meager world to me, and with my vow of poverty all I could think of was how I might get ripped off while I was with her.

When we were seated again I asked if I could speak to her son. Doris seemed to resist my seeing him at first. "Frederick doesn't like to talk about his sickness."

"I just wanted to say a prayer for him," I said, thinking that wouldn't be a problem. She waited a moment and then led me down a dingy hallway into a tiny room where the patient was half sitting, half lying down on a small cot.

This room was their kitchen. With a small old-fashioned stove in a corner, a broken-up linoleum floor, and an old table with three chairs, it was a scene from Appalachia. Doris drew up one of the chairs for me near Frederick and stood back near the wall. "This is Reverend Paul, Frederick. He's come to visit you...and pray." Her voice tapered off.

My hand reached out. "Hello, Frederick..." I forced a smile. The man was enormous: about six-foot-three, with powerful shoulders and a neck thick like a boxer's. His hair was cut very close to the scalp. Clad only in faded pajama bottoms, his feet were like an elephant's. Frederick was the kind of man who would scare me into crossing to the opposite sidewalk if I saw him coming toward me, even on a brightly lit street. Yet out of this giant figure came a surprisingly soft voice.

"Because of the pain in my legs," he explained, "I've got to sit up like this for twenty-four hours a day."

"I'm sorry you are so sick."

"I don't like to talk about it," Frederick said while showing me a large, hard mass protruding from his abdomen. "A soft-tissue cancer, the doctors called it. It gets me depressed." I'll bet it does. It looked to me as if he had swallowed a Walkman.

Frederick shot a childlike glance at his mother as he spoke. Was this camouflage? It could make you forget the virile toughness of a street-wise dude who had learned survival in a New York City ghetto. According to the social worker, he had spent fifteen of his thirty-nine years in prison.

"Doc? . . . " he continued.

"I'm not the doctor. I'm a priest . . . a pastor. I am here to support you in your faith at this time, to say a prayer with you if that would be all right." Out of the corner of my eye I saw Doris nodding. I extended my hand. Frederick allowed me to take his big bear's paw almost as a child would, and I recited the Lord's Prayer, finishing it up the way Protestants do, " . . . for thine is the kingdom and the power and the glory, now and forever, Amen." Doris said it along with me.

"That helps a lot, Reverend," said Frederick. "Come anytime, y'hear?" Grinning because we had made a connection, I shook his hand goodbye.

At the doorway Doris and I gave each other a little awkward hug. "I'll give you a call in a week or so," I told her. She was watching from the window when I got into my car, and she waved as I pulled away.

Finding a bench under a shady tree in the Queens Botanical Gardens a little while later, I sank my teeth into the liverwurst sandwich my stomach was growling for. My eyes took in the old retired couples. Women with babies lolled on the benches among the gorgeous red and yellow roses in this well-kept part of town. It was strange to go back and forth between the varied economic zones in this huge metropolis, to see the different lifestyles.

Frederick was still on my mind. Something about him, something about men being reduced to powerlessness by this disease, was especially touching to me. Maybe it's because men are so identified with bodily strength, and because the childlike helplessness we show when we are physically weak seems greater than women's. Black men even more so. Although we emasculate them socially and economically, we hold their image in our psyches as the embodiment of masculine strength.

Despite this tension and the danger in places like Frederick's, I was glad to be going into poor homes where people had so little opportunity compared to me and my family. I was going to bring God to them, I thought. In a strange way that I couldn't put my finger on yet, I was discovering that God was there before me.

A few weeks later I phoned Frederick one evening to make an appointment. At the team meeting earlier in the day we had been told that he had moved back with his girlfriend, Tina. "I'm hurting, Reverend," he groaned when he picked up the phone. "I'm really hurting."

"I'm sorry, Frederick. . . . I'd like to come over and visit you tomorrow."

"I'm hurting so bad man, I feel like doing something to end it." His voice was slurred and morose. "End what? . . . What do you mean?"

"It wouldn't be the first time I tried."

"Frederick, are you thinking of doing something to yourself? . . . anything in particular?"

"Pills, I got plenty man."

"Will you wait until I come?"

"Yeah."

"Is anyone there with you now?"

"My girl, Tina. . . . I need to hang up now, Reverend."

"Frederick? . . ." The phone went dead.

Looking back on it now, I suppose I should have done something immediately, but I had become rather callous lately. It was almost nine o'clock at night and I was bushed. He said he'd wait till I came. I'd visit him in the morning. Pushing his threat out of my mind, I made some other calls and went to sleep early, asking God to take care of him for the night.

The next morning I arrived early at Tina's high-rise. According to the nurses it was a heavy-duty crack area. After circling the block for ten minutes to find a parking place, I was finally forced to settle for an illegal spot and take my chances that the trusty meter maid wouldn't find my car for the hour or so I would be with Frederick. A grocery store on the corner would be a place to get some lunch later. Two teenage boys sat on milk crates in front of it drinking beer.

The thirty-two-story project looked like all the others in New York City: unimaginative towering blocks of brick with small windows where people hung out for air or a view that might offer some hope, a courtyard below with a row of benches on which people rarely sat because of fear.

Kids on bikes and skateboards bombed in and out of scraggly trees that dared to survive in this concrete jungle. Even if the outside seemed calm enough, you knew the inside stairwells were scrawled with profanities. Danger lurked, not least for the residents, many of whom were trying to raise children as single parents. At the other end of the spectrum, some finished out their days in old age here, held captive by a handful of their own people who used the projects to sell dope. A quick death was the promised reward for anyone who would turn them in.

The elevator took a long time coming. When it finally lumbered open and I pressed the button for the fourteenth floor, I almost gagged because someone had recently urinated in it. When it opened upstairs, the long tiled corridors were deserted, and I walked swiftly, feeling my stomach tighten when I passed the darkened stairway. No name was on the door. I took a deep breath and knocked, hoping Frederick was still alive.

A young black man in his early twenties opened the door an inch. Clad in a T-shirt and jeans, he was barefoot. "I'm Father Paul. I'm here to see Frederick." He gazed at me intently and then gestured noncommittally for me to enter as he swung the door aside.

"He's back there," he pointed down a darkened hallway. He shut the door and bolted it, disappearing into a side room. Quickly taking in the sparse furnishings, I made my way down the narrow corridor to the room he had indicated. There in a straight-backed chair sat Frederick — *thank God!* — holding an oxygen mask to his face. In a hospital bed next to him lay a woman in street clothes. A window beyond her suffused the room with a gray light. The woman's arm covered her eyes and she didn't stir. On a dresser in the corner a TV spilled out a soap opera.

"Frederick! How are you?" I tried to act relaxed. Feebly he took my hand, removing the mask and moving as though to give me his chair; there were no others in the room. "No, I'll get another one."

"The kitchen..." he gasped. Frederick sounded depressed.

When I returned with the chair, I placed it alongside his and sat down facing him. He looked worse, a pair of shorty pajamas revealing his long bony legs. His face was almost ashen and his upper torso more emaciated, except for his abdomen which was visible through his open shirt. He could see himself in the mirror that faced him on the dressing table. An array of medicine bottles was lined up on it. "You don't look good, Frederick."

Immediately he opened up about his pain. Pulling the oxygen mask off and on as he spoke with difficulty, Frederick explained matter-of-factly that he had planned to take medicine to end his life the previous evening,..."...until you called."

"It hurts that bad?" I couldn't remember ever feeling so desperate myself.

"It's taking away my manhood!" He said this as though I should understand.

"What do you mean?"

Frederick described how the pain in his belly was so bad that he has been reduced to begging for his friends and his family, even his enemies, to take it away. A man begging, I thought, and begging for help to stop the pain from those he may once have treated arrogantly — that would be its own special hell.

Tina stirred in the bed next to him and looked up sleepily. A slightly built and youngish woman, she brushed aside her disheveled hair and I recognized a ravaged face I had seen before on ghetto-dwellers. "Oh, company...I didn't know."

"It's the Reverend from the hospice," Frederick informed her.

"Oh, hi." Rubbing her eyes, Tina excused herself and went into another room.

Frederick continued, "Sometimes the pain is so bad I can't help but cry." His bloodshot eyes pleaded with a mixture of fear and suffering.

Tina's sudden departure made me aware of the intimacy of the setting. Nervous, but moved by his plight, I told him, "Those are a man's tears, Frederick, and they are nothing to be ashamed of. Even Christ cried out in agony," I went on, searching for a way to help him accept what felt like weakness. "His tears and yours are strong... even beautiful." But my words felt stupid to me. They wouldn't take away his pain. Frederick pulled open his pajama top to show me the tumor again, his voice quivering as he recounted the relentless pain in his side. It was as if he were showing me some pet animal that had locked onto his body and was eating the life out of him.

I had an urge to reach out and hold this big brother who wouldn't look me in the eye, who seemed like a child in some strange way. If only I could relieve some of his pain, bear some of it myself, I would. "May I touch it? Pray over it?"

Frederick agreed, but first said he needed to take some medicine. Glancing toward the door through which Tina had disappeared, shakily he stood and made his way over to the dresser, took a swig from one of the bottles, and then returned to his seat. While I registered the possible medicine abuse, Frederick leaned forward with his hands on his knees, exposing his back. There I saw what looked like a small crater at the base of his spine.

Remembering the lessons the nurses had given us about "therapeutic touch," I tried to relax and let myself be completely present to Frederick and his pain. I asked God to use me as a channel for his healing power of love. Very gently I placed the fingers of my right hand on his tumor. Slowly I moved my hand back and forth, caressing it in my palm. I felt shy doing this, but good too. It brought the spiritual and physical dimensions of pastoral ministry together in a way that I loved. Earlier during morning prayer I had prayed to Jesus to be with me in this visit to his dark brother, to let the love energy that I feel as a celibate man come out through my touch.[6]

Closing my eyes, I asked God to let energy come through the touch to shrink the tumor if he wished. Gradually I allowed my hand to move across the width of Frederick's abdomen, stroking the depression on his spine with my other hand. Relaxing now, I ignored the question in my mind of how he might react and kept this up rhythmically for some minutes, letting God's love come through my hands. "Ooh, that feels so good," Frederick murmured, as though he sensed my need for feedback.

With ever-growing confidence I massaged his large bony shoulders, then his neck, even his head. All the while Frederick remained still, soaking in this touch with the greatest trust. When I had finished, I stood silently with my hands by my side. The room was filled with a presence. Frederick leaned back, a look of sweet contentment on his face. "Thanks, Reverend. I feel comfortable now."

"Frederick!" Excitedly I drew my chair around to face him. "It seems like you need to be touched more. Sometimes when people are sick or hurting, others shrink back from them just when they need it the most. You should ask people to touch you."

"Tina rubs my legs with ointment," he offered, looking me in the eye now. I glanced behind me through the door, wondering where she was, wondering what she would think about me praying over Frederick in such a physical way or about him chugging the medicine.

The mood changed and became almost folksy. Frederick began telling me stories of his life, his years in prison, which began when he was thirteen. "The scars on my back are from gunshot wounds years ago. There's still a piece of bullet in there they couldn't take out," he bragged. With that he climbed into the bed and propped himself up with pillows. "I have a son," he went on eagerly, "a twenty-one-year-old boy, Frederick, Jr. In two months he'll be getting married. And he even has a bank account," he added with pride.

"Is that the man who let me in this morning?"

"No, that's Tina's son." Frederick then described for me how he had been released from prison one time when his son was six years old.

"He was living with one of my girlfriends. One day when I was visiting her I saw him try to grab onto a truck as it was taking off at a red light. 'Come over here, boy!' I yelled to him. He gave me a nasty look, but came to me anyway. I whupped him on the head and told him, 'Never do that again or you're gonna get killed, y'hear?' Reverend, you know that kid badmouthed me! 'Who're you?' the little bastard said. 'I'll tell you who I am,' I shot back. 'I'm your father, that's who!' That boy almost pissed in his pants. But you know what we did that afternoon, Reverend? He and I made a deal. I told him that I would stay out of jail if he would stay off the trucks." With his rheumy eyes wide with the memory, Frederick concluded, "I haven't been back to jail since."

Frederick told me he feels retarded because he can't remember the words to the Lord's Prayer when he is alone. Laughing, I advised, "Just say it in your own words, like 'Father, help me!' or 'Lord, have mercy!' when you are feeling the pain." I hadn't addressed the suicide threat directly yet; I'm not sure why. I guess I felt that if Frederick really wanted to take his life, I couldn't or wouldn't stop him. Maybe I sensed that our interaction might be the best invitation to live.[7]

"You couldn't have called me at a better time last night," Frederick said at one point. "I been so frustrated with this cancer."

"Yeah, I'm sorry."

"You really connect with what I feel like," he said. As I looked at his exhausted face, Frederick seemed like an old man to me. We could have gone on talking for hours, for he was surprisingly talkative despite the pain. I was making signs to go when he offered me some of his nutritive drink from the refrigerator. "It's good real cold, and the vanilla is better than the chocolate," he confided as though he were selling me an ice cream soda. I went to get us both one.

Sitting in this drab high-rise, sharing a can of vanilla Ensure with this former inmate whose gunshot wounds I had just massaged, listening to him brag about the scraps of excitement and success in his life while cancer wracked him with pain, I felt strangely happy. A sense of peace arose in me, a hope even that the black and white antagonism in our city could be overcome and that when we are dying it isn't really important what we have achieved in life so much as what we have accomplished against the odds we've been given. It couldn't have been better at the Waldorf Astoria!

"Call me Sparky," Frederick said, finishing his drink with a smack of his lips. "Uncle Sparky, that's what everyone calls me."

"Uncle Sparky! Okay." I could have kissed him. Some moments of silence passed. "I think I'll go now so you can rest."

"Okay, but come back again, will you?" he said through puffy lips.

"In two weeks . . . " I was thinking of the list of patients I had yet to see. "But I won't be able to see you at all if you take an overdose."

"Don't worry, I'm okay now." As we shook hands goodbye, I made a mental note to tell Joanne about the suicide talk and Sparky's use of medicine and at the next team meeting to agree on a plan to deal with the situation.

Tina was not in the other room, so I let myself out, noticing a faded picture of the Last Supper on the kitchen wall. Would I see Sparky again? I wasn't sure, but I did feel the presence of God in that apartment. I felt it, in the midst of crack dens and welfare families, in a neighborhood where one could be as easily shot as asked for directions. I felt it in Sparky's handshake, in his willingness to have a white man caress the painful tumors that had reduced him to crying like a baby, and in my own letting go of fears long enough to love for a morning in Brooklyn.

Within the next two weeks it was decided that Sparky would be transferred to St. Rose's, a nursing home for indigent terminally ill people run by nuns in lower Manhattan. Supposedly this was Sparky's wish, but we heard that Tina was furious. In the courtyard of the project a few days before she had yelled at Joanne, "You ain't taking my man nowhere!"

When Joanne, whose husband is a former New York City cop, had reenacted this encounter at the team meeting, we had all roared; but we heard Tina's feelings too and wanted to help her. An ambulance would be transferring Sparky, and there might be some trouble, so Joanne and I agreed to meet that morning at Tina's apartment to assist.

Joanne and I met at the corner grocery store and rode up the elevator together. Tina let us in. She was cool to us, but evidently dealing with the transfer. "She cried all night," Sparky informed us when she left the room for a moment. In his jeans and a flannel shirt with his boots unzipped, he looked uncomfortable. A denim jacket was draped over his shoulders. All his belongings were stuffed in two shopping bags by the bedroom door. Since he was agitated, Joanne gave him a dose of morphine to calm him down just as the ambulance crew was phoning from the lobby. "I don't think I'm going to like this place I'm going," he said to me in an aside. When I asked why not, he didn't elaborate.

With difficulty the two husky Hispanic ambulance attendants got Sparky strapped onto the stretcher; all the while he was moaning. Just as they were about to wheel him out the door, the phone rang. All of us waited as this hulk of a man spoke like a child to his mother before he left home, probably for the last time. "Yeah, Mom, I'll be okay...will you come see me?" She had better hurry, I thought when he hung up.

There was room on the elevator only for the stretcher crew and Sparky, so Joanne, Tina, and I walked down the fire stairwell. On the eighth floor, Tina cut off to see a friend. They already had him in the ambulance when we got down to the street. Gloomily he peered out from the shadows while the attendants jotted on their charts. "It's going to be a nice place, Sparky," Joanne assured him. "Just try to relax. I'll be in to see you later this week." Sparky just gaped at her with his bulging eyes.

I climbed into the back of the ambulance and sat down next to him. "Hey, man, remember this," I said. "You'll never lose your manhood as long as you've got your soul." He took my hand limply. Joanne slid the bags of his belongings under the stretcher.

Tina arrived sporting dark glasses, with alcohol evident on her breath. Joanne helped her in so that she could ride beside Sparky for the trip. We needed to check in on her too now that her man was gone.

The heavy doors were slammed shut and the ambulance headed out to pierce through the traffic, its hysterical sirens wailing out the chaos inside it. Joanne and I looked at each other, little grins of solidarity on our faces. Seeing a patient together, we agreed, was something we should do more often. It didn't feel half so bad when someone shared these goodbyes with you.

Thirteen days later Sparky died of pneumonia at St. Rose's. I felt very bad. In the short time I had known him I had grown fond of him and had a visit planned for the next day. It seemed we had only set the groundwork for him to really communicate about his relationship with God. Death, I kept discovering, doesn't always wait until everything is tied up neatly.

When I phoned Doris to offer my condolences, she invited me to the funeral. Normally I would not go to the patients' funeral services — there are too many! There was something special about Sparky though. Since I had missed seeing him when I had promised to and needed some closure myself, I agreed to go with Joanne. And I was curious about how Baptists celebrate a funeral.

About fifty people were at the Bell Funeral Home on Classon Avenue when we arrived shortly before 10:00 a.m. Milling around on the sunny sidewalk, talking together in small groups, they were dressed up as though it were Easter. We didn't recognize anyone.

"Reverend Paul!" Doris's low voice called out. Dressed in a chocolate-colored lace dress and matching coat with a big brown hat, Doris kissed me when I went up to embrace her. She was genuinely glad to see us. We made small talk until a distinguished gray-haired gentleman came out of the building and announced that the service was ready to begin. We all filed under the canopy and through the doorway, Joanne and I waiting until last. Tina was nowhere to be seen.

Inside what I thought was only a business establishment I was surprised to find a chapel, complete with stained-glass windows depicting biblical scenes. Adorning the vestibule were large portraits of black people, Martin Luther King, Malcolm X — all men except one of Sojourner Truth.

Up in front was the open coffin surrounded by flowers. Behind it at an organ on a pedestal, facing us, sat a man in a black suit with dark glasses who looked like Ray Charles. While we found seats in the folding chairs that were arranged in tight rows, he began to rock back and forth while he nursed a melancholy hymn out of the electric organ.

To me it sounded like soap opera music. But then the man began to sing. "Mmm, Mmmmm, Da da da da dahhhh...." Gradually he built up volume... "Dooweeeeeee, bah, bah, bah, BAHHHH!!!" Soon a full-throated Gospel-blues was rising: "Lawdeeeee! deeelivah yo chillunn!... can't yo see dat der SPIR-RRIIIIIT!... is dyin' to be freeeeeee...yeaaaah!" He breathed this ending onto us like a challenge. As though he had plucked a communal heart-chord, handkerchiefs and sniffles began to appear in the congregation.

I felt jealous at the way black people were able to combine their pain and their faith so powerfully. My own Irish ancestors had suffered deeply too. We bragged about it in all the tear-jerking ballads sung in Irish pubs throughout the world. Yet somehow we had not learned to join this pain with our faith.

It is as if to us God were some kind of disembodied being who expects us to jump across our pain to the place where faith in him truly dwells — the realm of the Spirit, a Spirit we had grown up to believe was far from the drinking, dancing, fighting, and baby-making Irish bodies!

Sure, the Irish and other Europeans glorify Jesus' suffering. In Roman Catholic churches, in America at least, we sing "O Sacred Head Surrounded by Crown of Piercing Thorn" as if it were our national anthem. Yet our suffering, our desire for love and justice, are borne stoically as though the risen Jesus could read our minds.

I never hear us wailing and rocking out our needs to God in church. Faithfully we go there to celebrate the Body and Blood of Jesus but leave our own bodies at home. This is "soul" to us while the opposite is "soul" to black people. No wonder most of them have never found a home in my church; and no wonder they attract me. They stir up this lost part of me. Their suffering seems to break them out of their powerlessness, at least when they express it in their faith. To be whole, I needed to touch and be touched by this energy.

"Joanne," I whispered in one of the back rows where we were seated, "this is how I want my funeral celebrated." She gave me a knowing look.

The funeral director stood solemnly at the lectern until the hymn was completed. All were caught up in the spirit — the men in their suits; the women with their big hats; Doris and the family up front; old and young folks; children, even a baby carried by someone. Joanne and I were the only white people.

It was then that I noticed Sparky's girlfriend, Tina, in the row across from us. Standing by herself, she was sobbing into a handkerchief. I tried to catch her attention but she was oblivious. Up front a woman minister began to proclaim a passage from the Gospel with great animation.

While Jesus was at Bethany in the house of Simon the leper, a woman carrying a jar of costly perfume came up to him at table and began to pour it on his head. When the disciples saw this, they grew indignant, protesting, "What is the point of such extravagance? This could have been sold for a good price and the money given to the poor." Jesus became aware of this and said to them, "Why do you criticize the woman? It is a good deed she has done for me. The poor you will always have with you, but you will not always have me. By pouring this perfume on my body, she has contributed to my burial preparation. I assure you, wherever the good news is proclaimed throughout the world, what she did will be spoken of as her memorial." (Matt. 26:6–13)

"Amen, sister! Amen!" the people responded. Another minister then recited a prayer in a dramatic fashion followed by another hymn. This one Joanne and I knew and we sang along. When we were seated again the minister spoke about Sparky: when and where he had been born, his parents and brothers and sisters, his aunts and uncles in Alabama, the school in Brooklyn he had gone to, and when and where he had been baptized. He spoke with increasing emotion about Sparky's long illness and his suffering in recent years. When he mentioned the efforts of his mother, in particular, to care for him at home and how her son had appreciated this, people next to Doris leaned and spoke to her.

"Yes, this is the ointment of love of which the evangelist speaks," he said with a tremor in his voice. "This is the good works the Lord Jesus promised will never be forgotten." Murmurs and nods of approval came from the congregation.

"Tell it, brother!" a man behind us called out.

Buoyed by the people's response, the minister continued. "Oh, yes, some would say you are a fool to expend the ointment of human kindness, that it is a waste of time and money to care for those who cannot be cured, that you should think about yourself and the living instead. But we know that's a lie!"

"Yes, Lord!" "That's right!"

"Sisters and brothers, you know and I *know* . . . " — his voice reached a crescendo and he did a little dip with his knees — "that the same people who offer this advice don't, no they don't care one *hoot* about the poor. No, sir, they just want the money for themselves!" He flicked a sideways glance at the funeral director, who was twirling his fingers nervously. The minister paused. He had us in his palm now.

"Frederick Jackson will not forget the love you gave him in his darkest hour." Tina was facing forward but seemed lost in thought. "The precious ointment of your care will be remembered always. By Frederick your beloved son, yes! *and* by the Lord and Redeemer in whom he believed; Jesus is the one in whom you can trust!" He was pounding on the lectern.

"Yes, Lord!" A lady's voice rose from the crowd.

"Jesus is the one who will not forget you!"

"Amen, brother!"

"Jesus is the one who will bring us justice!" His hands shot toward the ceiling in a victory sign.

"HALLELUJAH!" The minister was bowing now, beads of sweat gleaming on his bald head. "You tell it, Reverend... amen, Lord." The little flock helped him down from his ecstatic height.

"God bless you!" He bowed and took his seat.

I wasn't prepared for what happened next. The funeral director was at the podium. "There is with us today," he intoned, "a friend of the Jackson family, a Reverend who was with Frederick during the last weeks of his life." He made a gesture toward me and heads swiveled. "Reverend, would you be so kind as to say a word?" Nervously I gave a wave of my hand and then clumsily climbed over the people in our row and went up to the lectern.

In a daze, I searched for a few words. "It's a blessing to have known Frederick, and as a Catholic to be able to be here this morning to pray with you...." The heads nodded. Dark heads, dark faces like Sparky's, including one tall, strapping man in the front row who could be Frederick, Jr. What else could you say?

It struck me that the minister had skipped from the beginning of Sparky's life to the end, as though the middle was too painful or disastrous to mention. I stole a look at the coffin. So strange to see Sparky all dressed up in a suit and tie! A memory of a morning with Sparky flooded through me and words came up from another place.

" 'Call me Sparky,' he told me one day. 'That's what everyone calls me... Uncle Sparky!' " The congregation murmured.

"All right, Uncle Sparky," I looked over at his body surrounded with flowers, "that's what we'll do." The young man who looked like his son smiled. Doris leaned over and said something to a lady next to her.

"I don't know if he ever told you this," I began slowly, "but Sparky shared a marvelous story with me one day while he was lying in bed, barely able to speak through an oxygen mask."

Gaining courage from their faces — Tina had removed her sunglasses — I continued. "Yeah, he was telling me about his whole life... including all the years he spent in jail." The silence was intense.

"Sparky said he got out of jail one day and went to his girlfriend's house. There he saw his son who was six years old. The kid was trying to hop onto the back of a truck for a ride. 'I whupped him,' Sparky told me, 'warned him not to do it again'" A look of recognition began to stir on Frederick, Jr.'s, shiny face.

"'Who're you?' the boy yelled back. 'I'll tell you who I am,' said Sparky. 'I'm your father!' He thought that would end the argument. 'Oh, yeah?' answered the kid, 'I don't even know you!'" The congregation turned wide-eyed toward one another. Frederick, Jr., wiped the corner of his eye. There was no way I could stop now.

"So do you know what Sparky said?" I paused for effect. "'Look, I'll make you a deal, son. You stay off the trucks and I'll stay out of jail. We made that agreement,' Sparky told me with a great deal of pride, 'and you know what, Doc?' — sometimes he called me 'Doc' — 'I never went back to jail since that day.'" Frederick, Jr., was beaming. Tina nodded.

"Amen, Brother!" someone shouted. Another, "Praise the Lord!"

"Yes," I continued, feeling looser now, "Sparky was so proud of his son. He saw him doing things he never had the chance to. That's what will live on in his memory. And those of you who stuck by him at the end, who anointed his feet with your care," I glanced down at Tina, "these are the things that will rise to the Lord as a pleasing fragrance, a prayer of forgiveness and mercy for Frederick Jackson."

I was about to sit down when one more thought tumbled out. Seeing Joanne in the back, aware of the black faces around me, and remembering the neighborhood we were in, I said, "One thing that I am grateful for especially. Getting to know Sparky and Doris, and feeling their acceptance and love, has helped me to be healed from some of the racism I have in me. It's enabled me to believe and hope that black and white people in this city can begin to see our common humanity and live together in peace.... Thank you for this, Sparky. May you rest in peace."

When I took my seat they were applauding. Joanne squeezed my hand.

While the minister recited a closing prayer, Tina reached out a hand to Joanne before she hurried down the aisle and disappeared into the foyer. A recessional hymn began. The congregation rose to pay their last respects to Sparky. All of them, children included, filed slowly past the coffin, gazing down at a son, a father, a lover, a street-buddy, friend, or neighbor, maybe even an enemy. The organist laid back his head and poured out their Gospel faith with passion:

> Precious Lord, take my hand,
> Lead me on, let me stand,
> I am tired, I am weak, I am worn ...
> Through the storm, through the night,
> Lead me on to the light,
> Take my hand, precious Lord, lead me home ...
>
> When my way grows drear,
> Precious Lord, linger near,
> When my life is almost gone ...
> Hear my cry, hear my call,
> Hold my hand, lest I fall,
> Take my hand, precious Lord, lead me home ..

~ Dominic ~

DURING THE PREVIOUS SIX MONTHS, Natalie's husband, Dominic, had continued his histrionic behavior over her illness. Somewhere between his sardonic humor and his raging at a God, whom he believed could end his wife's illness whenever he wished, he showed flashes of real grief. All of this he expressed to the visitors, including myself, though not to his wife, whom he continued to relate to as though she were temporarily sick. Dominic expressed surprise when I told him one day that Natalie had spoken about her dying. It seemed that this denial on his part was for him, not her, even though he described it as a way not to trouble her.

One day Dominic spoke of suicide to me, though he quickly brushed this threat off: "But I gave away my gun, and I'm afraid of heights!" I didn't believe that Dominic really was considering suicide, yet given his history, which he recounted in the same conversation, it was not completely farfetched. His own father had hung himself as Dominic's mother lay dying of cancer when he was eight years old. After she died a short time later, Dominic was raised in an orphanage. Only recently had his sister told him how his father died.

Because of Dominic's almost childish ways of expressing his feelings to the team, we ultimately had confidence in him. Sure, we joked about his crazy comments and actions, but unlike really depressed people, Dominic got his feelings out; he didn't let them fester and eat away his spirit. "If tragedy strikes me," I told the team one day, "I hope I can let my feelings out with as much abandon as Dominic does."

The first time I had visited him and Natalie, he remarked to

108

me as I was leaving, "Y'know, Faddah Paul, all this suffering has changed me. I'm no longer such a shallow guy."

Joanne said she had told him, "Remember you've got yourself to live for when Natalie dies." Dominic was as much our patient as Natalie was.

He also had problems with Natalie's family; she had a daughter in her twenties and an older sister. Natalie's mother had died only in the past year; her father years before. The family members would visit her unannounced and only very briefly. Dominic would make caustic remarks about the Jewish faith. For example, he said that the family's claim that the Jewish religion emphasizes life more than death was why they were ignoring Natalie now that she was no longer vivacious.

"Are you sure that's what they mean?" I asked him. I didn't know, but I could see how the family might look at this gruff Italian as a recent intruder into their family and not care much for having to go through him and his moods to see their mother and sister.

In the middle of one of these tirades at the end of a visit, Dominic broke down and cried as he described how Natalie was slipping. "She was the most beautiful woman you ever saw. When she entered a room, an energy came with her; everyone noticed. And now she can barely talk, barely recognizes me." I placed my hand on his. Yes, Dominic, let the more vulnerable feelings out, the ones that the anger is hiding.

When he had finished crying, Dominic brought me in to see Natalie. He left us alone. She was awake and sitting up, aware of me, I thought. With her hand she grasped mine tightly but otherwise was noncommunicative. We sat there a while like that; I looked at her occasionally, while she stared straight ahead at the large blank TV screen that stood out against the peach-colored wallpaper. The blue ring, I noticed, was pressed even tighter against her swollen finger.

Now and then Natalie would lay her head back on her pillow and hum or croon a lullaby to herself. I didn't know whether the tumor had spread to her brain in a way that made verbalization impossible or whether she grasped anymore what was actually going on. When I asked if I could pray, she nodded yes. I reminded her of God's promise to be with us through anything. Natalie just lay there expressionless.

Then I called Dominic back into the room and we anointed
Natalie with oil; I had told them it was both a Jewish and Christian tradition. Lovingly, Dominic rubbed the oil on her face with
both hands, and she seemed to relish this. Though tears glis-
tened in his eyes, Dominic purred, "Hey, Baby, y'know your hair
is growing back? . . . It's a blond crew cut!" Natalie made kissing
gestures and sounds to him.

It was difficult to know from such interactions what was
really going on inside Natalie and between them. When Dominic told me on the way out that she had bitten his finger
recently and drawn blood, I encouraged him to use moments
like that to invite her to voice her feelings about what was
happening. "Don't wait until it's too late."

The next time I visited, Dominic wasn't there. Instead a
friend of Natalie's let me in, a beautifully coiffed blonde in her
late thirties with perfect make-up and long pink fingernails. Her
lipstick was moist, as though just applied. In tailored white
slacks and a matching sweater, she was a knock-out. Cissie,
from Long Island.

"Hi, Natalie!" I said cheerily when we entered her bedroom,
but this day she was even less communicative. With Cissie
seated in a chair next to her watching me inquisitively, I read
a passage from the Gospel of John:

> I am the good shepherd: the good shepherd lays down his
>   life for the sheep. . . .
> The Father loves me for this: that I lay down my life to take
>   it up again.
> No one takes it from me; I lay it down freely.
> I have power to lay it down, and I have power to take it up
>   again.
>
> —John 10:11, 17–18

I thought of Natalie and her dynamic personality so at home
in the fast-paced world of New York, her sense of freedom and
accomplishment, her circle of glamorous friends. "It must be so
hard on you," I said to her at one point. A frown appeared on
her face. Dominic arrived and gave her a smooch. As we left the
room, I promised Natalie I'd see her again in two weeks. I kissed
her on the cheek.

In the living room, Cissie, Dominic, and I got into an involved conversation over belief in God in light of suffering such as Natalie's. "I don't know if I believe in God anymore," said Dominic. "I think he's a jerk." Cissie seemed interested in the Gospel passage, what it meant about someone freely laying down one's life.

"I don't know exactly," I offered, "but I've always liked those words of Jesus. They make me feel like he wasn't just some doormat... 'I lay my life down of my own free will.' "

"Yeah, but he had a choice!" Dominic protested. "We don't."

"Maybe it's an attitude," said Cissie, her elegant fingers accentuating her words. I liked that idea.

"Yeah, Christians are supposed to sacrifice for instance. We feel guilty if someone suggests we are doing anything for ourselves. But if it's an attitude rather than something we have to do...." Dominic jumped in on another tangent about how God is supposed to be all-powerful.

"Remember Natalie's words?" I said, " 'Pray that I understand before I die.' "

"Yeah," said Dominic out of the side of his mouth, "he better hurry."

I kept feeling more at home with this family and hoped I could be there for them when Natalie died. When I left ten minutes later, I gave Dominic a carnation that I had brought for Natalie. With their coaxing, I took some Italian pastry, which Cissie wrapped up as a gift.

Natalie continued to deteriorate in the following weeks, less and less aware of the team members' presence — in large part because of the drugs she was taking. Once she snored as I sang "Whatever Will Be Will Be." Joanne reported that Dominic was trying to lose weight and remained cynical about God. One afternoon he phoned the office and asked if I would like to come over the next morning for breakfast with them.

"Breakfast!... How early?"

"Eight, nine o'clock?"

"Eight."

"It's a deal."

The next day began with a bright Manhattan morning. The seagulls squawking overhead reminded me that all of this commotion, these millions of people coming and going with such intensity, was all happening on a little island at the edge of the Atlantic Ocean. I liked to think of that when things got too busy, to throw my head back and see if I could smell the salt air.

With a honeydew melon tucked under my arm I headed to Dominic and Natalie's. It felt good to be drawn into a meal with these folks, though I was a little squeamish over how it would be with Natalie trying to eat. I took the subway down to Eighty-sixth Street and made it to their place in less than an hour. When I arrived, Dominic was in the midst of trying to maneuver the hospital chair through the bedroom door. "Hey, you're just in time, Father Paul!"

He wanted to have Natalie join us in the living room for the meal. When he finally got the chair out by the kitchen table, he went back into the bedroom and emerged with Natalie in his arms — holding his wife's swollen body chest to chest with his as he would to dance, her thick legs dangling out of her nightgown to the floor. Natalie was barely awake, lolling her head to the side in the drugged state she had been in for the past two months. Dominic plopped her in the chair.

With the air of one at a holiday cookout, Dominic proceeded to cook bacon and eggs for the three of us — plus a portion for the toy poodle! — while Natalie dozed in the chair. We talked about many things, but not about Natalie. He had recently admonished me again not to use the word "hospice" in her presence.

Dominic spoke his usual lovey talk to her as though she were fully alert: "How ya doin', Baby? . . . Father Paul is here to see you. . . . You want a wrap on your neck?"

Natalie, whom Dominic had urged me to turn so she was facing the window — "So she can see the world out there" — didn't respond, except by an amazing appetite. Dominic fed her huge portions of scrambled eggs, bacon, honeydew, orange juice, toasted baby bagels with strawberry jam along with freshly brewed coffee. "It's unbelievable how much she can eat!" I exclaimed, forgetting how her medicine caused this voracious hunger.

At one point he asked if I wanted to feed her, and I did, chuckling at the memory of how I used to feed my little brothers and sisters in their high chairs . . . "One for you and one for me!"

By nine o'clock I had to leave for a meeting at the office. "Relax! relax!" Dominic urged, but I insisted. On a cue from him, Natalie made pursed lips to kiss me when I said goodbye. It occurred to me that there was something both eerie and holy about us eating a meal together. My normal role was becoming blurred. I was becoming more like a friend with them than a pastor. This could be a help as well as a hindrance. They both might be playing a denial game, and I could be playing into it. Dominic could really crash! Yet God seemed near, perhaps in the juxtaposition of death (Natalie's near "vegetable" state) and life (we had just partaken of a delicious meal). Real Jewish, it seemed. It had a quality, I thought later, of a "Last Meal." I saw them only one more time while she was alive.

Dominic telephoned me at the office one morning at the beginning of April. He had a scared note in his voice, saying it was possible his wife had pneumonia. He wanted me to make a visit. I said I could see him in an hour and found out from the office before I left that Joanne had left earlier to see them with a plan to have a suction machine delivered that day.

When the Home Health Aid opened the door to the apartment, I could see Dominic was very distraught, pacing up and down in the hallway. He greeted me with a warm handshake and then alternately wept or raged at his wife's condition. "If there is a God, I hate him!" he spit out with fury. "He could stop this at a wish. Why create such misery . . . humans who can die?" I took him into the living room and we sat down.

Experiencing tremendous frustration at his inability to do anything to help his wife, Dominic likened it to standing on the shore and listening to Natalie cry, "Save me!" "All I can answer is, 'Baby, I can't swim!'" His pain and its convoluted expression was palpable when he added a few moments later, "Once, early on in her illness when she was acting out, I . . . I wished . . . she'd get hit by a car and die."

Dominic was glum-faced and sunk into the chair as he confessed this. Remembering how a friend had reassured me once when I had a similar feeling about my mother, I told him in a firm voice, "You aren't causing her death, Dominic; God doesn't act on such fleeting feelings of ours."

I spent some time with Natalie alone, stroking her arm and, though she seemed to be in a coma, talking to her about her ancestors, her great successes in life, and her husband's love for her. Later Dominic showed me a clearer reason for his guilt: he needed to make a decision about discontinuing her medicine because it was the cause of her gaining so much weight. If he did, the brain tumor could go unchecked and thus cause Natalie's death more quickly. His sister, Gina, had arrived and volunteered that if it were her decision she'd discontinue the medicine as their doctor had suggested.

"I'm wavering," said Dominic, appearing to want someone else to help him.

"Why don't you wait and talk with Joanne about it," I suggested. "She'll be here shortly." We sat in silence for some moments, all of us taking in the words that had been spoken, thinking of Natalie. Outside we could hear an airplane passing overhead, maybe people going off to some balmy spot for a vacation. The dog stood up on its hind legs, looked over the top of its pen in the corner, and whined.

"I had to cut the ring off." Dominic was talking. "It was so tight it was hurting her, so last night I cut it off with a pair of pliers." There was nothing to say. The three of us just sat there. When I made a move to leave, Dominic got up to get my coat.

"Thanks, Father Paul," said Gina.

"Anytime . . ."

"Can I ask you a favor?" Dominic asked. "Would you say something at Nattie's funeral?" His face was close to mine, eyes tired but wide and pleading, like the animals my brother and I would come upon caught in the traps we had set in the woods when we were small. His request caught me by surprise, and I shook my head affirmatively.

"I'd be honored to, but I better give you my home phone number just in case . . . call me there anytime if you need me."

"Thanks." He took the card, and I reached up to hug this bear of a man goodbye.

Outside on Broadway as I waited at the traffic light, I thought of Dominic cutting the ring off, of what that would mean to the two of them, of what he might have said to her in her coma. I thought of his words, so simple and yet so forthright, about her funeral.

Such moments are so gripping — to make decisions that at last acknowledge the reality of a mate's impending death, to speak words held off against all odds, as though even to think them would be a betrayal, to give in at last to death or to God, who has been waiting like an enemy just outside your walls to rush through such a weakness and destroy forever the one you love. And destroy you in the process.

" . . . Till death do us part," spouses promise. But then what? When one of them dies, the other may feel abandoned or guilty afterward, depending on who let go first. And should you let yourself love again? Can anyone take your beloved's place? Love doesn't die, does it, just because one of the partners has to let go?

The light turned green and I let myself flow with the afternoon crowd through the traffic.

> Let me not to the marriage of true minds admit impediments.
> Love is not love which alters when it alteration finds, or bends with the remover to remove.
> Oh, no! It is an ever-fixed mark, that looks on tempests and is never shaken.
> It is the star to every wandering bark, whose worth's unknown, although his height be taken.
> Love's not Time's fool, though rosy lips and cheeks within his bending sickle's compass come.
> Love alters not with his brief hours and weeks, but bears it out even to the edge of doom.
> If this be error and upon me proved, I never writ, nor no man ever loved.
>
> —William Shakespeare, Sonnet 116

~

By the time I got home hours later, I felt very restless. It was Friday night, what used to be party night. After dinner one of my religious brothers came to the door of my room and noticed me stalking around. "What's up?"

"I feel like I'm going to explode."

"Go out!" he advised.

He was busy. I preferred not to go out alone, but I changed into some jeans and a big sweater anyway and grabbed a subway downtown around nine o'clock. I knew I would have some adventures there, even if it was just to be distracted by the array of people wandering among the vendors of second-hand goods for sale on the sidewalk at Astor Place.

After listening to some street musicians on Seventh Avenue, I turned into St. Mark's Place, where the shops are open late. I bartered with a man selling old comic books until he parted with a Conan the Barbarian for two dollars, a gift for Elmo the next time I saw him.

Feeling the pressures of the day subsiding by the time I reached Greenwich Village, I turned back in the direction of the subway, letting the splendid displays of flowers, fruits, and vegetables in front of the all-night delis catch my eye. A twinge of jealousy hit me as I passed a young couple arm in arm, laughing at some private joke. When I got to Bleecker Street I noticed the tempo picking up; the night was barely beginning for most people down in this part of town, even though it was after eleven o'clock. The sound of a piano interlaced with voices singing a show tune drifted through a pub window. I considered going in, but headed for the subway instead.

A half hour later at Union Station I took my seat in a deserted car of the subway back to the Bronx. A black man about thirty years old was sitting across from me. He was clumsily counting coins he had poured out of an old cardboard coffee cup. I pulled out my comic to read.

When the train jerked around a curve, one of his coins dropped and rolled across the aisle, plunking to a stop by my foot. The man got up to retrieve it. Glancing down, I could see his hand on it and remarked, "Damn! I'd have had that penny if you hadn't found it!"

Caught by surprise at first, his cloudy eyes rolled, and then he laughed. He returned to his seat and he began conversing with me, mumbling among other things that I looked like a professor. I pulled my glasses down the bridge of my nose another notch; ostentatiously I spread open the comic I was reading so he could see the barbarian on the cover.

"Ha! Ha! Ha!" Another guffaw burst out from him, yet all the while he meticulously counted his coins.

"What's your name?"

"Dwayne."

"Mine's Paul." We reached across the aisle, shook hands, and then went back to what we were doing. Peering over the top of my comic a few stops later, I asked him where he lived.

"I been homeless for three months, but I'm doin' all right. . . . I sleep in the subways." I noticed his tattered jeans, and his beat-up sneakers untied. As I mulled over whether to give him some money, the train screeched to a halt at the 125th Street Station in Harlem. Suddenly Dwayne stood up to get off.

" . . . But there's one thing they can't take away from me," he called across the aisle as he scooped the coins into his cup, "my faith."

Surprised, I nodded in agreement.

"My man upstairs," he motioned with his gloved hand as he moved toward the door, his broken teeth flashing. "Yeah, I got faith in him." He said this very surely and then shuffled out onto the platform. The doors slammed shut and the train lurched forward. I turned to watch Dwayne searching for a bench to sleep on with his faith, wishing I had not thought so much about giving him some change.

How can Dwayne show such unashamed belief in God in the midst of such vivid loss? Maybe it's because of it. I was glad to be getting a glimpse into his world. Maybe his faith could teach me something.

—

"Your mother has had a massive brain hemorrhage," the doctor announced to my two sisters and me in the waiting room. "we have to operate."

Just a few hours before I had gotten the phone call from Sally. Her panicked words still ricocheted in me like a gunshot: "Paul! They found Mama unconscious on the floor of the hospital! They've got her in intensive care now! Her left side is paralyzed! She's in a coma! . . . "

It had been barely ten days before that she had gone in for observation because of incessant headaches. Most of the family had been in to see her since. It was so uncharacteristic for Mama to be the one being taken care of. Daddy and I had laughed aloud when she told us how she had reprimanded the others in her ward for leaving their dirty dishes in the sink. The last memory I have of her from that time was of her exhaling from a cigarette in her funny way as she remarked ruefully, "Imagine! Nora Morrissey in a psychiatric ward!"

It was almost midnight when I got to the hospital, joined there by two of my sisters. With a trembling hand I had signed the required release form for the craniotomy as if it were her death warrant. We stopped the nurses as they rushed by us with her on a stretcher toward the elevators. "Wait! That's our mother! We want to say a prayer!"

Kneeling down in the corridor with Maura and Sally to bless her, we watched Mama breathe in and out like a steam engine fighting to get up a hill. Her silver hair flying, a slash of red lipstick on her unconscious face, they rushed on with their possession. "God be with you!" I yelled toward the doctor.

Hours later when we heard the click of footsteps coming toward us as we lay curled in fetal positions on the waiting room chairs, we dragged ourselves out of the stupor of our dreams to see the operating team in their green pajamas peer over the artificial flowers. The brain surgeon announced: "The operation is over. The tumor has been removed. We will not know for seventy-two hours whether it is malignant or not. Your mother is resting now upstairs in Room 672. You may see her if you wish but she is still unconscious." The row of tired eyes stared at us. "Call me each morning for a progress check," the doctor added. He smiled grimly. They turned and left.

She's still alive! We looked at each other, so grateful for this reprieve.

The sixth floor was quiet and only partly lit at the early hour. As the elevator door crashed closed behind us, the polished floor stretched forlornly to the nurses' station, which brightened the far end of the corridor like a bus stop. Passing by the various rooms, we arrived at 672 and looked in. They must have gotten the room numbers wrong because someone else was there. We went down to the nurses' station to check. They assured us that Mama was indeed in 672. As we retraced our steps, the mixture of hope and dread in our hearts told us that from now on our lives would be different.

With the dawn light streaming in eerily like a thief, the three of us clutched each other as we approached the small figure wrapped in a sheet. Her puffy, tube-filled face was swathed in bandages, her bed surrounded by machines — beeping monitors, feeding tubes, a respirator mechanically wheezing air into her lungs. *Oh, Mamacita, you never knew what hit you!*

"That's not Mama!" Maura cried, bolting from the room. Sally and I ran quickly after her. Sobbing and storming about in the hallway, Maura shook her large mop of dark hair violently and protested, "There's no way they're going to make me believe that's Mama. . . . It's just a vegetable."

What horrible words to hear or even think about someone, but to hear your youngest sister crying them out about your mother, the source of her life and yours, is enough to smash your faith, all dreams of immortality. Sally and I, weeping and aghast at the sight ourselves, tried to comfort her, but in vain. There was no way. Maura stayed outside while we went back into the room.

It was Mama. We held each other for support and then found her hands, which were the only part of her body visible and free. We each took one, hands that had held us so often, a little afraid to touch them now that they were so limp and lifeless. Sally looked over at me with tears in her eyes, biting her lip. We said a familiar prayer while the tubes and machines fed food and air to this person who had always seemed so impregnable while she nursed us into life.

For some moments we watched in silence, stroking her hands lightly. My mind was numb, revolted at the disfigurement. I turned and saw Maura by the door, rubbing her eyes. Instinctively, as though to fill the void, I began to murmur, "Mama, it's Paul . . . I'm here with Sally and Maura . . . you've had a very tough operation and we've been here all night with you . . . praying for you. . . ."

Sally forced a little grin and said, "Mama, you don't look very good with all those bandages on you, but we know you are giving it the old Morrissey fight . . . " Her words trailed off.

I felt empty but went on anyway, building energy by the words, "C'mon Mama, we're all pulling for you . . . get well!" Inside me a voice accused, "It's too late Paul; you never did enough."

My imagination went under the bandages on her head, searching for something familiar underneath the swollen whiteness. Her mind is gone, she can't hear a thing, I thought.

Groaning inwardly, my heart insisted, Yes, she can! You can't kill her spirit!

"We'll be in to see you later today, Mama." I nodded to Sally, "Let's go!" She and Maura and I drove home to face the family.

~ Henri ~

E VENTUALLY, much of the shock and fear of the early days of the hospice ministry subsided, at least to the extent that now I had some idea of what I might encounter when entering the home of a person who was terminally ill. A man in a diaper or a woman showing me her breast tumor no longer put me off. Sure, nurses' talk of "disimpacting" constipated patients while we sipped our morning coffee still tended to gag me, but I had learned to laugh even at my own sense of delicacy. There was no one, I believed by now, who could help me approach the naturalness of dying as the hospice nurses could, to trust my ability to enter into this process with my own special gifts.

Ruby's continued encouragement to "Just be Paul!" freed me up to do almost anything to help a patient: sing a song, stand on my head, play maracas. Despite my activist nature, sometimes I would simply sit and hold a patient's hand. It finally came down to this rule of thumb: don't be afraid to make a fool of yourself. This is what I taught the student chaplains too.

To symbolize this approach to pastoral care I hung a clown on my office wall in the form of a cross. This is how the patients must feel, I thought: nailed to a bed. Even Jesus never experienced the pain of being confined to a bed as life inexorably is drained away by some debilitating disease. His heart must be close to these brothers and sisters of his who go through this anguish. To express this even better, I fastened a small doll's mattress behind the clown on the wall. Looking up at that figure before I went out in the field to visit one of these "fools of God," I hoped I could learn to be one myself before it was too late.

One of the things a clown reminds us of is our need for forgiveness. A clown trips on his own feet. Seeing our own stupidity

121

in his antics, we laugh and have a little mercy on ourselves. The tear on a clown's cheek complements his exaggerated smile, mirroring our own sorrow at hurts done to us and hurts we have caused, even while we put on a good front. With such a buffoon we can be gentle instead of harsh, discover how wonderful it can be to forgive and to say I'm sorry. When this miracle happens, the world feels lighter and one's heart purer.

Cicely Saunders, the pioneer of the modern hospice movement and the founder of St. Christopher's Hospice in England, said that there are some important things people need to do when they are dying. "We must not lose the chance of making good on a great deal of untidiness in our lives," she says, "or of making time to pack our bags and say, 'Sorry, goodbye, and thank you.'" Three things to communicate. I would add a fourth: "I love you." It may be that the hardest of these to say and truly mean is "I'm sorry." Is it because this acknowledges our need to receive one more thing before we "check out," as Ruby calls it? Forgiveness, the one thing we cannot give to ourselves?

> A clean heart create for me, O God,
> and a steadfast spirit renew within me.
> Cast me not out from your presence,
> and your holy spirit take not from me.
> Give me back the joy of your salvation,
> and a willing spirit sustain in me.
> —Ps. 51:12–14

One of the most dramatic examples of this need for forgiveness occurred with a patient named Henri. One of our volunteers asked me if I would be willing to see a man with AIDS who was not in the hospice program. A friend of hers who lived with this man in a condo on Central Park South, a posh locale in Manhattan that overlooks the park, had called her asking if she knew a priest because Henri wanted to talk to one. Since I had originally gotten into the hospice ministry through a desire to do something for people with AIDS, I was delighted and took his number.

A young man answered the phone when I called. "This is Kevin . . . you wish to speak with Henri? . . . just a moment."

A low voice with a French accent got on. "Allo? This is Henri."

Introducing myself, I told him why I was calling. He was pleased that I was willing to come to see him, and we agreed on a time and day.

"Late mornings are best for me," said Henri. "I get drowsy in the afternoon."

The next day was my regular day off. "I could see you tomorrow."

"Excellent." He thanked me in a gracious manner, giving directions to the apartment including what to say to the doorman. As I hung up I found myself intrigued by the thought of meeting a wealthy person on his own turf. Yes, I needed a break from the poverty and danger of the ghettos.

The next day I didn't get up for morning prayers with the community, but decided to sleep in for a change — which felt delicious! My appointment with Henri wasn't until eleven so I turned over and burrowed into the pillow. I didn't need to catch the subway until ten, and I rose in time to take a stinging hot shower. I decided to wear my gray turtleneck shirt and black slacks. Yes, that would be formal enough without resorting to a tie and shirt. After a leisurely breakfast of pancakes and bacon, I threw on my charcoal trenchcoat and tweed cap to head downtown, a book of psalms in my pocket.

The day was so gorgeous that it begged to be savored, so I didn't buy a newspaper. The Number 4 subway was mostly above ground through the Bronx, so I took it instead of the "D." I got on the next to last car where there were only a few passengers.

Already the sun had climbed high enough to bathe the dull gray apartment buildings in a brilliant orange glow. Shafts of light pierced through the coils of razor wire set up to block potential intruders and sent shadows dancing across the rooftops. Spray-painted graffiti proclaimed the names of "Zap" and "Mojo" along with a multitude of other local youths on the chimneys and walls that jutted up like bunkers from the asphalt below.

Apartment buildings formerly occupied by Jewish and Irish families stood like bombed-out shells amid the vacant lots of the South Bronx strewn with broken glass, garbage, and old mattresses. Outside some makeshift shacks people burned scraps of wood in trash cans to keep warm. Some of these abandoned buildings had crude replicas of window shades or flower pots painted on their boarded-up windows to give the illusion to vandals or passersby that this neighborhood really wasn't dying. It was. Yet people really lived here, raised babies, told each other jokes, turned to each other during the night and held on.

The train provided a respite as it ducked underground after the Yankee Stadium stop. Sparing the riders a street-level view of Harlem, it soon screeched with relief into the Eighty-sixth Street Station. From now on you could ride with as many white people as blacks or Hispanics. I jumped off at the Bloomingdale's stop at Fifty-ninth and Lexington so I could stroll by Central Park. How blessed I felt! Such a fantastic day to be alive!

The park was full of magnificent clusters of trees: oaks, elms, willows, maples. Calmly they floated down their leaves, like messages from the gods, upon us poor rushing mortals below. Already they had begun their transformation into the stunning golds and reds of autumn. An oasis of ponds and playing fields, meadows to fly a kite in, shady paths to get lost with your lover, all in the heart of the busiest metropolis in the world. As I checked again the name of Henri's apartment house, my gaze was drawn to a pair of swans gliding past two elderly ladies conversing on a sunny bench. I promised myself I'd sit by that pond for a while after the visit.

Marble columns supported a wrought iron grating above the heavy glass doors to the foyer of the Regency. My shoes sank into a pale blue oriental rug. A middle-aged Hispanic man in a maroon uniform and cap was polishing the brass railings. He glanced up with indifference. "May I help you?"

"Yes, I'm here to see Henri Vallou . . . he's expecting me." While the intercom rang, the man calmly surveyed me, smiling slightly when I returned his gaze.

"He's ready to see you. The elevator is there behind the partition to your right." He followed me around to it, an ornate old-fashioned model, while I wondered what kinds of visitors he had seen Henri receiving and whether he knew that Henri was dying of AIDS. "When you get off at the fourteenth floor, the door is on your right." He flashed a friendly grin.

"Thanks." With my heartbeat more noticeable I rode the elevator up to what I envisioned as an interesting adventure. I did not know how profound it would be.

As I waited after ringing the bell, the mirrors and antique tables in the vestibule caught my attention, furnishings that would have been extravagant in the living rooms of most of the people I knew. They would be ripped off for sale or even firewood in the Bronx! With such astonishingly different lifestyles existing so close together, it was a wonder to me that the contrast didn't cause an explosion. All of these people lived in the same city to be sure, but not in the same world.

The polished wooden door opened and a pleasant-looking young man appeared. In his early twenties, he had curly brown hair and pale skin; he was dressed in pressed jeans and a starched long-sleeved sportshirt. "You must be Father Morrissey," he said cheerily. "I'm Kevin, please come in." We shook hands.

While I took off my coat in the darkened entryway, Kevin lit a lamp on a lovely antique table. "Henri is very glad you are able to come, Father. He's been quite sick this past week." Before I could respond he added, "You don't look like a priest. I'm a Catholic and am used to seeing priests, well . . . looking different." He eyed the turtleneck shirt.

"Oh? . . . I thought Henri might be more relaxed this way."

The young man smiled as he took my coat, while my gaze drifted through an archway to the room beyond us. There the sunlight streamed through gigantic windows that stretched almost from the floor to a ceiling studded with beautiful wooden rafters. Graced with a candelabra, an ancient table stood on one side near the doorway like a monastic altar. Throughout the rest of the room were plush sofas and chairs with a similar design.

"This way," called Kevin, turning in the other direction. "Henri's in the bedroom." I followed him down a long corridor hung with exquisitely framed Impressionist paintings, my psalm book in hand.

We entered a large room, itself a work of art with carefully placed statues of Greek gods and heroes. A polished turtle shell the size of a man's torso was braced upright in a stand on a table by the window, while from a spotlighted picture on the far wall the flaming cape of a matador was flung in macho triumph at the horns of an enraged bull.

The room was bathed in a soft light. In counterpoint to the vivid portrayal of masculine strength surrounding him, the one whom I had come to visit was perched upright like a fragile teacup among fluffy pillows and a pink satin quilt. Classical violin music floated over all this.

"Henri, this is Father Paul," Kevin announced softly. A middle-aged man with thinning brown hair cut conservatively and a narrow aquiline face stared at me with large, expressionless eyes.

"Fathaire," he caressed the syllables, "I am so glad you could come." He offered his hand. "Forgive me, I am so weak today." The hand touched his breast gracefully. "Sit down, sit down." Henri motioned for Kevin to pull up a chair for me next to the bed. After saying he would bring us some tea, Kevin excused himself.

Henri and I sat surveying each other for some moments. I noticed his carefully pressed pajamas, his manicured hands, the many medicines located on the small table next to him. On the wall behind his bed, a jewel-encrusted crucifix hung suspended by a woven silver cord.

"May I call you Father Paul?"

"Of course."

"You see, I have great respect for priests. I am Roman Catholic and was raised in France in a very religious family. In fact, I thought of being a priest myself then, but... " he waved his hand with a flourish, "that was long ago. I suppose you don't want to hear of that."

"Whatever you'd like to talk about."

Henri then began to tell me about his history. He had come to the United States when he was nineteen and met up with a wealthy businessman who took him in. He had many opportunities in those days, he explained, but did not take advantage of them. He did not say so explicitly, but I presumed that he meant he had a sexual relationship with this man, who was quite a bit older than he.

"I was handsome in those days," his voice trailed off wistfully, "and it was easy to trade my charms for a place to stay." I wondered if this was the situation with him and Kevin now. "You don't mind listening to this sad tale?"

"Is it so sad?"

"Well, you see, Father Paul," his gaze dropped, "I've wasted my life."

"How so?" I would have liked to convince him otherwise, but Henri plunged on with his tale.

"I am near death as you can see, and I care more about the things I am leaving than the people." He gazed at the artwork around the room and then back to me. A silence enveloped us. I could not believe what I was hearing, embarrassed for him to be so naked in front of me. Never had I heard anyone make such a devastating judgment on himself. Breathing deeply, I just sat still and tried not to interrupt.

"You don't believe me, do you? You think, 'Surely, he is exaggerating.' Well, I am not, I tell you. I am bored with life, sick to death of it. I have seen everything, done everything, gone everywhere I wanted. Look at all of this!" He swept his hand around the room. "It will be a relief to die. There is no one I feel bad about leaving, do you understand? All I care about are these magnificent things I have collected over the years. Don't you see what a waste that has been?" His head slumped down on his chest.

Slowly I nodded, shocked at the horror of what I was hearing. Strangely, though, Henri spoke of this unemotionally, as though he were speaking about some other person.

Kevin appeared with the tea. A china pot and cups with elegantly curved handles were arranged precisely on a silver tray. The young man set it down on a table next to the bed and poured each of us a cup. I was glad for the respite.

"Call me if you need anything," he murmured in Henri's ear as he adjusted his pillows. He beamed a smile back at me as he closed the door behind him.

"Do you take sugaire?"

"No, thank you."

After a period of silence Henri said, "I like your shirt, the way you are dressed...very nice." He blew on a teaspoonful of tea.

"Well..." I was about to apologize, but he went on.

"I can't stand the way Americans are so casual." The word "caaaasual" was stretched out as though it were a despised enemy. I was beginning not to like this man, beginning to understand why he loved things more than people.

"Everything in this country is reduced to extreme familiarity," he sneered, "as though familiarity were the chief good when we know it breeds contempt." He spoke then of being a historian, of loving the period in history when kings and queens reigned.

"I was born at the wrong time, Father Paul. I believe everything and everyone should be in their proper place. That is why it will be a relief to die. 'Caaaasual' is the way everything is today, and this is the enemy of everything I stand for." The two of us sipped our tea; I now felt completely different from him.

"Thank God they sent me a normal priest, not one of those left-wing revolutionaries who have wrecked the church." I almost choked on my tea, but kept my face blank. "Where do you celebrate Mass?"

"At our parish...up in the Bronx," I added to get his goat, imagining his image of that borough. "I'm a religious order priest, an Augustinian."

"Oh! Do you wear a religious habit?" His interest was piqued.

"Yes," I said, even though I wear it only once or twice a year for some liturgical event. "It is a black tunic and cupuche with a leather cincture." This impressed Henri, and he was about to go off on it. But I wanted to get back to his great sense of failure, somehow to link that with confession.

"Henri, you said you feel you have wasted your life. Do you speak to God about this?" For a moment he sat speechless, sipping his tea. Then he began to tell how he imagines God as the "Lord in Majesty." He uttered this with such drama and reverence that it unnerved me, because I related to God more familiarly.

Maybe Henri is right, I thought. Maybe God is sitting on a majestic throne in glory somewhere, expecting us lowly creatures to quiver in awe before him. Maybe God does despise my being so "casual" before him. Nevertheless, Henri's description put me off. I sensed how this kept him feeling like dirt before this grand "Lord in Majesty."

"The greatest tragedy that ever happened," he pronounced these words with fervor, "was when the Vatican Council changed the way of addressing God in prayer from the more respectful 'Vous' to the more familiar 'Tu.' I do not speak to God except in formal prayers."

"But Henri!" I interjected, "if God is so majestic, why doesn't he do something about your sickness? Don't you think he cares?"

"The Lord in Majesty cares, but do you know what I am dying from? — AIIIIIDSSSSSS!..." He hissed this through his teeth as if it were poison. "I am only getting what I deserve."

Oh, God, the man hates himself, and to such a depth that only God could reach it. Yet he keeps God so far above the hell of AIDS that forgiveness is impossible. "You think God made you get AIDS?"

"I am dying of AIDS because I was casual with sex."

"Oh!..." It dawned on me. "So that's the 'casual' you hate?" Henri stared at me blankly. Finishing the tea, I replaced my cup on the tray. "Look, Henri," I offered, "AIDS is a medical illness. It is caused by a virus. It isn't a punishment for sin. Otherwise little babies wouldn't have it, would they?"

With a pitiless tone in his voice he said, "The sins of their parents..." Damn! This "majesty" he speaks of is in him. That's what's destroying him. That's what makes him look down on others whom he deems as too "casual," less than perfect. But that's why he hates himself now. He cannot bear the shit he sees in himself and will die despising it. I decided to go for broke.

"Henri, I don't know all about your sex life, what you may have been looking for all these years — a place to stay, companionship, getting your rocks off, even love. But from what you say now I hear you looking for forgiveness from God, and I think it is for something deeper than having sex or AIDS."

"And what could that be, Father Paul?" Henri stifled a bored yawn.

"You tell me! What did you ask me to come here for? Why did you just tell me about wasting your life?" Silence...

Moments later he spoke in a gentler voice. "I want to go to confession. The priest I used to go to in the parish would not understand." His hand went to his forehead. "But I am getting tired."

Over an hour and a half had passed already. It would be better for him to make a general confession at another time when he was fresh; it would give him time to think over the specific things he was sorry for. He would have more actual feeling than I heard in his voice now, be better prepared. I could be better prepared too. "Suppose I come next week and we have the confession then? We know each other better now and you'll be more rested . . . okay?"

"That would be fine."

"May I read you a psalm before I go?"

"Certainly." Getting down on my knees next to his bed, I read a psalm aloud:

> O Lord, hear my prayer,
>   and let my cry come to you.
> Hide not your face from me
>   in the day of my distress.
> Incline your ear to me;
>   in the day when I call, answer me speedily.
> For my days vanish like smoke,
>   and my bones burn like fire.
> Withered and dried up like grass is my heart;
>   I forget to eat my bread.
> Because of my insistent sighing,
>   I am reduced to skin and bone . . .

I glanced upward at Henri; his eyes were closed . . .

> But you, O Lord, abide forever,
>   and your name through all generations.
> You will arise and have mercy on Zion,
>   for it is time to pity her,
>   for the appointed time has come.
> For her stones are dear to your servants,
>   and her dust moves them to pity . . .
>
> —Ps. 102:1–15

Later as I sat in the park, I mused on our conversation while I watched the swans circle effortlessly around the lily pads and the shadows from the willow tree wash over them. What a world Henri lives in! What strange values. What a sad life. And most of all, what a confession! What a bitter thing to have to admit about yourself as your life ends — that you've wasted it.

I felt depressed, drawn into Henri's morose spirit. I did not want to feel that way, and I kept trying to hold on to the differences between us: the possessions, the lifestyle, the strange view of God.

Tears brimmed in the corners of my eyes. I looked around to see if anyone could notice. Damn, in certain ways I am like Henri! More than I'd like to admit. Something of the same majesty in me, or at least a fierce demand on myself that I be perfect before I let God or anyone else love me. Hidden under that majesty, that pride, is a sense of myself as a pile of garbage, as worth despising. I just manage to hide the self-hatred and the pride better than Henri does. How cruel! *How pitiful! O God, won't you help me?*

Something broke inside and hot tears began to flow. Bitter bile arose from my heart at the pains I felt in my life: the failed relationships, the blaming of God and others for this, and most of all for a hopeless sense of war I felt within myself — one figure with a shotgun forever blasting away at another pathetic one who kept trying to be accepted. "Lay the goddam shotgun down!" I growled under my breath. In a while my fists unclenched and a smaller, warmer voice pleaded, "Won't you two please come together?"

At the far end of the pond the two swans circled toward each other and turned their black-beaked faces toward me. On the street off to the left, the clip-clop of a horse and buggy faded off into silence. Yellow leaves drifted from a nearby tree, barely creating a ripple as they hit the water As I wiped my eyes, a thought came — *but Henri confessed this!* An astounding grace, so his life is no longer a waste! I can do the same.

I felt exhausted but shaken together into a new beginning. Yes, "Man upstairs," it is time to arise and have mercy on Zion ... for her stones are dear to your servants, and her dust moves them to pity. . . .

~

After dinner that night, I watched *Wheel of Fortune* with some of the other friars. We joked about how Vanna White says "Bye-bye!" as she waves out to the viewing audience with her big, sweet smile. "It sure makes my day!" I mimicked her as I got up to go to my room, "Bye-bye!"

"Well, if that makes your day, you're in trouble," remarked one of them with a laugh. His ribbing stayed with me as I climbed the dingy staircase, threw my mail on the table, and checked my answering machine. Changing into sweat pants and a T-shirt, I slipped a Barbra Streisand cassette into my tape deck and flopped down on the floor to relax.

In a while, faces of my patients came to mind: Isha and Candida, Henri, Elmo, Natalie. Some were already dead... Sparky, Gertie, Pedro. Feeling an old loneliness come up on me, I wished I had someone beside me, someone to hold me. Then I began to remember my friends and family members, some still in my life, some long gone. "Bye-bye!" Vanna's cheery wave came to mind. I smiled sadly and stretched.

> Midnight.
> Not a sound from the pavement.
> Has the moon lost her memory?
> She is smiling alone.
> In the lamplight, the withered
> leaves collect at my feet,
> and the wind begins to moan...
>
> —"Memory," from the
> Broadway musical *CATS*

The window was open. It felt chilly on the carpet so I reached for a patchwork quilt from the chair, placed it over me, and pulled it up to my neck. One of my sisters had made it for me one Christmas before her husband died. I thought of her, her husband gone now because of a car accident, with her two young children to care for by herself. I remembered friends I had broken up with or who were far away. Missing all these people, I felt their loss deeply... oh, where is a friend when I need one?

Usually this kind of thinking makes me sad, blue. At moments like this I often experience all of these relationships as "not here," and I feel empty because of this. But this time I learned something new. It was as though a voice in me said: "We are here! *We are not dead! Just call us in!*" So I did.

Starting with those I had just been thinking of — my sister's husband, my mother, my deceased patients, and then even my living family members and friends and patients — I drew their presence up around me like the quilt I was lying under, remembering their unique characteristics, their love for me and mine for them, even if just for a time...

> Touch me,
> it's so easy to leave me,

all alone with the memory,
of my days in the sun.
If you touch me, you'll understand
what happiness is.
Look! A new day has begun...

I know it sounds strange, but I felt those people *living* beside me on that carpet, hugging me and holding me as the music washed over me — some I am presently related to and some long gone but once dear. For once I didn't feel lonely, even though I had no one to hold me just when I desired it. For once the loneliness had not focused only on the "not here" of my relationships, but had called forth their indomitable presence within me. I lay there for over a half hour as this "friendship quilt" knit itself over me. How very consoling and lovely it was! I decided to try this again as a way of healing myself at the end of a difficult day.

~

A week later I made a follow-up visit to Henri to hear his formal confession. Kevin received me again. I began to understand from how Henri and Kevin interacted — the tender ways Kevin touched him, the twin beds in Henri's room — that these two men were lovers. Kevin told me in an aside that he had recently gone for the AIDS test himself and was anxiously awaiting the result. The horror of this dread disease struck me — not only killing many young people in their prime, but dragging their partners into the whirlpool with them, as though their love itself was a death sentence. I could imagine the blame and guilt if one of them caught it from some promiscuous encounter and then gave it to the other in an act of love. That any of them stuck by each other in the face of this was a testimony to their depth of love and the mercy of God. I felt myself being drawn into this whirlpool myself as I spoke with them.

Henri was weaker, failing. An oxygen machine was set up near him. He was sitting up in bed, however, a burgundy robe draped over his bony shoulders.

"Fathaire Paul!" he pronounced weakly, "please sit down." Kevin stood near him, brushing Henri's hair back in place gently. Watching them together, the older man with his wealth and arrogance and his life draining out of him, the younger man a trifle too pretty but so selfless and sweet with his care, a stab of jealousy hit my heart. I wished I had someone to stroke me like that if I got sick.

"Are you ready for confession?" I thought I'd better start with that this time.

"Yes."

He turned toward Kevin who replied with a wink, "I can take a hint!" Then smiling, "Father Paul, Henri's got a lot of nasty sins to confess! And sometime you'll have to hear my confession too. I've got a lot of juicy ones!" With that he swiveled and disappeared.

What surprised me then was how Henri acted. After I placed a purple stole around my neck to signify the official Sacrament of Penance — or Reconciliation as it is called now — he blessed himself devoutly and proceeded to state very general ways he wished he could have been better during his life. Then he fell silent for absolution. But no specific sins were stated, as is called for in the sacrament, and the graphic statements of the week before about wasting his life were absent. You might say that his confession was "all cleaned up" in order to present it to the Lord in Majesty.

Even more unusual was what followed. With a conviction that seemed to emerge from the past few months of having touched patients' tumors while we prayed, I proceeded to lead Henri down into the pain in his soul, reminding him of his words to me the week before . . . " I care more about the possessions I'm leaving than the people."

With Henri following at first but gradually resisting, we ended up at one point with him crying out in tears with his fists clenched, "No! You've got to stop!" But I didn't. No, he had asked to be forgiven and it was now or never.

We went down into the hell Jesus had descended into long ago to redeem us.[8] Down into that cellar of arrogance and self-hatred — I knew the way now because of my own journey — until Henri had looked these demons full in the face. When all the poison and sorrow had risen to the surface and at last he lay back exhausted and sobbing on his pillows, only then did I hear myself say the absolution, "May almighty God have mercy on you, Henri, forgive you your sins, and bring you to everlasting life, Amen."

"Oh, oh!..." he gasped like a woman in labor.

Never had I "led" a confession like this before. It felt strange, even scary. Yet Henri seemed different now.

"Thank you, Fathaire...thank you," he whispered with his eyes closed.

I called Kevin and together we anointed Henri. As the young man's tears fell silently while he traced the oil on his lover's body, I told them of the Scripture story in which a woman had done the same for Jesus long ago and his words of gratitude about her: "I tell you, that is why her many sins are forgiven — because of her great love" (Luke 7:47).

~ Sofia ~

MY MOTHER never came out of the coma. After her operation for a brain tumor in that autumn of 1975, we hoped against hope and set up 'round-the-clock shifts in the corridor outside the Intensive Care Unit at Misericordia Hospital in Philadelphia. We prayed every prayer we ever knew while making bargains with God. We stopped our lives because the one who had given us life was in mortal danger and we would do anything to help her. What we did without knowing it then was to set up a "hospice" before the program existed, at least in Philadelphia.

The doctor had told us that they would not know for seventy-two hours after the operation whether the tumor was malignant. After the first day of shock my hunch was that he assumed Mama would die within a few days. In any case, I thought the hemorrhage had been so bad that even if the tumor was not malignant, it wouldn't make any difference. She wouldn't recover. I didn't know that for certain, but I sensed it.

It felt like the end of the world. Mama had been the center of communication for the whole Morrissey clan. All important phone numbers, for instance, were logged in her head like a computer. From the family home in Upper Darby, Mama had presided over this gradually scattering brood as though from the hub of a big wagon wheel. Without serious warning, one day the hub became disconnected from the rest of the wheel. The spokes and the rim flopped and floundered helplessly. The computer was "down" as they say now. We didn't know it, but all the information in Mama's mind was irretrievable. And the information was only a symbol of what we were so ill-prepared to lose: Mama

136

had cemented us together, made us a family, a home. Without her we were just a pile of bricks.

No wonder the first of the two weeks she lay in a coma was a time of terror and denial. Nothing in our lives had prepared us for this. Yet everything had. Coping skills emerged. We took turns falling apart and saw our individual flaws and strengths in greater relief. We would argue about her care, fall asleep from grief, laugh inappropriately, or fall silent in mid-sentence. The important lesson we learned in this: trust all your emotions in such moments of crises. All of them are yours and they are precious. None are "right"; they are just there. Given time and respect, they are your path to healing. A ritual enabled us to hold these varied pieces together.

Sally and I had phoned all of our brothers and sisters that horrible first night when it was determined that it was necessary to operate. To awaken each in the middle of the night with such bad news was like delivering a death sentence. As each one arrived at the family home the morning after, white-faced and solemn, the rest of us who were already seated around the big dining room table relived the initial moments of despair as our stricken faces met. Yet some imperceptible strength grew as we welcomed each one into the communal crisis.

When Daddy came downstairs, eyes red and voice shaking a little after 9:30 a.m., the whole throng of us rose and surrounded him as if he were a wounded stag. We could feel our hope rising in our bondedness. Yes, our desire for her life would pull Mama through. What do people do in such a crisis, we wondered, who have no family like this?

A system of visitation began evolving: Mama's youngest sister, Anne, a nun, would sit in the corridor outside Mama's room all day, coordinating the major part of the family's visits during these daytime hours. My sister, Sally and I were the night watch. We would sleep during the day and go to the hospital after dinner each night. We took turns sitting with Mama until about 8:00 a.m., when Aunt Anne would arrive to relieve us. After the first day, the family never left Mama alone.

Toward the end of the first three days, as we waited for the results of the biopsy, the family began dividing more or less into two camps. One camp, led by my oldest brother, Shawn, wanted to sue Mama's doctor, who had originally prescribed that she take up to twelve aspirins a day as a treatment for her persistent headache, never suggesting she be given a CAT-scan to see if anything more serious were responsible. This group was pulling for Mama with the most visible hope, almost like it was a football game they were rooting for or a war. Don't flinch, don't falter! Be furious at what is happening to us and we can overcome it!

I was part of the group that took the other approach. In my deepest heart I hoped for Mama to come out of the coma, to get well again, but I just couldn't believe that she would. Was this more realistic or defeatist? The dream of the year before was unfolding. Who knows, maybe I just couldn't bear that she would revive and not be the healthy, vivacious woman we knew only the week before.

As each day went by and the first weekend approached with no change in her condition, the brothers and sisters who lived further away began planning to go back to work. They would come back the following weekend or at an emergency phone call. I felt we should discuss what we might do if Mama didn't recover.

An idea came: the Sacrament of Anointing. I hadn't yet had the experience of hospice in regard to this ritual, but I felt it could help us gather around Mama's bed before we scattered, claim our faith at the very least by praying together, and accept — I hardly let myself think this — Mama's impending death before she died. No matter how difficult, it seemed important for us to say goodbye to her together while she was still alive. Our grief would be even greater if we waited until it was too late.

With the reluctance of a few, the family agreed to this way of coming together in faith and prayer around Mama while we were all still there. We would do this on Saturday night.

On the night of the anointing we all gathered in the corridor outside Mama's room on the fourth floor. I had gotten special permission for the whole family to go into the ICU for a brief service around Mama's bed.

When everyone had arrived, I explained nervously to them what we would be doing. "We'll anoint her with oil and pray for her health and forgiveness." I was trying to hold my own feelings in so I could get the family through this. Standing behind his wife, Shawn had a stony expression on his face, but I could see he was blinking back tears. Daddy, on my oldest sister's arm, was a mixture of grim determination and brokenness. His jaw was locked, his lips quivering. Aunt Anne had a face like the Rock of Gibraltar.

A nurse came over from her station and drew Mama's curtain aside, presenting her in the familiar posture — the bandaged head, eyes closed, the respirator breathing relentlessly. Slowly we circled her bed. There were almost two dozen of us crowding close, hoping not to trip over the tubes and cords. We were like parents trying not to wake a baby in its crib. Maura motioned to me, her lips moving silently. "Richie's not here." I looked around at the faces, faces I had grown up with over thirty-five years. Such an impregnable throng, we could never imagine being divided by death. Their faces searched mine, but mine was a mask.

All the faces brought back the same panorama from happier times. All those meals around the huge dining-room table as we grew up together. Mama would serve us out of a big stew pot while we fought for extras. Before we washed the dishes we'd pray the rosary, ending up with that syrupy hymn Mama got out of some old novena book that she had when she was a girl growing up in West Philadelphia. In the summertime our prayers would pour out through the screened windows of our corner house while we older ones cringed with embarrassment.

"In the Name of the Father, and of the Son, and of the Holy Spirit..." I began from my place behind Mama's head. At times like this I was grateful for the old formulas to fall back on. Our feelings could tumble out in them like trusty containers. We all made the sign of the cross, that Christian way of claiming Christ as Lord and of professing our willingness to die on a cross like him if necessary for the faith. But no one ever explained that the cross could look like this!

I traced a cross on Mama's forehead with the sacred oil while everyone craned to see. The family recited the Hail Mary, a prayer we had said a thousand times, but without ever hearing the words as clearly as now: "...Holy Mary, Mother of God, pray for us sinners, now and at the hour of our death. Amen."

Done. All was quiet now except for some sniffles and the respirator. We were awkward in the silence, and it wasn't clear what we should do next. Catching Daddy's eye, I said, "Well, Mama, here we are. Your family. You and Daddy taught us well. We are here together praying for you to get well."

Sally leaned over and whispered, "Let's sing 'Good Night Sweet Jesus.'"

"There is one more thing we'd like to do for you Mama..." The nurses said that hearing is the last sense to go, so I kept speaking to her as though she could hear. "We want to sing you one of your favorite lullabies so you can get a good night's sleep, okay? You can sing it along in your mind with us if you want to."

> Good night, sweet Jesus,
> Guard us in sleep,
> Our souls and bodies,
> In thy love keep...

One at a time we picked it up, faltering at first until we forgot ourselves. Soon our voices had swelled into a chorus, gratefully joining in the old childhood hymn we had hated.

> Waking or sleeping, keep us in sight,
> Dear gentle savior, good night, good night,
> Good night dear Jesus, good night, goooooooood night.

Gradually we drifted away. Some touched Mama's hand or kissed her. Others offered words of encouragement: "You can make it, Mama!... Give it the old Irish fight!" We hugged one another, moist cheeks rubbing together. We weren't sure what to do next.

I could feel the relief, though. Shawn made a quip about us sounding like a bunch of alley cats howling for our supper. The nurse said she had coffee and cookies prepared in an adjacent room. Bonded together in a new way, our family followed her there.

~

In the Roman Catholic tradition the anointing ritual used to be called the Sacrament of Extreme Unction, though now it is used not only for people close to death but also for those who are sick and hope to recover.[9] When traditional Catholics saw the priest arrive in his black suit to "anoint" them, it was as if the Angel of Death had come to tap them on the shoulder — "ready or not!"

When the patient and family are truly at peace with an impending death, this reaction isn't bad. But other times, when there is fear in people's eyes, it is difficult to have to represent God the Judge arriving to claim their loved one's soul. Nonetheless, this tradition can be used quite fruitfully to bring into consciousness a reality the family hadn't quite accepted.

In a nonsacramental form the ritual had helped others who weren't Roman Catholic: Isha and Lilianne, Natalie, Pedro and his mother. Once after I had anointed a young woman from Zaire with her husband and five children gathered around her bed, her husband told me with tears in his eyes, "My children will have that ceremony stamped on their minds for the rest of their lives."

Human beings are embodied spirits. Not just skin and bones, emotions and intellect, we have something called "soul" or "spirit" that is deeper than all of these and unites them. That is why we communicate most deeply when we use our whole beings — body, heart, mind, and spirit — to express ourselves to one another. Every culture and religion have developed symbols and rituals that speak from this deep part of ourselves. Without these symbols and rituals, the tribes, nations, and religions of this world are only collections of individuals.

Rituals were becoming much more a part of my pastoral repertoire. Even the hospice team began to see their value and would enter into discussions about them at our weekly meetings — not quite as likely to be prescribed as Duoderm or morphine for sure, but at least they were respectable now. No longer did I have to apologize for pastoral care as though it were some sort of pap for the unsophisticated. And it gave me a secret chuckle to know we were weighing the pros and cons of such spiritual interventions in the heart of the secular city. With a glint in my eye I would tell the friars back at the rectory, "You know that red light you can see blinking at night on the top of the Empire State Building? That's my chapel!"

As if to help me tap into the astonishing wideness and depth of the soul's passion, I was asked to celebrate a ritual later in the month that was both touching and humorous. It had started out as a joke at a team meeting. Everyone had laughed when Ruby said that a memorial service was needed by a patient even though she hadn't died yet.

"I'm not kidding," Ruby insisted. "Mrs. Banores is heart-broken about her pet dog dying. I think it would help her a lot to have some kind of service." She turned toward me with a sly smile as if to say, "Okay, Father, friend of the grieving, whaddaya say?"

As youngsters, my brothers and sisters and I buried pet white mice and goldfish in our backyard. I love animals and consider St. Francis one of my heroes. But a formal memorial service for a dog? C'mon, you guys! That's the social worker's department. Let Beverly do it! I could hear my religious brothers razzing me. "A funeral for a dog, Paul? . . . a dog?"

The team's eyes were still glued on me. "I'll be glad to do it. What's her phone number?"

I found many excuses not to call Sofia Banores. Finally, after Ruby had reminded me for a couple of weeks, I called and got her husband, Teddy, on the phone. "This is Father Paul from the hospice program," I began.

"I hear we're going to have a service," announced Teddy. Aha! It was one of Ruby's plots. He described how Sofia, who had a malignant brain tumor, was grieving deeply over the loss of her dog, Zeus, who had died a month before. As if I did this kind of thing every day, I suggested that he and Sofia try to think of a way we might symbolize what Zeus meant to her, and even some kind of ritual by which she might let him go. Teddy thought that was a good idea, and we agreed on the next afternoon.

On the subway as I headed toward their place I reviewed the patient's profile. Sofia was a forty-five-year-old Greek woman who had worked for twenty years as a teacher in the New York City public school system. She had been married to Teddy for the past fifteen years and the couple had no children. They were members of the Greek Orthodox Church but were not active in their local parish. Teddy was aware of her prognosis, but Sofia was not.

When I arrived a half hour late at their apartment in Astoria, a stocky man with a friendly face swung the door open. We shook hands and he brought me over to introduce me to Sofia, who reclined in a hospital bed against the side wall of the tiny, sparsely furnished room. There was no carpet, one floor lamp next to a small couch, and a portable TV on a bookcase.

I spotted a framed picture of a large brown dog with its tongue hanging out.

Sofia, an obese, olive-skinned woman clothed in a hospital gown, had an ugly tumor protruding from the top of her bald head. She was in the midst of eating a meal from a tray in front of her. Some of the rice was stuck to the side of her mouth. Taking my hand, she smiled but didn't seem able to speak much. She said with difficulty, "Thank you . . . for coming."

"Sit here," said Teddy, patting the raggedy sofa next to him. I had wondered at the narrowness of the room, but now I was able to see a plywood barricade that blocked off a large portion of the room. Behind it I spied a very large black dog, which was pacing nervously back and forth.

"That's Crunch, my dog," Teddy said with pride. My stomach muscles tightened, but I managed to be friendly toward Crunch, who was over four feet high and eyed me like I was his supper. Damn Ruby! She never said a word about this.

"Hi, Crunch . . . nice doggy!"

The couch on which we sat backed up against this barricade. I moved up to the edge of it, to distance myself from the huge creature, which had been panting his bad breath on my neck.

I began to speak of why I had come. I mentioned the loss of Sofia's dog and that we wanted to speak and pray about him. Teddy spoke endearingly about Zeus, the nine-year-old brother of Crunch, and how he had died of a tumor on his behind. In lurid detail he described how the tumor had bled profusely and the various ways they had tried to stop it. Finally it had been necessary to put the dog to sleep. "I feel guilty about this," said Teddy while Sofia listened glumly.

Teddy continued on about how the two dogs had saved their lives from muggers any number of times. He even described the unique personality of Zeus as he handed me his picture. I encouraged them, nodding and murmuring in sorrow.

Teddy went into another room and returned with a beat-up metal dog dish. "This was Zeus's dish." Mournfully he looked over at Sofia. "His favorite spot in the house was exactly where you are sitting." I glanced down, aware that we were into the ritual now; you might even say I was seated on the altar. But moments later, when Sofia began to cry, I was deeply struck. These dogs are every bit as much a part of their family as the children they never had.

When Ruby had first asked, I thought how weird it would be to speak religiously about a dog. I would be willing to cloak their grieving needs in spiritual trappings, though, because it was what I knew best. In desperation the night before I had hunted up a prayer of St. Francis. It spoke about how the least of God's creatures praises him simply by its existence. Clumsily now, I began to speak of this to Sofia and Teddy. "God is the Creator of all, right? He creates things in his image, so every creature must be like him somehow. . . . "

In the course of this explanation, Teddy let his dog out from behind the barricade. The monster must have outweighed me by fifty pounds. With saliva foaming from his jowls, Crunch nervously sniffed me all over before Teddy dragged him back next to his feet with a chain choke collar. "Don't be afraid," he reassured me. "I think he likes you."

You *think!* Sure, this beast is made in God's image! I faked a smile. "May I say this prayer of St. Francis?"

"Sure, Father, go right ahead."

O Most High, Almighty, good Lord God, to thee belong praise, honor, glory, and all blessing. Praised be my Lord God, with all his creatures, and especially our brother the sun, who brings us the day and who brings us the light: fair is he, and he shines with a very great splendor. O Lord, he signifies thee to us . . .

Sofia continued to weep. Instinctively my hand reached out to console her. Midway through this gesture, Crunch flung himself taut on the chain with a roar, AAAAARGH! Oh, God! I froze in midstep, unsure whether to go forward or backward.

Praised be my Lord for our sister the moon, and for the stars, the which he has set clear and lovely in the heavens. Praised be my Lord for our brother the wind, and for air and clouds, calms and all weather, by which thou upholdest life and all creatures. . . . (from "Canticle to the Sun")

"Down Crunch! Down!" Teddy commanded. With the choke collar my only hope against disaster, it was amazing how quickly my love of all God's creatures vanished.

Calmly Teddy informed me, "He attacks some people, but as long as you're with us you'll be all right." Teddy wasn't worried, no! But I was. Especially when he added — all very sweetly — "Crunch is a mixed-breed Doberman, Great Dane, African Police Dog... usually they go for the throat." Meantime, Sofia had tears coursing down her cheeks.

With the calmest voice I could manage, I asked her, "May I say another prayer?" Sofia nodded yes. Ever so gingerly I edged across the carpet toward her, making an act of faith as I did so. This prayer was as much for me as for them. Teddy ordered Crunch to stay where he was while he joined me at his wife's bedside.

"O God, bless Sofia and Teddy," I began. "Especially help her in her grief over her dear dog, Zeus." Sofia bowed her head, exposing the grotesque tumor in the lamplight. Zeus's dish lay upside down in her lap. "And, Lord, help her with her own illness too." It had been unmentioned up to this point.

Teddy chimed in, "I wish to pray also." Tenderly he placed one of his rough hands against Sofia's neck, the other one on my shoulder. He paused for a moment and then offered from the heart, "Lord God, I pray for us... that we have the courage to go on in the future, believing in your love for us... no matter what. And Lord?..." There was a note in his voice as though he were checking to see if God were still listening, "I also pray for Zeus... for his soul, wherever he is." Trying to imagine Zeus's soul, I began to sing a hymn.

> All creatures of our God and King,
> Lift up your voice and with us sing...

From behind us as if he understood and wanted to join in and as if connected to some great wellspring of creaturely grieving, Crunch reared up on his hind legs and draped his huge paws over our shoulders. As I continued to sing, Crunch howled.

> Thou rising morn in praise rejoice,
> Ye lights of evening find a voice:
> Oh praise him, oh praise him,
> Alleluia, Alleluia, Alleluia...

I left that house with a new understanding of the universality of love and grief and how ritual can unleash the feelings that our words often hide. All of creation groans for redemption, St. Paul tells us (Rom. 8:22). We don't need simply to talk about this, do we? With symbols and gestures we can love and grieve to that place deep down inside of us "where the dogs are." This is the ultimate faith and acceptance, where in God's good time new hope can be born again with the sweet, mad freedom to love again.

~ Alberto ~

URING ONE of our recent team meetings, we listened to updates on nineteen patients. Some had intricate social problems, like Candida Perez and her son, Angel. With others, a financial crisis was the main thrust of the discussion. Isha had been in the program for over a year and a half now and we were caring for her gratis. Joanne reported that Dominic continued his denial about Natalie's condition while in her presence, yet vociferously acted out about it with the staff. I described my recent visits with Elmo.

After these updates, we would deal with the three or four new admissions a week. At some point during each meeting there would be one patient who would touch just the right chord. This morning it was the last patient, one of Ruby's.

"Alberto Cruz is a forty-five-year-old Dominican man with cancer of the prostate," she began. "He and his thirty-nine-year-old wife, Rita, and their sixteen-year-old daughter, Lydia, live in a comfortable and clean second-floor apartment in Washington Heights. Alberto has been diagnosed with this disease for two-and-a-half years. He has had two rounds of radiation and one of chemo. Eight months ago he had an orchiectomy. His appetite is fair, but he hasn't had a bowel movement for over a week."

She went on to describe a whole list of medications he was taking — Halcion, Colace, Xanax, Dilaudid, Compazine, MS Contin — a litany I was beginning to recognize as if they were old friends. According to Ruby, his chief complaint was severe pain when he urinated, as well as pain in both hips and across the abdomen.

"Alberto is Roman Catholic," she continued. "Rita is a Santeria."

147

"What's that?" I asked.

"It's a type of spiritualism that combines African rituals with traditional Catholic beliefs. Talk to Yolanda; she would know more about it." I scribbled on my pad.

"And how is the sixteen-year-old handling all of this?" asked Beverly.

"I think she's got problems, and . . . " Ruby hesitated.

"And what?" asked Doc.

"Well, you've got to understand . . . there are, uh . . . some problems." Ruby liked to tease us along this way and spice up the team meetings if she could. "Alberto speaks very little English. The same with his wife. He's got a friend though, a Mr. Madera, who is always there. Practically all communication with Alberto has to go through him. And whenever I've been there," she rolled her eyes, "Mr. Madera sits on the bed next to him." Ruby made a limp-wristed gesture with her hand and the team burst out laughing.

"Ruby!" Kate didn't like the innuendo.

"What I'm saying is," Ruby went on, "there are some unusual family dynamics. I think a social worker ought to go in. And Paul too, if they'll let him."

"What do you mean, 'if they'll let me'?" I asked, noticing on his sheet where it said he's an inactive Catholic.

"He was raised Catholic in the Dominican Republic," explained Ruby, who usually talked very little about formal religion. "I think he had problems with his church, and now he worships in his own way. But he's very spiritual, and if he'd talk with you I think it would help the family."

I enjoyed the challenge of patients who were estranged from their churches and had also learned by now that the religious label, such as "Catholic" or "Baptist," that people accepted for themselves said very little about how they interpreted such a religion for themselves. You had to get much closer to them before they would reveal that. "Okay, I'll try and see him with Yolanda some time next week." I would need her as an interpreter.

While the team debated medical options, I found myself looking forward to this visit more than usual. The family dynamics and religious mix would surely be a fascinating experience, and I didn't know which issue would be more crucial.

"Keep us posted on Alberto," said Doc with a twinkle in his eye as the meeting broke up.

"You bet."

Later when I spoke to Yolanda to set up our visit, she explained that there were followers of the Santeria religion among the droves of Dominican and Puerto Rican immigrants packed into the apartment houses in Manhattan. When I thought about it, it seemed to me that a Hispanic network followed the Number 1 subway as it snaked its way out of Midtown all the way to the northernmost tip of the island, where the Cruz family lived. Their storefront Pentecostal churches, which provided more personal and dramatic expression of their fight against evil than the mainline churches offered, were a common sight. Here and there in the dense barrios of the West Side above Harlem, crowded with families living side by side with drug-dealers and addicts, one could be steered to a "botanica," a neighborhood shop that sold amulets and incense to ward off evil spirits. Alongside these were displayed the statues of bleeding saints, rosaries, scapulars, and holy pictures that were more acceptable within the traditional Roman Catholic upbringing of most of the people.

The official Catholic Church frowned on mixing these sacred symbols with what it considered superstition, but I was curious. Across the Harlem River in the Bronx where I lived, occasionally we would find a chicken with its throat slit on the front steps of our church. A mile down the road from us, a storefront church conducted weekly exorcisms. This was the kind of liminal space where people's dream world and external reality could become blurred. When these people told you about "devils" and "voices," you didn't write them off as simply psychotic; they lived in this spirit world. "New York City is the capital of the world," a visitor told me once with awe as he pointed out the towering buildings and the international make-up of the crowds crossing the street. In a place such as this, you encounter many kinds of spirits.

The following week, a gorgeous spring day, Yolanda and I rode the subway up to Washington Heights, the brilliant sun warm on our faces. The smell of fresh earth was in the air as we passed a small plot of ground near a church, strolled past the vegetable stands that jutted out onto the sidewalk, and turned a corner into the apartment-lined street where Alberto lived. Yolanda, diminutive but savvy in these Spanish-speaking neighborhoods, relaxed me by her presence even as we cut diagonally across the street past clusters of unemployed men who hung on the doorsteps and eyed us.

I forgot that Ruby had said there was no buzzer on the street-level door. We had to backtrack to a pay phone to call Rita Cruz and tell her we were there so she could come down to let us in.

"Buenos días . . ." A woman's accented voice sounded low and protected, but intimate too.

"This is Father Paul, Rita. We are downstairs . . . Okay?"

"Okay." She sounded pleased.

Moments later an attractive woman with a smooth, round olive face came down the stairway. Soft brown eyes averted my gaze through the glass doorway as she acknowledged our presence with a half-smile. Shyness, I supposed, and found it attractive. Rita wore slacks and a flowered blouse; her dark hair was pulled back in a bun.

"I am Father Paul . . . Ruby and I work together."

"Yes, I know," she said, accepting my handshake lightly. The two women exchanged pecks on the cheek; she already knew Yolanda, who had been there before with Ruby. We were led up a rickety stairway to their second-floor apartment.

When Rita swung open the door for us, a long, narrow corridor lined with small statues and vases interspersed with pictures became visible. With Yolanda leading the way, we edged ourselves carefully through this mini-museum, passing a few bedrooms with doors partially ajar. The corridor opened into a well-furnished, dimly-lit living room, not the kind I would expect in this neighborhood. Satin drapes decorated the windows, and comfortable furniture was arranged in conversation nooks. An Oriental rug and vases of dried flower arrangements completed the eclectic ambiance. I recognized the two marble statues closest to me: a fierce-looking Moses clutching the ten commandments, and St. Lazarus on crutches with a dog licking his wounds.

From the kitchen beyond where we stood appeared a tall, slender man with features like a hawk. Pale and balding with a thin gray moustache framing his lip, very politely he offered his hand. "Hector Madera."

I introduced Yolanda and myself and turned toward Rita for a signal. But it was Hector who motioned for us to go back down the hallway to Alberto's bedroom. Rita, it seemed, would remain in the living room. I told Yolanda to ask Rita if we could speak with her later.

We were ushered into a warmly decorated room where a man with curly gray hair was sitting up in a double bed with a peach-colored quilt carefully draped over his legs. His eyes were closed, but he opened them with great weariness as we entered, keeping his gaze on us as Hector moved up close beside him and introduced us in a soft voice.

"Alberto! . . . " Yolanda said something to him in Spanish. His response was a shrug with a sort of "What the hell?" gesture. Yolanda thought this was funny. "He said it probably wouldn't hurt to talk to you." There was a slightly wary look on his handsome brown face. After Hector got two folding chairs and placed them at the foot of the bed for us, he half-reclined on the bed next to Alberto.

With Yolanda translating, I decided to cut right away through the religious ice. "Alberto, how are you doing spiritually?" I made a gesture with my hand toward my heart.

"He says he was a strict Catholic at one point," Yolanda said, "but he doesn't connect with the church anymore." I didn't think it opportune to ask what caused this change at just that moment, whether he had some bad experience as often happens, so I nodded. Alberto went on to say how he is very spiritual. Staring at me intensely, he seemed to be sizing me up.

Hector jumped in as translator at this point. "He says he used to be an altar boy and went to all the religious services."

Noticing a large framed painting on the wall next to the dresser, St. Michael the Archangel slaying Satan, I remembered the image of God I had learned as a boy: an almighty, totally good Being who overcomes all evil.

"You know, I don't care whether you've gone to church all your life or not; I'm not here to check on that, but to encourage your way of relating to God at this time, whatever that is."

Shortly after this Hector got up and left the room. I suppose he trusted by then that I wasn't there to browbeat his friend about religion or about death.

Yolanda's soft voice broke into my thoughts, "He says his back hurts."

"We could say a prayer. And would it be all right to place my hands on your back while I did?" Alberto had been eyeing me quite suspiciously up to then. His eyes seemed to mellow, and he nodded in agreement. Yolanda and I moved up beside him; she took a seat on the bed while I stood next to him on the other side. He leaned forward and I placed my hand on his back, the flannel pajama top warm to the touch. After a silent prayer in this fashion, he leaned back on the pillows again. I took a cue from Yolanda who was holding one hand, and I held his other hand.

Alberto began to tell us of his desire to see his sister who lives in a small village outside of Santo Domingo and was also sick. Her husband, according to Alberto, is not sensitive and keeps her from speaking directly to him on the phone. Also, she would have difficulty getting a visa. In spite of his prognosis, I inquired whether it were impossible for him to go there to see her. He hadn't thought of that, he said, but was interested.

"Soon it will be Holy Week," I said, trying to fish for where he stood about Catholic rituals. "Is there any special way you want to celebrate it this year?"

"No."

After I had described it though, he was willing for me to come in and have an anointing service with the family present. "But Hector is not a Catholic," Alberto added, "so do not ask him to attend."

As he spoke, Alberto would occasionally draw his manicured hands away from ours, gesticulate to make a point, and then replace them in ours. Once he smiled at something Yolanda said, but she didn't translate.

When Alberto began to speak in a very weak voice, I took the opportunity to probe what he thought was happening to him. Yolanda looked gravely at me as she gave his response, "He says maybe his time is coming to an end. But he doesn't want to die; he wants to get better." Her eyes filled up as she said this.

"Have you told God this?" I asked, always hoping to get people into some kind of communication with God. Alberto shook his head.

"If you wish to speak to God, you might not want to wait until you are too tired or too drugged to do so." Carefully, his brown eyes searched mine.

"The same with your sister," I said as I looked at Yolanda.

"Ask him if he could write her a letter expressing his love, not necessarily telling her how sick he is, because she is sick too, but at least to say to her what he wishes while he can." Alberto seemed to think this was a good idea even if someone had to write the letter for him.

We fell into a peaceful silence. I could hear only our muffled breathing and an occasional airplane or car horn from the street below. Alberto said something to Yolanda and she studied him; the love she had for him was evident on her face. She turned to me. "He would like it if you would just hold his hand." Surprised by this request, I nodded my willingness though I was already grasping his hand.

"I'll be talking to Rita in the other room," Yolanda said, "so take your time." She gathered her things and left us alone.

The lamplight bathed the quilt in pink light, reflecting shadows off the side of Alberto's face. Nervous at first with just the two of us there and no way to communicate, I continued to hold his hand. "Just hold his hand," Yolanda had said. Oh, you dummy! He's tired of talking; that's why Yolanda left. Shifting my weight, I knelt, resting my arm across the bed. I could feel the pulse beating in Alberto's warm hand.

After a few minutes I thought I should leave so Alberto could rest. I began to slip my hand out of his — but no! — Alberto kept holding tightly onto it. Oh! You want me to stay! I didn't know. . . . "Just hold his hand."

I settled back onto the floor. Alberto was looking straight ahead, as though far away. I watched him, wondering what he was thinking. I relaxed and stroked the back of his hand lightly. As I looked at him this way, with a slight smile on my face in case he turned my way but at the same time not wanting to distract him, I considered his plight. Alberto was a relatively young man, with a charming wife and a sixteen-year-old daughter. He has a friend who sticks by him in his illness, and a sister he can't get to or speak to. All the while the damn cancer is eating away at him and there is nothing he or they can do to stop it. This warm vibrant man, having to get ready to die and not wanting to . . . I felt a tear on my face and brushed it away. Alberto turned and looked at me.

This wordless interaction felt awkward, yet it also felt good, like a silent prayer. Alberto's hand remained tight in mine for five, maybe ten minutes, it didn't matter. Something passed between us more than perspiration, something bigger and deeper than the two of us.

Gradually Alberto's hand relaxed. This time I knew it was okay to leave. Slipping my hand away, I stood and backed slowly toward the door. The two of us smiled at each other in the mellow light. "Alberto!" It was the first word spoken since Yolanda had left. "I'll see you again within two weeks."

I don't know if he understood me, but when this brother clasped his hands together and moved them back and forth in a gesture of solidarity, I did the same.

When I joined his wife and Hector in the living room with Yolanda, I asked Rita how she was doing.

"Fine." She said this with a smile, but still with that heavy voice.

Hector said, "Rita is not speaking honestly when she says she is feeling fine. Hispanics are much less likely than Anglos to speak openly about death and other difficult feelings with anyone other than close friends."

"So you are not feeling fine?" I asked. Rita smiled back, but cast her dark eyes down and didn't want to speak further. I appreciated Hector's directness, but we'd have to go slow in getting to Rita's real feelings. She did register surprise when I mentioned Alberto's willingness to have an anointing service. Soon it was time for Yolanda and me to depart. Since Hector seemed interested in my returning, I gave him my card. "I'll be back in two weeks," I told them, the next time intending to speak more at length with Rita and Hector.

When he went to get my jacket, I studied the family pictures in the bookcase. There was a photo of Rita and Alberto when they were younger, she even more beautiful, with her head resting on his shoulder. There was also a large picture of their daughter, Lydia, in her First Communion dress with a big white bow in her hair. After saying goodbye, we walked down the long hallway past Lazarus and Moses and left. Tired though I was, I felt energized, recounting excitedly to Yolanda about the silent time with Alberto.

"Spanish people like touch, Paul," she remarked with a hint of suggestiveness. We threw back our heads and laughed. After we hugged each other by the corner vegetable stand, she headed down into the subway for the long ride home to Brooklyn. I crossed the street to the Uptown side for the train to the Bronx as I sang, "There is a rose in Spanish Harlem, a red rose up in Spanish Harlem..."

Before the next two weeks elapsed I phoned Rita and discovered she could speak more English than Alberto, or in any case was willing to try conversing with me without an interpreter after I told her she spoke well.

"My daughter and my husband alike...both keep their feelings inside...they use to talk to each other all the time...now even that stop...Alberto push her away." In a lowered voice she added, "He even jealous of the time she and I together." The team was right. This family needed help in separating.

"Father Paul?" she continued, a question in her voice, "in the middle of the night Alberto wake me up and ask why I call him...but I no call him." Rita sounded very tired and emotionally strung out from all of this. "Maybe it is a bad spirit."

"You know, Rita, what is going on with Alberto is very common when someone is seriously ill." I told her about what the nurses call "advanced confusion," the often strange kinds of behavior that patients begin to exhibit when they are preparing themselves for death. "The patient may hear someone calling him at night, or he may see things we don't see. To us, or even to him, it may seem crazy; but it isn't always."

"No?..." Rita's voice was like a child's.

"No. This talking with people who aren't visible is often the soul of the patient communicating with those who will help him to go over to the other side of death when it is time. We shouldn't ignore this or mock it or drug it away if possible; rather we should listen for clues to what the patient needs...who they can expect to be a bridge for them at the moment of death. It could be Jesus or Mary, maybe Moses or a relative who has died."

"Ohhh..." She let out a long sigh.

"So talk to him about these things, Rita," I encouraged. "For instance, ask him what he hears you calling to him at night."

"Ohhh, okay." She sounded relieved. "You come next week, Father Paul?"

"Yes."

In a low, drawn out way she said, "I...love...you."

"Get some sleep yourself too, okay?"

"Okay." We hung up, but I sat there with growing concern over how this family was going to hang together through Alberto's death. And I was also concerned how I could help, since I did not really know the Spanish culture.

One afternoon I decided to take a colleague with me to see Alberto. Carlos, in his mid-twenties, was one of the young Hispanic seminarians who lived in our rectory.

I had asked Carlos to work with me for the summer because he had a naturally sensitive way with people. Also, I wanted to get to know him more. Carlos would be perfect for Alberto because they could talk without an interpreter, meet without the culture gap.

While we waited on the subway platform, I showed Carlos the on-call sheet that listed all the information on Alberto. After some moments of studying it, I asked him, "What do you see?"

"A very sick man," said Carlos, " . . . and one estranged from the church." A train rumbled up to the station and we hopped on, right behind a couple of tall black teenagers.

"What's this?" I asked after we were seated, pointing at one of the entries under Alberto's medical history — an orchiectomy.

Carlos scrutinized the strange word, "ork . . . ek . . . ti . . . me," he tried, grinning.

"Or-ki-ek-to-me," I enunciated carefully, repeating what the nurses had done for me when I had asked the same question a few years before.

I waited some moments for effect and then whispered in his ear, "It's when a man's balls are cut off!"

"Nooo!" Carlos protested, his face flushed.

"Yes!" I assured him, wagging my head up and down. "When the cancer spreads there, that's what they do." I wanted him to appreciate what Alberto was dealing with and also to feel free to discuss anything with me.[10]

With the utmost seriousness, this young man informed me, "Father Paul, in the Hispanic culture a man's balls are very important."

"Noooo!" It was my turn to protest. Grinning from ear to ear, I mocked, "In every culture a man's balls are important!" Carlos's jaw dropped.

Surreptitiously I glanced over toward the black teenagers who were sprawled against the subway door. "Want to ask those dudes if their balls are important to them?" The two of us laughed until tears rolled down our cheeks. Later the thought came to me: as celibates we're more like Alberto than we may think.

When Carlos and I reached the hospital where Doc was monitoring Alberto's pain management for a few days, it was lunchtime and the patients were being fed. Everyone was in the room, and I introduced Carlos to Rita, Lydia, and Hector. I came up close by Alberto while Carlos remained by the door. They explained how he was in much pain, especially his head, his right side, and his abdomen. I saw that his face was noticeably swollen and pale; the cancer must be getting to his brain. Awake, but in a daze, Alberto took my hand. There was a strange look in his eyes. "Carlos, come here." He grasped Carlos's hand and I could see that they would hit it off.

Hector went to get some special food for Alberto, while Rita and Lydia remained with us. The two of them looked worried and very tired. Rita was seated on a chair by the window, while her daughter stood by the foot of the bed. A mature looking sixteen-year-old with large dark eyes and sensuous lips, Lydia's glistening black hair tumbled out over her shoulders. "Sit here, Father Paul," motioned Rita, wanting to give me her seat.

"No." I indicated that I would sit on the edge of the bed. Carlos stood on the other side and he and Alberto began to converse in Spanish. Though the patient continued to hold my hand, he was engrossed with Carlos. Gradually they became more animated and I could hear the tone of affection in their voices. Try as I might, I couldn't understand what they were saying.

In a while, a strange feeling arose. They don't need me; I may as well not be here! I wanted the two of them to strike up a friendship, needed it in fact. But this was too quick, too "disposing" of me. I was jealous of this young kid usurping "my" patient.

Glancing over at Lydia, I noticed that her eyes were moist. I looked at Rita, but there were no feelings I could recognize there. Maybe they feel the same way toward us! I had never thought of this before: that a family might actually resent our team's quick and intimate involvement with their loved one. No matter how helpful it was, maybe they too felt discarded for some "special" caregiver who hasn't borne the heat of the day with the patient and who comes in like a savior to drop pearls of wisdom.

We can pray with beautiful words, even hold a hand with love, but we leave when we wish and do not feel the emptiness of the house and the surviving spouse or child's life because we just go on to the next patient. Maybe that's why some of them don't want us to come into their homes. I let go of Alberto's hand and went over to speak with them.

Rita explained that the doctor will try liquid pain medicine first. If that doesn't relieve Alberto's discomfort, he will give him injections. "He eats and eats," she said, expressing amazement at such an appetite in someone so sick.

"The medicine does that," I explained. Lydia kept staring ahead at her father. "What about the two of you?" I placed my hand on the girl's. "How're you doing?"

"We stay up with Daddy at night," she said huskily. Her voice alternated between what sounded like a calm adult awareness at what was happening and a barely concealed panic of a teenager whose world was about to crumble. "I'm going to school, but I can't concentrate for nothing...I can't believe this is happening." Peeking sideways at her mother, she went on, "Mommy wakes him up when he falls asleep at night."

"What?" Rita was staring at the floor. "What do you mean?" Lydia waited for her mother to explain.

Sheepishly Rita described how she stays up with Alberto at night and wakes him up whenever he falls into a deep asleep. "I'm afraid he will die," she said, her lips pursed together.

"So you don't want him to die?" I shook my head in a mock reprimand. "But he will and you will if neither of you get any sleep!" Laughing gently, Rita promised not to do this again. My hunch was that Ruby would have to reinforce this.

The door swung open and Hector appeared with huge bags of food. "I hope everyone is hungry," he announced. "I bought enough for all of us." Soon we were all diving into cardboard containers of egg-drop soup, pork-fried rice, broccoli with a delicious garlic sauce, and a shrimp, chicken, and cashew nut combination.

I sat next to Carlos and he filled me in on his conversation with Alberto. Hoping to get in a few words with Hector, I got my opening when he passed around second helpings. "Hector, may I speak with you privately?"

"Certainly." We took our cups of tea into the corridor. I saw no visitor's room where we could be alone, so I led him over to two chairs placed by a large potted fern at the end of a hallway. Its curving boughs overhead suggested coziness.

I had not found a time during my other visits to speak with Hector without the family around, and I wanted to see if he would open up. His avowed atheism didn't allow much of an opening. Yet even if his age and superior bearing made me feel uncomfortable, I decided the time was getting short.

We talked about Alberto's condition, and Hector spoke of it all very fatalistically. "You do everything you can while you are alive. You live life to the fullest. I've travelled to India and China, had a good life, been a friend of Alberto's these many years. We've done all we can, and now we have to accept . . . no one lives forever."

"No, but how are you dealing with it? How are you going to cope without him?" The graceful fingers drummed on the arm of the chair. His raised eyebrows and faint smile were all I could see.

"I have an apartment; it's being painted right now. What can you do? This is the way life is."

His tendency to intellectualize encouraged me to risk being more pointed about their relationship. "Hector . . . " I laid my hand clumsily on his wrist, "do you know how Alberto described you to Carlos in the room just now?" He crossed his legs, one hand under his chin, surveying me as one might a book or an interesting painting.

"How was that?"

I paused before telling him what would touch him to the core if anything could. "Alberto said, 'Hector es mi madre, mi padre, mi hermana, mi hermano . . . mi amigo.'" The faded eyes blinked once or twice. Then his mouth crumpled and the man bent his head. He covered his eyes.

Slowly I repeated it in English with emotion. "Hector is my mother, my father, my sister, my brother . . . my friend. You really love each other, don't you?" A muffled cry came from his belly. His head nodded and the tears came. Above us a fern branch sagged, as if struck with a pang of mercy for a fellow living thing.

Before we returned to the others, Hector offered additional information that made him what we called a bereavement risk. A friend of his, a sixty-five-year-old gay man, was recently killed when struck by a sanitation truck. Hector said he did not intend to go to the funeral because the man's family is antagonistic toward him.

Alberto's eyes were closed when we entered the room. Carlos was still next to him holding his hand. Spasmodic light breaths came out of him while Lydia sat transfixed in a chair watching. Rita had her back to us, looking out the window. Quietly I slipped up to Alberto with Hector by my side.

"What an appetite! You're going to get fat!" I said when he opened his eyes. Alberto didn't smile. Instead he stared with glazed eyes and said something in Spanish that Carlos translated.

"He says he wants you to help him be born."

"Ask him what he means by that." Then I remembered how it said in Scripture that you must be born again if you want to enter into God's Kingdom (John 3:3ff.). Taking out the holy oil, I indicated to him and the family that we better not wait for him to come back home for the anointing service we had planned.

"You want to be born, Alberto? . . . " I reached to touch his hand, but he held it out as though to someone else in front of him. He was still staring, but now right through me.

"Ask him who he sees, who he wants to help him be born," I said.

"He says no one is there," Carlos said. But still Alberto reached out toward something. I motioned for Rita, Lydia, and Hector to come closer. The women did, but Hector remained in the back by the door. I sat down on the bed, and with Carlos's assistance, reminded Alberto of his faith, encouraging him to trust God. I asked Lydia to read a passage from the Old Testament, and she began, "There is an appointed time for everything, and a time for every affair under the heavens. . . . "

After I made the sign of the cross on his forehead and hand with the oil, they all took turns placing their hands on him. Rita wanted his other hand, hidden under the sheet, to be anointed too. That's when I told them about the former custom in the Catholic Church of anointing all the senses — eyes, ears, nose, mouth, hands, and feet — "to pray for forgiveness for anything we may have done wrong through our bodily senses and also to offer to God everything we have done good through them." Hector came up behind us at this point. I held out my hand with the oil; he took a drop and touched Alberto's cheek with it.

While Lydia was in the midst of the Scripture passage, Alberto yawned and she paused. Rita said something in Spanish, and Lydia said that her mother felt that his yawn was a sign there was an evil spirit in the room. This spirit did not want us to be there, Rita explained with wide eyes. They looked at me. With my hands I made a shooing gesture toward the walls to show them we were chasing this spirit away. Rita seemed satisfied and Lydia finished the passage.

"Through this holy anointing, may the Lord in his love and mercy help you with the grace of the Holy Spirit." I said the blessing from the prayerbook.

Alberto mumbled something. Carlos said, "He says he doesn't want to die." "Tell him the sacrament will help him get better... or, when he is ready, to let go to God." Were we rushing him? From Alberto's looks I didn't think so.

We sat quietly with him for some moments. Finally, I peeked at my watch. "We've got to go... Alberto, it is time to say adios."

I felt such love in my heart for this beautiful man with such a great warm smile. I wanted to wrap my arms around his wooly head and hold him against my chest, to tell him how much he had gotten inside me and would remain so always. But I couldn't; it would sound so foolish.

I stood to go. Carlos was taking Alberto's hand, kissing it gently as though it were a chalice. Oh, Paul, you idiot! What are you waiting for? I leaned back down and gratefully did likewise.

"Gracias, Padre." Alberto whispered.

"Gracias, Alberto." When I turned to look back at him from the doorway, Alberto's eyes were closed. *Lord, help him be born into your kingdom... mi madre, mi padre... mi amigo, Alberto Cruz.*

When Hector shook hands with us and Rita and Lydia hugged Carlos and me in the corridor, I was grateful that a ritual had been able to bring our differences together for once instead of driving us apart.

I had heard that the family planned to cremate Alberto's body, and I told Carlos this as we walked toward the subway.

"Cremated!" he protested, "I don't like that."

"Yes, I know it is strange to Catholics, but it is allowed now. Too many bodies in the cemetery!" He glanced at me to check my seriousness. "They plan to throw his ashes off the George Washington Bridge...wanna come?"

"Oh, my God!" he said in his innocent but resilient way.

"C'mon!" I poked him in the ribs. "You've got to get into the fun parts of this ministry. The worst that could happen is that his ashes might blow back in your face!"

Chuckling together now, we came to a red light, the traffic plowing past us as we waited. The young man turned and looked back at the hospital tower, then over toward the sun, setting like a golden rose behind the skyscrapers. Yes, Carlos was initiated now. He had taught me something too. To hell with my jealousy toward my patients. Just show each one my love while I can.

~ Gerri ~

O my Father: ancient, hallowed,
   Lonely, disappointed Father:
   Betrayed and rejected Ruler of the Universe:
   Angry, wrinkled Old Majesty:
   I want to pray.
   I want to say Kaddish.
   My own Kaddish. There may be
   No one to say it after me.

I have so little time, as You well know.
   Is my end a minute away? An hour?
   Is there even time to consider the question?
   It could be here, while we are singing,
   That we may be stopped, once for all,
   Cut off in the act of praising You.
   But while I have breath, however brief,
   I will sing this final Kaddish for You,
   For me, and for all these I love
   Here in this sacred house.

I want to pray, and time is short,
   Yit'gadal v'yit'kadash sh'me raba...

> —Excerpt from Leonard Bernstein,
> the symphony "Kaddish"

DOMINIC had made the difficult decision to withdraw the medicine Natalie had been taking to curb the spread of cancer in her brain. The doctor told him it could hasten his wife's death as well as curb her insatiable appetite. He didn't make the decision easily. Weighed against the guilt he felt

163

for giving up was his anguish at seeing his beloved Nattie suffering day after day. But Dominic was closer to accepting it now. Though he continued to rant and rave to the hospice team, we sensed that he was finally ready to let her go.

But she didn't die. Instead, Natalie slipped in and out of a coma for weeks, and Dominic now had to deal with her inexplicable hanging on.

One of my teachers, an extraordinary nurse named Cathy Fanslow, said that dying people and their loved ones go through stages of hope. The first is the hope that the diagnosis is wrong or that the disease can be cured by treatment or even by a miracle. During the second stage there is the hope that life will be prolonged and that the suffering will not be too great. The final stage is the hope for a "good" or peaceful death and, for believers, the hope for a better life beyond death.

The first stage is usually encountered more vividly before patients come into the hospice program; it is accompanied by second medical opinions and by aggressive treatment such as chemotherapy and radiation for most cancer patients. The second and third stages usually predominate in hospice patients, though the hope for a cure may yet emerge in waves until acceptance is finally reached. Woven like a purple thread through all of these stages is the waiting.

It seems glib to describe anyone else's experience of waiting for anything — let alone waiting to die — as sometimes beneficial. Yet this is what I have noticed in many of our patients and caregivers.

The time of waiting is an opportunity for many things to happen. I've already mentioned the "tasks" of saying thank you, I'm sorry, I love you, and goodbye. Yet these are only words. It may take a little longer for the deeper meaning related to the words to sink in. That is where the real healing takes place. The unfinished business that a patient or family members may have can keep some patients hanging on long after their mere physiological state would otherwise allow.

This was certainly true of Elmo, who had become very dear to me. At age sixteen, his waiting, his acceptance of death was ambivalent. Something must be built into their psyche that allows young people to see only life, even in the face of clear signals that they do not have much time left. The kid had barely lived yet. Talk about unfinished business!

In some ways though, I suppose Elmo's response was simply an accentuated expression of the ambivalence we all have toward death, preferring the known to the unknown even when the latter would put us out of our misery. A dying child accentuates these feelings of ambivalence in the caregivers too.

After almost a year of visiting Elmo — first at his foster home and then at Queens General Hospital — I got a telephone message that he was being transferred to St. Mary's Children's Hospital in Bayside. He had been waiting for a bed, and finally there was an opening. This special hospital, sponsored by the Episcopal Church, treats children of all religions: some with chronic diseases that left them crippled and unable to be cared for at home, some who were recovering from serious operations, and some like Elmo who would not recover from their illness.

At first he would be on a regular ward, although in a private room. As soon as his mother signed the "Do Not Resuscitate" papers, he would be transferred to the hospice section, which they called the Palliative Care Unit. The hospital chaplain, Father Chadwicke, would be chiefly responsible for Elmo's spiritual care. I decided to continue to see him as a friend.

The first time I visited Elmo at St. Mary's he seemed glad to see me. "I'm hungry!" was his chief complaint. All he could think about was a pizza. Like a little tyrant he ordered me to get his box of toys from under his bed, turn on the TV, and buy him some batteries for his Walkman. His grandmother had visited, he told me, and Father Chadwicke too.

Elmo surprised me by asking if I knew any Bible stories I could tell him.

"You got any favorites?"

"Yeah ... Joseph."

"Which one?"

"The one who had the rainbow-colored coat."

I recounted this tale from the history of Israel (Gen. 37) as well as I remembered while Elmo played with his robots. Every now and then he stopped to listen. "What part did you like the best?" I asked when I had finished, imagining he would say when the brothers fought about throwing Joseph into the well.

Without glancing up the boy responded, "When he got back together with his father."

I remembered that comment as I drove home later. Elmo's mother was a drug addict, and she had farmed him out to a foster home. He told me he saw his father only a couple of times a year. Fathers! Such an important relationship and so absent or distant for so many people. It is as if motherhood has at least some primal instinct to cut through the normal problems we have to deal with in growing up. But there is such a weak follow-through from so many fathers after they have planted their seed. No wonder we call God "Father"; heaven has to make up for what so many of us are missing. Did Elmo like that part of the story because he yet hopes for something from his father?

The hospice patients "hang on" for many reasons. Some wait till a member of the family finally gets there or to celebrate one more Christmas or birthday. Some seem to wait until they get their financial affairs in order or even to get well enough in one last rush of the life-force to get on a plane and go to the Caribbean with a spouse. Some seem to wait until they can die alone.

When a loved one is dying, some families may hover over the patient incessantly. They want to be there for those last precious moments of existence, as if to sum up their deep involvement with this person during life. Or to make up for the lack of it. "Why don't you take a break?" I've heard nurses suggest to some caregivers. People need to have the option to die in private. Dying is so intensely personal that some patients don't want to be surrounded even by their loved ones. They may also wish to spare the family the grief of actually witnessing the moment of death. Consciously or not, we have more control over the timing of our death than we think.*

~

Gerri was a feisty sixty-three-year-old efficiency expert. Dying from lung cancer, she manifested reasons for waiting when even she might not have known why. She told Joanne at the first interview, "I'm a renegade Catholic... but don't put that down

---

*See *Final Gifts: Understanding the Special Awareness, Needs, and Communications of the Dying,* by hospice nurses Maggie Callanan and Patricia Kelley (New York: Poseidon Press, 1992).

on the form." She represented many — regardless of their religious affiliation — who have become disillusioned with the easy answers of their religion. You could say she had "lost her faith."

Gerri had said she was willing to see a priest. Maybe Joanne had done one of her sales pitches for me; I wasn't sure. She only said that Gerri would be helped by companionship, and she was a woman who liked to talk.

The patient lived in an apartment house in a decent neighborhood on the Upper West Side. Sharing the apartment was her seventy-five-year-old "significant other" who had moved in with her fifteen years before, a year after her first husband had died. When I telephoned, introduced myself, and asked, "May I come for spiritual support?" a scratchy but friendly voice answered, "Not today, honey...I'm too weak...tomorrow. Late mornings are best for me." We agreed on 11:00 a.m.

When I arrived at the apartment house, Gerri's friend Sol let me in. An elderly gentleman with a shock of white hair, he reminded me of my father. He was big boned and must have been handsome in his day, but he was stooped now with bleary eyes, and his weight had settled around his waist. On one level, he seemed as if you could sit around a kitchen table and trade stories with him, but in his eyes a glimmer of pain or disappointment stopped you from getting close enough to touch.

A small, slender lady in a pink nightgown lay in a bed breathing from an oxygen mask at the far end of the room. As I entered, she slowly turned her head on the pillow to see who it was. Her hair was mousy brown and dishevelled. Freckles were sprinkled like cinnamon over her bony pallid face. An equally bony hand with age spots clutched the oxygen mask, while over the top of it peered a pair of tired eyes with a sparkle in them yet.

After some preliminary introductions, Gerri asked, "Well, what's the answer, Paul?...do you mind if I call you Paul?" The corners of her mouth crinkled in a funny smile around the sides of the oxygen mask.

"The answer?..."

"You know," she yawned, "each of us dies, but life goes on."

"And you want to know the answer?" I smiled.

Sucking in air, Gerri continued to philosophize. "I suppose that's the answer, isn't it?...'Life goes on'...it's bigger than me, you, any of us." Sol was staring at the rhododendron plant on the desk.

Gerri lightened it up. She spoke of not having much interest in reading newspapers anymore, how difficult it was to keep her mail up to date. "I can barely get out of bed and walk to my desk," she croaked and then complained about how her mouth was so dry from having to breathe through it. Sol gave me a knowing look.

"What do think about assisted dying?" Gerri asked after a lull in the conversation. She seemed to be playing with me.

"You mean mercy killing? ... I'm against it."

"Well, honey, when you're falling apart day by day like I am, you may get a different idea." I had never discussed this topic with a patient before, and I would have liked to pursue it, but Gerri was already onto something else.

"Have you had anything to eat yet?" she asked suddenly.

"Thanks, I already had breakfast."

"Well, how about something to wet your whistle with then? ... Sol, get him one of those popsicles," she ordered. "A cherry, they're the best!"

When Sol returned the carton to the kitchen at her directions, Gerri remarked how he was very dependent on her. She didn't know how he would get on without her.

"Don't get me wrong. He is a dear friend, but I don't love him the way I loved my husband." When I looked at the pictures on her dresser, she started to tell me about her two daughters.

"Dorothy lives in Minneapolis and is very involved with my care. The other one lives in Virginia and we haven't talked for fifteen years ... since her father died." When I inquired more about this daughter, she said she didn't want to talk about her now. When Gerri began to nod off a little later, I made my exit.

On the way home I began to think of Gerri's controlling style, especially of how she might relate to time. As an efficiency expert she was paid to help businesses make every second count. Time is money; no wasted actions. It was revealing to me how one's temperament and profession could easily be carried into one's style of coping with dying.

"I want to die — it's enough already!" one of our patients had announced. Another, a ninety-six-year-old man with a voice like a child: "I'm ready to go home to Jesus!" A third: "It's too much,

all I do is lay here and suffer. . . . I'm praying to die in my sleep,"
while I noticed the sleeping tablets within reach on her dresser.

But willing to die doesn't always produce the desired result.
Though she seemed to have said it in jest, Gerri's comment
about mercy killing made me wonder. Tired of waiting for death,
some people think of "doing something" to hasten the inevitable
process. Loved ones may feel their compassion turn in this direction. Who wants to watch someone you love suffer while
together you wait? And for what — biology, God, fate, electricity to be turned off? There are so many difficult cases you hear
about in the news.

Yet who knows what we'd be short-circuiting if, impatient
with the waiting, we were to choose to hasten death? Is "eternal life" something we have no right to rush, even if the hope
for this afterlife is precisely what allows us to let go of this life
in peace? Though the patient (or caregivers) may feel that the
time is up, can we imagine such a thing as God's unfinished
business? What might God have to teach us yet through our
suffering?

Our hospice philosophy is to "walk with" our patients and
families in the midst of their shifting hopes, while providing
care on every level we can so they can be as pain-free as possible. The philosophy doesn't include actively enabling them to
end their lives. On the other hand, who of us can judge a long-
suffering, terminally ill person like Gerri who might take "God's
time" into her own hands through actions that could hasten her
death? Whose life is it ultimately?[11]

The differing approaches to these questions — the aggressive
care up to the end taken by hospitals and the more natural approach to dying taken by the hospice movement — dramatize
the difficulty of these decisions that patients and families of the
terminally ill must make.

A week later I heard that Gerri was failing. I got Sol on the
phone. "Yes, come tomorrow," he said. "It might cheer her up,
but we are planning to send her to Calvary Hospital." It is hard
to know what is best in situations like this. Moving her to the
hospital would provide better care than Sol could give her now,
and yet she seemed so far gone that if he could last another few
nights she could die at home as she originally had wanted.

When I arrived the next morning Sol met me at the door, his

eyes all puffed out and red from sleeplessness, crying, or both. In an undertone he confided, "I can't go on another night with her here. If I do, I'll die myself... and I think I've got a few more years. So we'll take her up to Calvary.... They'll be here any minute."

We went over to Gerri's bed. She was much more debilitated than the week before, and her lips were dry and cracked, though her eyes still showed recognition.

"Honey?..." Sol whispered in a haggard voice as he leaned over her, "We're going to take you to the hospital." You're just telling her!

"Is that what you want?" I asked her.

Gerri shook her head ever so slightly. No.

Sol interjected, "It's just for a little while. When you get better we'll bring you back." In an aside to me he added, "Her daughter made the arrangements."

"Maybe she won't come back, Sol." I hesitated and then spoke aloud for both of them to hear. "This place has a lot of meaning to both of you. Maybe you better say goodbye to Gerri, at least to your memories in this house...while you are both here." Gerri's gray eyes were fixed on mine, but the spark was gone.

The old man took her hand. "Honey, we've had a lot of good times, haven't we? I'm gonna miss you very much. I...love you." A tear trickled down his rough cheek. "Every day I'll come visit you at Calvary," he promised. I went over by the sofa so they could be alone.

Soon a buzzer sounded. The ambulance crew was in the lobby. I went over and asked Gerri if she would like to be anointed. She shook her head no. Five minutes later they had her on a stretcher going down the elevator with Sol and me right behind.

Out in front of their twenty-story apartment building, Sol turned and said, "Everyone in this place knows her; they ask me about her every day."

I imagined these neighbors peeking out of their windows above us. They would see an incredibly spunky efficiency manager wrapped in swaddling clothes for her last ride through town. Now completely vulnerable, she had to let go of everything she owned whether she had finished the paperwork or not. No more control; somebody else's wishes were being followed now.

Gerri even needed an ice chip stroked on her lips to get a sip of water. The old man and I hunkered into the back of the ambulance next to her as it roared up through Harlem toward the Bronx.

~

The next time I saw Elmo was different. The nurse called me over to the station before I went into his room and told me he had been depressed the night before, that the night nurse had found him crying when she made her rounds. When I entered his darkened room, Elmo was half asleep, staring at a plate of food on his tray. The TV was on.

"Hi, Elmo."

"Paul," he said weakly. He looked up at me glumly. "They keep shoving this food in my face. . . . I don't want to eat, I want to leave."

"But how're you gonna stay healthy if you don't eat?"

"Paul," he pleaded with his moon face, "my face will explode."

Father Chadwicke stuck his head in the door at this point. "Elmo, how're you doing?"

"No good."

"What?"

"I'm a sad case. . . . I've got no home."

"Elmo, *this* is your home," he said cheerfully. "In fact today we are going to get you into a wheelchair so we can give you a tour of this place and let you meet the other children." But Elmo was inconsolable.

As the nurses prepared him for this tour, Father Chadwicke whispered to me in the hallway that Elmo was refusing to eat or take his medicine. "He's feeling guilty, he says, over being too much a burden on others. . . . He wants to go to heaven." The priest rolled his eyes.

Glancing over my shoulder into the room, I saw them hoisting Elmo by a sling into a wheelchair. The skin on his legs and buttocks was beginning to break down. He was coughing up mucous. I shook my head. Wants to go to heaven! If I were Elmo, I would too. The chaplain and I went downstairs for some lunch.

Later I listened while three nurses and a doctor tried to per-suade Elmo to take his medicine and eat. They were warm and concerned, but he had shut down. I tried a different tack. "Hey, y'know what? It's your choice whether you eat or not.... No one can force you. If you want to live, you'll eat." Elmo just stared straight ahead.

I kept trying. "Besides, your face doesn't look that bad to me, just like you've been mugged." He gave me a look that said my humor had bombed. By the time I left they had returned him to his bed, where he looked more peaceful. I didn't say a prayer because it would have been one more spoon-feeding in his life. I said I'd see him in a couple of weeks.

Three weeks later Elmo was transferred to the Palliative Care Unit on the top floor. His mother had finally consented to sign the necessary papers. After Father Chadwicke took me for a tour of this bright, cheerfully decorated wing of the hospital, he left me, and I stood at Elmo's door. He was playing with his toy boats in a basin of water set up on his food stand. The comics I had brought him were hidden behind my back. He looked well cared for.

"You look great, Elmo! How do you feel?"

"Good." He was matter-of-fact, like a little professor. "What do you have for me, Paul?" I flashed the comics and his face lit up.

"Hey! Let me see!" I handed them over and he gobbled them up. Meanwhile, I started fooling with his toy boats in the basin. Elmo stopped me.

"Oh, so I bring you comics, but you won't let me play with your toys."

"A grown man!" he said in mild exasperation.

"I feel like being bad today," I said with a glint in my eye. "I'm tired of being nice."

The two of us sparred like this for a while, interrupted at one point by a nurse coming in to give him a bath. When I re-turned, he was in a mood to order me around and told me to go downstairs and get him an orange soda. The money, he said, was in his top drawer. When I came back with the soda, I gently challenged him about thinking only of himself.

"What makes you say that?"

"You didn't ask if I wanted a soda."

"Oh, Paul!"

I sounded to myself like his father. "You're feeling better, though, aren't you?" I said, sitting on his bed.

"Yep!" Slurping the soda, Elmo asked if I wanted to play a game.

"Sure!" I grinned, glad to be finally accepted as a play-partner. It was a game of tick-tack-toe played with blocks.

At first I thought I'd let him win, but decided not to. Instead I had to fight for my life, and he beat me on his own. "You're right, Paul," Elmo said with utmost seriousness. "You'll have to learn to play more."

We sat together in silence, watching the breeze ripple through the sunlit curtains. "You look so much better than the last time," I said.

"Yeah, but I'm bored."

"Bored? You got all these toys! You've got nurses falling over each other to take care of you!" He flashed a shy smile, and confided with excitement.

"Next Thursday I'll be seventeen."

"No kidding!" His grandmother had been in to see him a few days before and had promised him a remote-control racer. Elmo was excited over this and made me promise to take him outside to run it.

"I can't make it Thursday, but I'll be in on Friday." I wanted to bring some religious dimension to the visit and asked if I could tell him a Scripture story.

"Okay." I began to tell him in my own words the story of Job, while he turned to play with his boats in the basin.

"This guy had a huge family, lots of animals and servants, and a fantastic house.... He was on top of the world. One day a servant came to him and said some of his cattle had died from a disease. Job was sad. Later, another servant told him his camels had been stolen. Job got mad...." Elmo glanced up from the basin and then back to his toys again.

"His friends told him God must be punishing him, but Job said, 'For what? I've done nothing wrong.' Instead he said a prayer to God to give him strength and went back to work. One day a servant ran up to him and told him some of his children had been killed in an accident. Job screamed in sorrow. His friends told him he should curse God, but Job said 'For what? God gives us good things, so why not bad things too. . . .' "

Elmo interrupted, "Paul, I don't like this story. . . . Tell me another one instead."

"What don't you like about it?"

"I don't know. . . . It just frustrates me."

"Tell me one you'd like then."

He screwed his face up in thought for a moment. "Daniel in the Lion's Den."

Daniel in the Lion's Den — the story of how God saved Daniel when he was thrown into the lion pit by the king! This kid knew what he needed more than I did. I fumbled through the story and wanted to conclude with a prayer. Elmo said that would be okay, but when I asked him if he would lead it, he said he knew only grace before meals and the goodnight prayer.

"Say grace then," I countered. Elmo shook his head. We were still sparring.

Reaching over into the basin, I took his hand and held it dripping while I offered a spontaneous prayer about him, telling God about the boredom and excitement of his soon-to-be-seventeen son. Elmo looked even more bored. I went on. . . .

"Save this young guy as long ago you saved Daniel, Lord. . . ." Then imagining what it might be like in a sixteen-year-old body, whether sick or not, I blurted out, " . . . and help him deal with his feelings of wanting to make love." Not knowing where this prayer had come from, I smiled in surprise. Elmo smiled too.

"I don't think of that, Paul."

Playfully I retorted, "How could you lie in the middle of a prayer?"

"I don't have those thoughts anymore," he insisted.

I grinned down at him skeptically. "Oh, yeah! Why not?"

"'Cause I'm broken."

This kid felt more and more like a son to me, and his words stabbed my heart. I needed to save him from such a miserable idea about himself and ransacked my brain. "Broken?" I muttered. My fists clenched. "Is your heart broken? . . . or your mind?"

Wide-eyed and timid, he stared up at me. "No."

"Well, *that's* what I'm talking about!" There was a fierceness in my voice.

Elmo wanted to say a prayer for me then. "Bless Paul, Lord ... he's a great guy!"

I held that conversation in my heart when I attended Elmo's wake five days later in an empty funeral parlor in a rundown neighborhood of Bedford-Stuyvesant. Yes, the tumor finally got to his brain and shut down the life of Elmo Washington. He never made it to his seventeenth birthday.

The message was on my answering machine the day I had planned to visit him again. Father Chadwicke's voice was gentle: "Paul, I'm sorry to have to tell you this way, but Elmo died early this morning. He went peacefully. Call me for details about his wake. God bless."

I was scheduled to visit Gerri at Calvary that same day. The nurse told me that she was very alert but barely able to speak. The "good" daughter from Minneapolis was sleeping in a room upstairs. I slipped up to the patient's bed in the very cheery room. An oxygen tank was helping her to breathe. Above her on a stand, an IV bag fed her with liquid nutrients — "Standard procedure," the nurse had told me, "unless specifically declined."

"Gerri," I murmured, taking her limp, cold hand, "it's Father Paul." A faint flicker passed through her eyes. I talked aimlessly for some moments before her daughter came in. Dorothy, a yuppie career woman in her early thirties, was quite lively. She even made sly little jokes about her mother. The two of us stood there talking about Gerri, who lay between us, trying to include her, but it was difficult because she couldn't talk.

When Dorothy went to get some water for her, Gerri mumbled something. Leaning closer, the faintest whisper came out. "Why...is it taking...so long?" The water? What does she mean?

"What's taking so long?" I repeated.

With great effort she got out the word, "Leaving."

I thought of the IV bag above her giving her "three meals a day," according to the nurse. I wanted to say, "That bag is holding you here, Gerri. Do you want it?" But I didn't.

Later, when Dorothy returned, I asked about the other sister. "Does she know her mother's here?"

"Yes, but she doesn't know whether to come up from Virginia

or not," said Dorothy, who was carefully feeding her mother drops of water from a straw.

"Well, she better do so soon if she wants to see her." Below us, Gerri was shaking her head back and forth.

"Look," I said, "if people have an argument, they can make up face to face. And if they can't, they can do it in their hearts. So you can let go of any hurt or grievance you have now, Gerri. . . . You can forgive her in your heart, or ask her forgiveness if there is any need for that, okay?" Gerri was breathing very laboriously, as though any breath might be her last. I didn't know what was going on inside her, but thought this might help her let go.

I held one hand and Dorothy held the other while I prayed aloud for what we had been speaking about: I gave thanks for Gerri's life, her daughters, her friend Sol. Then I said goodbye. Outside in the corridor I gave my card to Dorothy and explained how I could be reached if necessary. She seemed pleased by the visit. I drove home feeling as if I had done a good day's work.

Before retiring that night I went up to the roof of the rectory. On clear nights it is beautiful there. The stars and moon hang over the city, and during winter when the people aren't on the street it is even peaceful. The moon was nearly full. I let my heart tumble out its feelings. . . .

Dear Elmo, already I miss you, but I'm glad for you too; your suffering is over. And Gerri, Natalie, Candida, Isha, all of you waiting for something — what's that like?

Someday that will be you too, Paul. Someday you'll have withdrawn from life, stopped eating and reading newspapers, drawn the blankets up over your head, maybe even gone into a coma after praying to die — and still you'll go on. What kind of suffering will that be? For yourself? For your loved ones? Even for your professional caregivers?

All that you are, all that you have known as worthwhile will be gone. "My only friend is darkness" (Ps. 88:19). Finally the unthinkable will have occurred, what you have ultimately fought against even on your most miserable days. The pain and suffering will finally be too much. You'll beg and pray to die!

Still, life will go on. You'll discover one more threshold of suffering beyond what you swore was the last. You'll wait, you'll exist while waiting for something or someone to finally extinguish the pain. Your will will be gone. You'll see that your willing was all a fantasy, that we cause nothing by our willing. If there is a God, you will discover this divine Spirit in you, waiting, suffering. Suffering for you even, suffering for all.

You surrender, let yourself join this Spirit, "offer up" your suffering, and possibly feel for the first time in your life an infinitesimal drop of pure love ... "Let it be done to me as you say" (Luke 1:38).

~

Joanne told me during a coffee break the next day that Gerri had died peacefully in her sleep the night before. A few days later I phoned Sol to offer my condolences. "How are you doing, Sol?"

"I feel her absence the most." The old man's voice cracked. "When I come home at night and I'm alone, I see her around every corner."

"That's tough. It'll take time, Sol."

"What can you do?" he asked philosophically. "Wives, parents, children die. That's just the way it is. I'm doing the best I can, going to the Y, keeping busy."

"That's good."

"By the way, Father, that last night before she died, her daughter from Virginia came up to see her. They talked and cried. I think this is what she was waiting for. Gerri died a little later when we went down for a coffee."

"Thanks for telling me this, Sol. I believe you're right. Take care now."

I hung up the phone. Good night, Sol. Good night, Gerri. What's the answer? Life goes on! I went to the kitchen to hunt for a cherry popsicle.

~

The young black man in a gray suit welcomed me into the funeral parlor on Utica Avenue, one of many such establishments in that neighborhood. It brought back a friend's words to me from twenty years before when I had worked briefly as a prison chaplain. Out on parole, this six-foot-two black man had walked with me through a similar neighborhood in South Philadelphia one summer day, giving me a tour of his home base.

"Check it out, Paul," Kenny had remarked ruefully. "There are three kinds of establishments in the ghetto: bars, storefront

churches, and funeral parlors. My people are either trying to
drink their troubles away, or pray them away, or it's all over, ain't
it?... time for the body-snatchers."

After I introduced myself, the funeral director informed me
that I could go back to the room where Elmo was if I wished; his
grandmother was due later. The place was as quiet as a church.
I peeked into the large rectangular room at the end of a long
hallway. A casket was up front with folding chairs arranged for
about a hundred people. Not a soul stirred in the late afternoon
twilight. I took a deep breath and entered.

Drawing closer, I saw Elmo's body in the casket. He was all
dressed up in a suit and tie and clutched a red carnation in
his white-gloved hands. I stood there for some moments gazing
down at him, the huge belly more subdued in the suit, his face
peaceful-looking with the eyes closed, his blond nappy hair, the
petulant lips. Elmo finally looked content. I took a seat off to the
side where I was able to see him.

It was strange to be in the large room with so many chairs,
a too-sweet picture of Jesus on the wall, quite a few floral bou-
quets, and Elmo's body — alone. I sat there for some time and
thought of all the times I had visited him, all the changes he
had gone through and I had gone through, and especially my
last visit less than a week ago. My heart filled with sadness for
this would-be cartoonist, but the carnation and the white gloves
made me smile too. He never stopped playing and was dreaming
of a remote-control race car only a few days ago.

I prayed for Elmo, who had been so abandoned during his
lifetime. I thanked God for him. His waiting was over; the body-
snatchers had him now. A deep sigh escaped: *enough* already!

His waiting was over, and my waiting with him was too.
Months ago Elmo had wanted to "go to heaven." So many people
wish the same but linger on. In the end their waiting, their suffering may be for those of us who remain. At the very least, by
patiently waiting with them we may learn to suffer and wait,
even to play and love better ourselves. *"I'm talking about your
heart, your mind...are they broken?"... "NO!"*

Standing to leave, I made the sign of the cross over Elmo,
touching him briefly on his cheek with my finger. At the front
desk I asked for a piece of paper and wrote a letter, which I left

for his grandmother, "Your faithful love for your grandson gave me a sign of God's unfailing love. Thank you."

As I escaped from that ghetto with its miserable bars and storefront churches, its funeral parlors and broken dreams, I felt tired and worn down. I needed a break. Yet a reason for the waiting came to me: Elmo's body might be broken, but he's one of my children. I needed to find a way to claim this fatherhood.

~ Eddie ~

HOSPICE WORK was so exhausting that I planned a weekend retreat for myself in the hills of upstate New York. In the silence and solitude of the wilderness, God would heal my soul from all the losses. Tomorrow I would drive off in the early morning hours even before the garbage trucks unloaded the dumpsters across the street from the rectory. I was near burnout. I was drained physically from the constant struggle to survive the aggressive madness of the city and spiritually from the recent series of deaths of patients I loved. I had my bags packed. All I had to do was get through one more day.

There were no patient visits on my schedule. Today would be a day to catch up on paperwork. I could even leave the office in the early afternoon to do some last-minute preparations for the trip to the country. When I arrived at work, Ruby was deep into paperwork. She offered me part of a large raisin muffin while we caught each other up on various patients. With our feet propped up on her desk, I noticed the white Oxfords with navy blue wing tips she was sporting.

"Check out the shoes! What a hot shot you are, Ruby!"

"Hey, Paul!" She wriggled her feet as though she were dancing. "If there is one thing I don't hold back spending money on, it's shoes. Shoot, all the walking around we do!" Her voice hung out there, accenting the obvious. "If you don't take care of yourself, honey, who will?" Ruby sipped her herb tea while I murmured assent. Hardly listening, I hoped the biting caffeine would stir a few of my brain cells into action.

"Get up!" she suddenly demanded. It was one of her games. Reluctantly I shifted out of the relaxed position and pulled myself up in front of her. "You need a hug." Ruby's strong arms

180

swiftly wrapped around my torso. With a surprisingly powerful grip she pressed me to herself and a muffled guffaw burst out of her.

"Oh, Ruby, you're so right!"

Reclining again, we continued to banter about her daughters' musical tastes — "Debbie loves jazz and blues but Anya is into rap music. I'm gonna get them to make a tape for you."

I told her about my weekend plans. "I'm not even going to think about this place."

"That's good, Paul."

Soon the office started filling up with harried-looking colleagues. When Ruby took a phone call, I headed to my office.

Absorbed in finishing up some patient records a half hour later, I didn't notice Ruby poke her head around the corner. "How about going up to visit Mr. Lara with me this afternoon?" Ruby rarely asked me to make a joint visit with her, so I just stared at her.

"I think he's about to check out, Paul. The family's very upset."

"Ruby? ... " I started to make an excuse. I had already gotten his parish priest involved with this Spanish-speaking patient a few weeks before. Something in Ruby's look, however — maybe it was just the earlier hug — made me waver.

"C'mon, Paul, have you ever been there when someone died?"

"What time are you going?"

"I'm meeting Yolanda up at the Burger King on 181st Street around one o'clock."

I thought I could make a quick detour there on my way home, and so I agreed.

It's strange, I mused after Ruby had left. Though I had ministered to hundreds of terminally ill patients, I had never been present at the actual moment of a patient's death. In fact, in my twenty-three years of priesthood — in hospital ministry, prison chaplaincy, even parish work in which I had celebrated dozens of wakes and funerals — never had I witnessed another human being's death.

Not the deaths of my grandfathers, whom I barely knew, nor my grandmothers, who had died in a nursing home nearby when I was in my twenties. Day by day they just drifted away in the cozy cleanliness of their hospital-like rooms where the family visited them on Sundays. The next thing I knew we were celebrating their wakes and funerals. Even my mother, the closest one to me ever to have died, had "slipped away" when we were out of the room.

The actual moment of death, and the mystery of what that is like for the one who is dying and for those left behind, was something I dreaded. At the same time I felt an attraction to it, as though to witness it would take the power and fright out of the deaths of those I love. Perhaps it could even defuse the fear of my own death.

A friend told me that once he saw the spirit of a person fly up through the floorboards of his room. His wife, a nurse, had been caring for a terminally ill woman in the room below. A moment after he saw this, she called up the stairway to tell him the lady had died. "I know," he responded. "I just saw her fly by while I was strumming my banjo, 'So long, it's been good to know you; so long, it's been good to know you. . . .'"

Different cultures have various practices to deal with death and have much to teach us. With my curiosity stirred by the upcoming visit, I took out a book I had been reading on the ways of Native Americans.

> Death to the Ohlones was a matter of enormous grief. In these tiny villages every person was well known and had a special place. Even before a man breathed his last, the villagers began sobbing and crying. When he finally died, the widow broke into a shrill, penetrating wail that rose in waves of anguish and filled the entire village. She screamed and screamed. She reached blindly for her pestle, beat herself on her breasts, and then fell to the ground still wailing and sobbing. Later she would singe her hair close to the scalp and cover her face with ashes and pitch.*

I took out the file on Eddie Lara, whom I had visited twice before. Only five weeks in our program, he was in the end stages of rectal cancer, which had spread to his pelvis and lungs. A fifty-year-old Guatemalan Indian, he was married, had two

---

*Malcolm Margolin, *The Ohlone Way* (Berkeley, Calif.: Heyday Books, 1978), 145.

daughters, a son, and three grandchildren. All of them lived together in the same building, some in different apartments.

Teresa, the daughter in her early twenties, was a single parent with two young children. When I had visited the patient three weeks before, she was caring for these children in an adjoining living room where they were watching TV. Besides these two tots, Teresa was watching the thirteen-month-old baby of her sister, Marianna, the eldest of the siblings. Marianna had recently married the baby's father, Fernando, and they lived upstairs.

"Poppa loves all of us," Teresa told me matter-of-factly, "but he loves Marianna the most." In fact it was Marianna who was more of a concern to our hospice team than the patient. She was so bound up with her father that we considered her a suicide risk. Marianna had developed all sorts of parallel illnesses that mirrored Eddie's symptoms: nausea, constipation, even pain in the same parts of the body that Eddie felt it.

Apparently Eddie and his wife, Gladys, had little feeling between them now. Marianna had become primary in his life. The last thing he would do at night before going to sleep was talk to his daughter on the telephone. Jeff, our social worker, was very concerned about this symbiotic relationship. He had been visiting Marianna weekly to help her begin to separate so she wouldn't go crazy when Eddie died. "If he dies," she had informed Jeff, "I want to die too."

Eddie was a short, ruggedly built man, a soccer star in his native country and black belt karate expert before he became ill. Like many Latino men, he was not a church-goer but was religious. The first time I had visited him he pulled up his pajama leg to show me the swelling that pained him so. Without embarrassment he also pointed out the colostomy bag attached to his abdomen. He said that I could return anytime, but that he wished to see a Spanish-speaking priest. That is when I connected him to his parish.

I had spoken to Marianna at least once on the phone. I had tried to arrange a visit with her after Jeff had said, "You might be able to help her choose life." Marianna was detained at the clinic on the day we had planned, so I had gone to visit Eddie instead. In the course of that visit — and assisted by his wife, Gladys, an attractive woman with a permanently sad expression — I asked him how he was sleeping.

"Better," he indicated. Gladys had told me earlier in the front room that he was becoming very anxious at night now because he was afraid of dying with no one around. Is it Marianna he's afraid won't be around? I wondered, but decided not to ask directly.

"Eddie, how do your children feel . . . about how sick you are?" I moved my hands dramatically as though I could get through to him in gesture if not word. With a blank face, Gladys translated. Eddie began to choke up, and he brushed away tears. He did not reply. Was I rubbing it in? Was I humiliating this strong man by implying that he was a cause of the suffering of his offspring? Gladys took a tissue and dabbed at the tears.

"It is good to let these feelings out." I placed my hand on both of theirs. Eddie wanted to sit up at this point; maybe he felt too vulnerable. One of the little children appeared at the doorway. She had a shy, questioning look on her tiny face. "Hi!" I said as gently as I could and opened my arms.

"Astra, come here," said Gladys. Hesitant at first, with a finger in her mouth and never taking her eyes off me, the little girl toddled over to us. She allowed Gladys to lift her onto my lap facing her grandfather. Eddie reached over and patted her on the cheek.

Temporarily this distracted him from his own pain. The TV babbled on with cartoons in the next room, and soon Astra returned to watch them. When Gladys left to go shopping, I decided to leave as well.

"Goodbye, Teresa. Tell Marianna I was asking for her." I saw Astra and hunched down to speak to her, a smile on my face. She was reserved now, half hiding behind her mother's head of thick dark hair. In the crib, Marianna's baby, Fernandito, gurgled back at me when I tickled him. I did it again, making sounds to cause him to laugh.

How wonderful to have children around someone who is sick! With their trust and spontaneity, the sheer power of life emanates from these little ones even though their vitality can make a patient's illness more apparent. Children and the dying: both are often in cribs and diapers, both need to be fed and bathed by others. Merely by their presence, children remind us of our original dependency and the naturalness of it. When we are dying, they can help us let go into a neediness we may have long forgotten. "Unless you change and become like little children, you will not enter the kingdom of God" (Matt. 18:3).

Oh, I wanted so much to gather these lovely kids into my arms and hug them close, absorb some of the sweet life from them to counteract the presence of death. But they weren't mine, so I just waved goodbye instead. Teresa walked me to the door. As I passed Eddie's doorway, I couldn't resist telling him what a wonderful family he and Gladys had raised.

That had been almost a month ago. I hadn't expected him to go so fast. It was almost noon. Gathering up my briefcase, I switched off the office light and headed for the subway. One brief visit and I could leave for the weekend I had planned.

At Thirty-fourth Street I waited for over a half hour on the crowded subway platform for the uptown express. The high school girl in front of me bit her boyfriend's earlobe as a train finally lumbered into the station on the local side.

"A fire on the tracks at Fourteenth Street, only local trains running!" crackled a voice on the loudspeaker. Everyone leapt forward to position themselves by a doorway, while the mob inside the train pressed up against the door to get out.

"Let them out! Let them out!" the accented voice demanded. Begrudgingly we opened a narrow passageway through which these people fought their way to the street.

I was poised between a huge bearded man in a black hat who was finishing some pizza and a lady with two stuffed Macy's bags; the three of us rushed for the open doorway at the same moment. We almost trampled a one-armed man who was shaking an old coffee cup in his teeth for donations. "Life sucks!" proclaimed his dirty T-shirt.

Elbowing my way past him like a subway veteran, I made it through the door before the others and dived for a prized seat, only to trip on a plastic bag of fortune cookies in the aisle. Everyone scrambled and screamed as I fell. The Chinese man who owned the bag howled in dismay as the bag came undone and his cookies flew in all directions: *AEEEEEEEE!!!*

Twisting, I landed on my back. Damn! A hundred accusing eyes peered down at me. The doors slammed shut while a lady clutching a baby slid into my seat.

Unhurt except for my pride, I slowly gathered myself up as the train lurched forward. I brushed off the dirt and the remains of the fortune cookies and tried to melt into a corner. The owner was still raving and glaring at me as he tried to retie the bag. Sheepishly I made my way over to him and asked how I could repay. We agreed on twenty dollars, all I had except for some change and a few tokens.

As I grabbed an overhead strap, I got a few furtive stares. The teenagers laughed and went back to their love-making. It did seem hilarious, and instructive. Life may suck, but where was I going so frenetically? If I were breathing my last today, what would I want to be doing? I tried to let go of the time and just relax into the moment. The train arrived at 181st Street before I knew it.

Ruby and Yolanda were waiting for me at the Burger King when I arrived. The streets were teeming with people, but through the window I could make out the two of them chattering like squirrels. Ruby waved.

"Take a load off, Paul," she said when I got to their table. "Get yourself a burger."

"I only want something to drink."

"Hi, Paul," said Yolanda as she finished some French fries, "nice tic."

"Thanks." I bought myself a large Sprite and then slid into the booth next to them. Feeling relaxed and comfortable with them, I took a deep swig from the cool drink, lay my head back on the cushioned seat, and sighed.

"What're you so content about?" asked Yolanda.

"He's going on some kind of retreat," mocked Ruby. "Paul's gonna go and get holy on us!"

"Not too holy I bet." Yolanda giggled.

"These priests!" said Ruby, "I heard about them." She leaned across to Yolanda and did a stage-whisper. "Some of them got a girl in every port!" She laughed wickedly.

"Is that right, Paul?" Yolanda feigned innocence.

"Yeah, sure!"

A little later, the intoxicating aroma of honey-roasted nuts wafted over us as we threaded through the blankets of the vendors who had spread out their wares on the sidewalk. "Check-idout! Checkidout!" they called as they peered up and down the street for the cops, who would bust them for selling without a license.

Snarled in a traffic jam in the center of the intersection, the burly driver of a huge moving van stared down with a deadpan expression at the honking cars trapped in the gridlock around him.

"Asshole!" someone yelled up at him. He spat a wad of tobacco out the window and sounded his horn. AAUUUHHH!

Trying to unravel this mess, a traffic cop shot her white-gloved hands left, right, up, down, as though she were leading an aerobic dance. Ruby, Yolanda, and I took advantage of the confusion and darted across the street.

"Yolanda and I have another patient to see this afternoon too," Ruby announced as we entered the lobby of the Lara family's apartment building, "so we'll try not to stay here too long."

My head was in a daze. I needed a good night's sleep. "That's fine with me," I agreed. Until the door opened I had almost forgotten what Ruby had mentioned earlier about Eddie being ready to "check out." The day turned out to be one I will not forget.

Gladys, solemn-faced and pale, stood in the doorway, her hair in disarray. It looked as if she had been crying. Behind her, down the long corridor leading to the living room, could be heard the sounds of a family in turmoil: wailing, shouting, and crying out. Wordlessly she motioned us in. The Angels of Death.

As Ruby embraced Gladys, the two of them communicated something by eye. This was the hospice nurse's domain and she took over; the rest of us followed. With all my experience I was completely unprepared for this.

I felt like a chip of balsa wood flung into whitewater rapids. The worst part of it was that I didn't know who among these many people to minister to, nor what to say if I did.

We came upon Eddie, who was thrashing in bed and breathing heavily. His family, grasping his hands and feet and trying to hold him down, called out to him in Spanish, but his gaze was elsewhere. So they looked upward in desperation and cried out.

"Don't leave us!" I imagined they were saying. "Don't take our father!" When Ruby told me to take Marianna aside into the living room, I was grateful. At least someone was giving direction to this chaos.

Marianna, an attractive woman with creamy skin and short black hair, was in a stupor. Her eyes were just slits. I sat her down on the couch and introduced myself. "Marianna! Marianna!" I clutched for a shred of hope. "Your love for your father will never die . . . nor will his love for you." Tears stung my eyes as I clasped her hands, which hung limp at her side, and repeated this to her like a mantra. Marianna gave no indication that she heard.

Across the room the family was mourning aloud over the departing Eddie, and this favorite daughter looked like she was about to depart this world with him. In the corner by the TV, a bearded young man in a bomber jacket and jeans, his face filled with fear, clutched the baby, Fernandito.

Marianna was on the brink. She could go insane for all I knew, and maybe anything I did would tip her over the edge! I reached into that catatonic place and whispered anyway, "Marianna, come with me. You need to tell your father you love him and say goodbye to him." Despite the risk, I felt it would be even worse if he died before she had done this.

Ruby had gotten them to pull his bed out from the wall so they could all stand around him. With Gladys and the other women wailing and clutching Eddie's hands, Marianna sat on the bed next to him and began to stroke him. All the while, Eddie flailed out at some unseen enemy.

"Papa! . . ." Softly Marianna spoke phrases to him now and then. You could hear the note of despair in her voice, and I glanced up at Ruby. Earlier she had checked Eddie's pulse and blood pressure. There is nothing else we can do, her gaze told me. Stay cool. It's only a matter of time. This is what we were trained for. This bedlam continued for almost half an hour.

More commotion at the front door. Two elderly women appeared with rosaries, Bibles, and bottles of holy water. They conducted a prayer service, reciting Scripture passages and shouting to God and to Eddie in Spanish. "María Santísima! María Santísima!" they called out to the Virgin Mary while they wiped the faces of Eddie and Marianna with the holy water. This seemed to make him even crazier because he curled up in a near fetal position, holding onto the side of the bed away from the women.

What should we do? Who's in charge here? I felt uneasy

at this, looking to Ruby and Yolanda for guidance, but their faces gave no reading. The family, in any case, responded to the prayers in a way that seemed to contain their hysteria.

Eddie's son, Sebastian, arrived, a stocky boy about nineteen. The family and others I did not recognize made room for him, and he began to shake his father's shoulders as though to pull him back into life.

"Papa? . . . PAPA!" he called out to him. The man in the bomber jacket — Marianna's husband, Fernando, I realized — joined him in this. Another young man, in his early twenties, came in and tearfully said Eddie had been like a father to him. Ruby encouraged all of these people to begin to say goodbye, to tell Eddie whatever they wanted while they could. The women wailed even louder.

Ignoring my fears, I got up by the head of the bed on my knees and stroked Eddie's shoulders. I told him to trust the Lord, not to be afraid. This calmed him for a moment, and then he would thrash his arms back over his head in karate chops. The guy's last fight, I thought.

"This is natural," Ruby assured them in an even tone. "It is not from pain, but a restlessness that happens . . ." Her voice trailed off. She went to call 911 and the funeral parlor. Moments later she returned and called me aside to hand me a slip of paper. "Call me at this number when Mr. Lara dies," she said matter-of-factly. "I have to see another patient right in the neighborhood." She and Yolanda left. I was alone in the madness.

Searching for a handle with which to guide them, I asked if they wanted to anoint Eddie. I particularly addressed this to Marianna. Still transfixed in front of her father, she came out of her stupor enough to nod yes. I gathered them around the bed, even calling in the ones in the adjoining room. Kneeling on the floor by Eddie's head with the oil in my palm, I was in an old familiar place. With Gladys and the daughters and son, the neighbors and friends looking on in fright, it hardly mattered if they understood what I said. They would understand the touch. Yes, even the babies in their parents' arms would understand, their eyes wide with a question that mirrored the adult faces around them.

"Bless this oil, O Lord. It represents our love, . . . your love for Eddie, your son, who is coming home to you now. . . . We touch him with it reverently, blessing his body with our love that will never die and with your love that is as close to him as this oil is on his skin."

Anointing him first myself, I indicated for them to do likewise — to make the sign of the cross on his forehead and hands and to say "I love you" if they wished. Amazingly, after Gladys stroked her husband's face and hands with it, Marianna reached for the oil. "Anoint his feet too," I encouraged, and she did so. All this time Eddie was breathing fitfully, but became more and more still as the different members of his family touched him and spoke endearing phrases in his ear.

The sight of the women all around him and of the little ones — Astra with Teresa, and little Fernando in his father's arms — reminded me of a few years before. One of my sisters had gotten permission from her doctor for me to be present when she gave birth to her daughter. Following my sister's labor rhythms, her husband and I had breathed with her until the baby's head had popped out. The incredible mystery of childbirth eliminated all pretensions of control. It was someone else's timing, someone else's doing.

"It is almost like labor pains he is having," I blurted out, "like when you are having a baby." The women stared at me. "It is the same at the beginning and the end of our lives, isn't it? . . . Our brother, Eddie, is getting ready to be born again." They stroked his legs in rhythm now, as my brother-in-law and I had done for my sister. A calmness came over the room.

Now we just began to watch him as he lay almost still, but with strong outward breaths that alternated with a long pause and then a shallower intake breath. At this point, Marianna was standing at the foot of the bed staring down at her father with glazed eyes. Oh, God, where is Ruby? I searched in my pocket for the phone number. But it was too late; I couldn't leave the room now. At any moment Eddie would die and the household would break out into an uncontrollable uproar.

Something needed to be said to Marianna to prepare her, but what? The neighbor women were saying the rosary aloud and they were between me and Marianna. I moved anyway, wriggling between them until I stood next to her. She was watching her father's breathing like an eagle.

"You see how he breathes out? . . . " I whispered in her ear, "and then in a while breathes in again?" She gave no notice of hearing me. "Well, one of these times he is going to breathe out . . . and then not breathe in again . . . that will be because his spirit has gone to God." Marianna continued to look straight ahead at him. "He will be okay . . . he'll be at peace." My voice was shaking.

Suddenly Marianna left the room. Perhaps she wanted to cushion herself from the sight of his death as I had described it. I didn't follow her at first, but soon noticed her crouching at the doorway by the head of Eddie's bed, her head in her hands, looking down. I went up and knelt beside her, wanting to be near her when he went, fearing that moment. As the rosary rolled on with its murmured responses, I leaned close and whispered to Marianna again, "Your love for him will never die, will it? *Never!* Nor will his love for you."

Her husband, Fernando, came up on the other side of her, their baby in his arms. He spoke to her, but Marianna only looked down. Frightened and blinking back tears, the man began to nuzzle their baby up against her face for a kiss. Nothing. I felt so badly for them, disaster all around. Then the baby reached out a pudgy hand and touched her cheek, his bright eyes oblivious to all but this one who had given him life. A beaming smile lit the child's face, but his mother didn't see it. Her mind was somewhere else.

But this called her back from the precipice. For the slightest instant Marianna leaned toward her baby and looked at him. It felt so important for her to have done that, if only for a moment to choose life, as Jeff had pleaded with her weeks ago: "But you need to live for your baby!" And Marianna's chilling response, "He has a father."

Gladys's scream ripped through the room. Pandemonium erupted. Marianna sprang to her feet. Flinging herself into the room, she shouted as if to summon back the departing spirit, "POPYYYYYYY!!!" In a frenzy, she threw herself onto Eddie's body while he heaved one last breath. Then his color changed rapidly. To everyone, including Marianna, it was inescapable: death.

While Fernando and I physically restrained her, she hurled herself over and over again toward him, yelling like an enraged animal for its stolen cub. Gradually she subsided, calling again and again to him in a pathetic voice, "Poppy? . . . Poppy?" . . . Poppy?" each of these calls interspersed with intense moments of waiting for a response. None was forthcoming. Eddie Lara was on the other side now.

Fernando wept openly as he clutched Marianna to his chest. Having lost his father-in-law, it seemed he was losing his wife now too. "Eddie is at peace," I repeated over and over to her as we drew her back onto the sofa. "He's not in pain, not suffering anymore. . . ." But Marianna was inconsolable.

All around us the family went berserk, as though each had to demonstrate her love for Eddie by the level of emotion. Soon tears flowed down my face too, from the grief all around and from sheer exhaustion. I wondered how much longer I could take this. Death felt like a whirlpool that would drag us all into it. Ruby! I went and phoned the number she had given me. When she asked how things were going I simply held the phone up toward the bedlam. "I hear, I hear," the voice said. "Hang in there, Paul. . . . We'll be over shortly."

There are other images that flash through my mind from that afternoon, ones that for all the tragedy make it an experience I would never have missed:

. . . Ramon, Teresa's little seven-year-old son being called out of school because of his grandfather's condition. Appearing in the doorway a half hour after Eddie had died, he had a frightened look on his face. By then some calmness had come over the room and all eyes fell on him. Without being sure what to do, I went over to the scared kid, took him in my arms, and walked him up next to Eddie's body. "Your grandfather is dying you know, and you must say goodbye . . . tell him you love him." With tears, the boy did so. Then as though that had released Eddie, I assured him that his grandfather was with God now and would be looking over him from heaven.[12]

. . . Ruby and Yolanda appearing, grim-faced but nonchalantly. At first they went up to Eddie to check his pulse, consoled Gladys briefly, and then went to Marianna, who still sat in a trance across from her father. While they sat on either side of her, they slowly rocked her back and forth. One of them — I couldn't tell who — was singing a child's song.

. . . Jeff, our social worker, arriving and standing in the middle of the room. He simply looked back and forth from Eddie's body to Marianna with such pathos in his face that it said everything. I caught his gaze, went up and hugged him, and told him what had just happened. "You hear that lullaby?" he asked as we watched the three women rocking. "It's the one Eddie used to sing to his children." It was Marianna who was singing it, maybe to herself now.

... Gladys bringing candles into the room and lighting them in front of a picture of Mary, the mother of Jesus, while Teresa took a red bandana from around her neck and tied up Eddie's jaw, which had been hanging open.

... The Emergency Medical Service paramedics arriving with a stretcher and a box of electronic equipment. They were intent on shooting voltage through Eddie's body to try to resuscitate him, apparently a city law unless a doctor has pronounced the person dead. We couldn't find the "Do Not Resuscitate" order, which might have stopped them until a doctor could do so, but Ruby intervened until we got Doc on the phone. He assured these sincere but legalistic men that given Ruby's word, indeed the patient was officially dead.

... The police appearing: one an older, heavy-set man who looked bored, as though he had witnessed this twenty times a day and it was nothing compared to murder scenes and drug busts; the other, a bright young rookie who lived with his wife and child in the suburbs, saying that if he had known how tough it was to be a cop he would never have joined the force. The young cop asked me who I was, and expressed surprise and friendly interest when I told him I was a priest. Later when he cautioned Eddie's son, who was a new police cadet, about the dangers of the police force, I said to both of them, "I've got forms for the priesthood in my briefcase if you want to switch!" They laughed.

I was on automatic pilot, but doing the best ministry of my life. Ruby and Yolanda had Marianna under control. The undertaker was due shortly. Jeff could take over with the family, so I decided to leave.

Near Eddie's body, which Gladys and the daughters were still watching, I knelt to say a prayer. To each of the family members I wanted to say goodbye, but what could I say that wouldn't be stupid? See you later? Hang in there? The specific words weren't important; I just wanted to acknowledge the grace of having been there with them through it.

Gladys, tearful and numb, let me kiss her on the cheek; Teresa held little Astra in her arms and I hugged them; Sebastian shook my hand. When I got to Marianna, who was still seated in a half-trance between Yolanda and Ruby, and assured her that the support of the hospice team would continue, she gave a glimmer of recognition. Who knows, maybe she would come through it after all?

I lingered a moment, needing someone to say "Good job!" or something. Ruby quipped, "Hey, Paul, get three bottles of wine for your retreat now — one for you, one for Yolanda, and one for me!" It was just what I needed. Exhausted as she looked after "a day's work," somehow this amazing woman was reminding me of priorities. Keep it light! We're in this together! Celebrate! Ruby's bravado in the face of death gave me hope. I felt such gratefulness for her and Yolanda, for Jeff and Doc and the whole hospice team back at the command center.

On the way out, I saw Marianna's husband, Fernando, in the kitchen. Sipping a mug of coffee as he leaned against the counter, he still held on to Fernandito as if the baby were a lifeline. With his intense, bloodshot eyes, he looked wrung out, though more at peace now than earlier. He smiled and I went up to him.

"You did well, Fernando." I grasped his shoulder.

"We both did." After a pause, "I think my wife will get better."

"I hope so."

"The family appreciates so much your being here."

I appreciate it even more so, Fernando, I wanted to say. How can I thank you? He must have sensed this because he pushed the little baby toward me, who planted a slobbery kiss on my face.

"The love coming from each of you is a sign of God's presence," I told him. "You've got to hold on to each other now and be confident that Eddie is with you in a new way."

His red-rimmed eyes blinked and filled up. Fernando took a step toward me and placed his free arm around to embrace me awkwardly, as men do. Fernandito looked up between us.

As I emerged into the sunlight and the frenzy of people on 181st Street, I squinted my eyes in disbelief. The tide of humanity careened around me as usual — shoppers and school children, loiterers and cabbies — all oblivious to the events that had just transpired in the apartment above us. This was the first time in my life I had ever witnessed the miracle of a fellow human being's death, and I felt tired but buoyant. In fact I was exhilarated and could have shouted for joy. It was life we had witnessed in that house, not death. Now I could leave for my retreat.

~ Goodbye ~

IF THERE WAS ANYTHING engraved on my heart from doing hospice work it was this: don't put off your dreams until it is too late. The patients who die in the most peace are those who at least have tried to accomplish their deepest dreams. Those who have the most difficulty dying are those who regret never trying. My dream was to write about the love and courage I had witnessed among our patients and caregivers in the hope that it would help many people.

There was no way I could get the distance to reflect about the deep things I had experienced while still immersed in them. In order to show my love for what we were doing, I would have to leave it. The team would feel wounded, betrayed even, as I had when Beverly left for another job a few months before. "She can't do that!" I had muttered to myself when she told me. This would be very difficult. It would feel as if I were breaking a bond of trust. Almost as if I were dying.

When I returned from my retreat, refreshed and relaxed, I announced to the team that I would be leaving the program. To choose to leave what you love is terrible and beautiful. It is very difficult to feel responsible somehow for the hurt you see on people's faces. Many excuses come to mind to make it easier: "It is just a job... Others have left and will leave... Nothing is permanent... Their love causes the pain, I don't... They'll get over it, I'll get over it." None of the excuses worked.

Just as the patients and their families must, the team has to deal with the pains of separation. We experience the same spectrum of feelings that they do and that we are supposed to know so well from our work — denial, bargaining, anger, fear, depression, grief, acceptance. The best thing I did was first talk privately to a few special friends on the team, and not try to hide my feelings by just announcing my decision to everyone in a group. This was new behavior for me.

"My partner!" responded my boss, Kate, when I told her first in my office. No one had ever called me that before. I began to realize then what I was losing. Ruby and Yolanda took me to their favorite soul food restaurant in Harlem. On a park bench in Queens Botanical Garden, Doc and I enjoyed sandwiches together and disbanded our "men's support group."

All in all, this was one of the most difficult and best times in my life. One part of me couldn't wait until it was over, yet in the six weeks or so I had to go, I could let the farewell take its own form and learn something about letting go. A few of my dearest patients were about to do the same. I still had things to do.

One of the reasons I felt that I could leave the hospice ministry was that Isha was "actively dying," as we say. Over the past six months she had gotten worse and worse. Unbelievably, Lilianne and she had moved during this period to a new apartment that was in a less crime-ridden area of Manhattan, one where Isha felt Lilianne would be safer after she was gone. However, it was a fourth-floor walk-up, and after the first month Isha, who loved to get out and walk around the block even when she was quite ill, could no longer go up and down the stairs. From then on her world was confined to the two-room apartment.

Isha's last months are all a blur. So many images mixed together: the flowers I would bring her, which she would carefully arrange and place on the window sill; the tea and quiche she had Eloise, the Home Health Aid, fix for us one day and insisted that I finish so I could stay strong; her gradually failing health — the painfully swollen feet, the fevers, the despondency, and flashes of anger. Once she demanded that Eloise give her a dose of morphine before the complete time was elapsed, and when Eloise refused, Isha snapped, "Me die, what matter?"

Isha kept growing weaker. Often in a drug-like stupor when I visited, she would force herself to sit up on the edge of the bed, sometimes with a blanket draped over her head for warmth that would not come.

"Why I not die like they say?" she asked one day. I didn't know what to say and joked that maybe I would die before she did. But Isha only looked at me quizzically with her emaciated face.

One day while I was visiting Ruby came as well and ordered Isha back to bed from the living room where she had dragged herself. Each of us took an arm to help her back to the bedroom. I was about to leave when Ruby placed a stethoscope on Isha's heart. She held up her hand for me not to move yet and then took my hand and placed it on Isha's distended belly. You would think Isha had a rock in her stomach, but it was the blasted tumor that was eating her life away. All of this was very touching, because something in Ruby's manner told me we may not see our friend alive again.

While I stepped into the other room to give them privacy, Ruby continued the examination. The phone rang. It was Lilianne, and I gave it to Ruby. While staring at me gravely, she told her, "Your mother's not going to make it this time, Lilianne. I need you to stay strong. Even Father Paul's taking it hard."

And you, Ruby! What about you? I knew how much she loved Isha and her daughter.

"Lilianne is taking it hard," said Ruby as she hung up. "She wants you to call her tomorrow."

We went back to Isha's bedroom to say goodbye. Ruby made a little laugh come out of Isha even in her far-gone state. "See ya later, sexy!" she quipped, rocking her head saucily from side to side.

When we got outside and spoke about the seriousness of Isha's condition, it dawned on me that I would need to prepare some of my long-time patients for the fact that I might not be with them to the end. This would hurt. It's not supposed to happen that way. People who are actively dying don't need to be left by another before their death, but it would be worse not to tell them.

I didn't intend to tell Isha because she was so close to the end, but I would have to tell some of the others. In a few cases, I hoped it might enable the patients to be in less denial, to deal in some way with the reality of their impending death by the feelings stirred up by my leaving. Candida, the Venezuelan woman with breast cancer who offered up her suffering for her sixteen-year-old son, was one of these.

Andy continued acting out his anger at her illness and what

he perceived to be her cooperation with it: staying out late at night with companions who appeared to be drug dealers, not going to school, getting sick himself. He wanted to break free from his mother even while she bound him all the more with cords of long-suffering love.

I felt ambiguous about my involvement with them. First of all, I had become not only Candida's pastor, but the family's counselor as well. Sometimes these roles conflicted. Moreover, the similarity between Andy's relationship with his parents and my history with my own parents made it hard to keep clear what I could do for them. My supervisor called it countertransference, the feelings of identification a counselor has with his clients' situations that can get in the way of relating to them wisely. I had to be careful not to relate to Candida as though she were my own mother.

One day I brought Candida Communion, which she received with her usual reverence. When I asked how she was doing, she surprised me by saying, "Much pain, Father Paul," indicating the difficulty she had in raising her right arm. She showed me her feet, which were becoming swollen too. Still, she sat up in a chair in the living room, dressed immaculately in a beautiful housecoat.

Her husband, Juan, was his effusive self. Taking my coat, he showed me a large chair to sit in between them, all the while speaking of Candida in his adoring way. "Her tumor is bigger, and she sleeps like a statue so she doesn't cause it to rupture." She was taking Tylenol and occasionally some Valium at night, but no codeine or morphine. While he spoke to me, his wife sat next to us smiling or praying.

At one point Candida got up with difficulty to make some tea. Juan then whispered to me conspiratorially about Andy's latest escapades. "He hasn't gone to school but instead comes home and speaks with glowing eyes of a millionaire who has befriended him and his buddies. I don't know," he said as though speaking of characters in a movie, "it's hard to believe this guy doesn't want them to do something wrong...drugs maybe, or he could be a homosexual...."

Candida returned with the tea and set it up on the coffee table which was arranged in its usual way like a small altar. A statue of the Blessed Virgin was surrounded with candles and flowers.

Juan continued, glancing at Candida as though for permission to speak of such troubling matters. I didn't see her nod, but some signal passed between them.

"Father Paul, two days ago my wife found our son in the bathroom with a roll of three thousand dollars!"

"What?..." I shook my head in disbelief.

"When she challenged him, he told her he was just holding it for someone...can you believe that?"

"No!" I realized now that Andy was in deep trouble.

Seeing my expression, Candida lifted her hand. "Please wait Padre..." She got up and returned in a moment with a belt-like contraption dangling from her hand as though it were a snake. "See what Angel has?" She dropped it into my lap. Any doubts I had about what she and Juan were implying vanished as I stared at the shoulder holster with its shiny six-inch steel blade!

After this meeting, I took it upon myself to talk to a detective at the local precinct. Friendly but not overly concerned, he agreed that the story about the millionaire sounded fishy and asked me to get the fathers of these boys to come in to see him about it. He thought that if Andy knew the police were involved, it might scare him enough to be good. I wasn't so sure. Later when I spoke to Juan about it he was in a different mood. He was actually beginning to believe his son's story.

This wealthy man, who lived in Connecticut, had already given Andy one five-hundred-dollar check. Juan showed the cancelled stub to me. He had promised to buy cars for the boys if they got their driver's licenses and to pay their way through college if they finished school. What could you say to this? All I felt able to do was tell Juan I had spoken to the police officer and encourage him to do the same; at the very least he should demand that this man meet him and Andy together. Juan, however, was very afraid of being seen as a snitch. He felt that if the police busted the gang, they would blame him and retaliate. It was the South American drug wars in Queens, New York!

When I visited them a few weeks later, Candida described for me in her broken English how her tumor had bled profusely on the weekend, but that she had prayed and the hole had closed up. "Like a fountain," she said wincing, dramatizing with her hands the flow of blood.

"And you weren't afraid of dying?" Candida held up her hand

for me to wait and then went and got her son who had been in his room so that he could translate for us.

Pale-faced, and meek, and wearing a pair of oversized pajamas, Andy explained that he had stayed home from school because of a pain in his stomach.

"It's good to see you, Andy." We shook hands. As he took a seat opposite his mother, it was difficult to know who would die first in this family. Candida was being kept alive by her ability to suffer for her son, while Andy, imitating her suffering even while he rebelled against it, was killing himself, if not her, by his behavior.

Remembering that he had told me they never discussed her sickness, I braced myself and plunged in. "Candida told me how her tumor has bled a lot this past weekend and that she prayed and the hole closed up." Candida fluttered her eyes closed and looked like a saint. Andy showed no emotion. "I asked her if she wasn't afraid of dying. . . . " I glanced over toward him, the kid so frail and vulnerable perched at the edge of the big sofa.

"Mamita!" he began, a tender note in his voice. Candida's eyes opened, a look of sweet love for him shining in them. Then he explained to her what I had asked. "No, she is not afraid to die," he translated her response without affect, "because she has prepared for so long."

I thought of what he might feel and then asked as though for him, "Do you ever get angry, Candida, at the pain and suffering?" Again Andy translated her words, this time with more tension in his voice.

"She says she doesn't get angry," he smiled ever so slightly, "because she prays for patience."

"I pray for patience too," I agreed, "but still I get angry sometimes. You know, in traffic jams, when things go wrong. . . . " I let the anger I felt inside be heard in my voice.

Andy turned to face me. "I get angry at her sickness," he said. "She prays for the bleeding to stop, but she never prays to get better." Candida's face remained placid. I didn't know if she understood him.

"Do you want to tell her that?" Andy hesitated and then said something to her that they bounced back and forth for a few moments with flashes of anger in both their voices.

He turned back to face me. "She says she'll pray to get better, if that is God's will."

For some moments, the three of us absorbed these words in silence before Andy said, "I'm feeling sick again." He stood and indicated he was returning to his room.

"Andy, thanks." He headed for the door. "Wait a minute! Here's something I brought for you to read." Reaching into my bag, I found the slender paperback I had been carrying for him for some time. It described how risking anger in our relationships can actually deepen them. Otherwise those we love, including God, are kept at a distance by our always being nice.

"Don't show it to your mom," I told him slyly. A faint smile crept across his face when he spied the title, *May I Hate God?** "Let's talk again sometime, okay?" I winked.

"Okay." Andy disappeared into his room. Candida and I sat quietly together for a few moments before I left.

Slowly but surely she deteriorated. The pain spread down her side to her feet. Candida was even using a walker the next time I saw her, explaining that her leg tended to buckle when she stood on it. Most notably though, she spoke of crying "mucho" during the past weekend because she was depressed at being so sick. This was the first time in almost two years in the program that Candida had ever indicated anything but gladness at being able to suffer for God. She said that she felt better after the cry and added that her husband had wept too when she was in so much pain the previous Sunday.

Juan told me that he keeps everything inside and has always done so. "Like Candida who suffers without question," he said with his eyes aglow. I had offered that it would be good if both of them could begin changing and to let each other know how they feel. Strangely, the crying indicated to me that Candida was getting worse physically, though better emotionally and spiritually.

Finally I broke the news to Candida and Juan that I would be leaving the hospice program in a couple of months. "Oh, Padre!" she said, grasping my hands tightly, "Why? Why?"

"I need a break," I told her, "and I want to write about this so that it will help people." I am not sure she understood but

---

*Pierre Wolff, *May I Hate God?* (New York: Paulist Press, 1979).

something was conveyed. A few weeks later when I phoned her about wanting to bring over a new colleague of mine to visit her, Carlos, who could both act as a translator and also eventually take my place, she said she wanted to speak to me about "things I never told the doctor, my husband, or my son." Amazingly, she said she was doing much better and was praying for a resurrection so that she could witness to people. Candida was even planning to go out to church that Sunday. Andy had promised to accompany her — "the best Mother's Day present he could give me."

The gist of her special communication to me through my assistant, Carlos, was this: Candida has had a long history of intense pain, most of which she tells no one about, rather offering it to God as a "victim of love" for peace in the world, for her son, for priests, everyone.

Candida mentioned that she was still deeply concerned about her son because he was planning to go to Connecticut for the summer to work at his millionaire friend's home. "Perhaps Andy needs to separate from you now one way or another," I told her. And maybe even the beliefs you represent, I thought.

Bowing her head down to her chest, Candida sighed deeply. "I believe God will take care of my son even after I am gone."

"Yes." I thought of the Powa exercise the Buddhists do to prepare for death.* "Close your eyes and imagine a ball of fire in your chest, breathe rhythmically, and let it go up to God when you are ready...."

Finally, and this was mentioned only after I asked if there were anything else she wished to talk about, she said, "I have doubts, Padre...doubts that God will find my suffering worth anything when I meet him."

I didn't explore these doubts enough at the time she mentioned them; I only said we can't be certain God will answer our prayers as we want. "When you meet Jesus, you can show him your scars and he can show you his." Candida liked this very much.

During my last meeting with her we conducted a home liturgy, a celebration of the Eucharist, which Roman Catholics

---

*See the "Ejection of Consciousness" Exercise in *The Tibetan Book of the Dead;* also in *The Sacred Art of Dying* (New York: Paulist Press, 1988), 76f.

believe is the resurrected presence of Jesus Christ. Her sister, Theresa, and her husband were up from Venezuela. He was a very silent man, she a charismatic person who was a less pious version of Candida. Candida was ecstatic that we would do this in her home and had invited some of her neighbors from the apartment building as well. Juan had taken off work. Andy had moved out.

I told the little group assembled in the Perez's living room how Jesus had celebrated this same meal with his disciples before he went away. "It was his way of saying goodbye, of leaving them something to remember him by." For a homily I paraphrased for them what Jesus might have said:

"Look, I will be gone soon. Please don't waste your time mourning over my remains, making relics of dead flesh. This body you see me in now is just a temporary dwelling place. It cannot begin to hold my spirit, which wants to fill this whole world. Unless I let this body go, my spirit cannot fully come. You see this bread on the table? This cup of wine in my hands? This will be my body and blood. You want to get close to me, hold onto me. I want the same, and with everyone. The only way I can get inside each of you, become part of everyone with my whole being, is to become nothing less than your food and your drink. I live and die for each of you this way and in so doing will live forever. Yes, this is my body, this is my blood. Take it, eat and drink now ... and when I am gone, do this to remember me."[13]

The Body and the Blood of Jesus. A very palpable and passionate reality, especially to those who join suffering and love. You can imagine what the Eucharist meant to Candida! When Juan finished translating what I had said, she leaned back and smiled to herself as a woman in love does.

At the offertory part of the service I asked, "Could we put Candida's medicine bottles on the altar so we can offer them up too?" Juan went into the bedroom and returned with an array of bottles. Carefully he placed them next to the bread and wine. Candida, who had been praying silently, smiled tightly and continued to move her lips. Theresa sang a fervent hymn in Spanish.

In the middle of this there was a knock at the door. It was Matilda, Candida's nurse, who had come to check on her. A look of surprise crossed her face when she saw us. Without any fuss she sat down on a chair by the door. I remembered that Matilda was a member of the Seventh-Day Adventist Church and I wasn't sure how she felt about getting roped into a Catholic Mass.

I broke the host in half. This is the key point of the Mass, which symbolizes the death of Christ. At the same time it shows our communion with him and each other in the sacred bread we are about to share: "Unless the grain of wheat falls to the earth and dies, it remains just a grain of wheat, but if it dies, it produces much fruit" (John 12:24).

After receiving Communion myself, I placed a morsel of the consecrated bread on each of their outstretched tongues, inspired by the simplicity of their faith, that they trusted these words and actions handed down from two thousand years ago.

Afterward we all remained in silence for a few moments of private prayer. I was sitting on the piano bench, the one Andy had sat on a year before when his parents had prevailed on him to play "Happy Birthday." Remembering his begrudging look — caught between a childhood wish to make his parents happy and his adolescent need to be his own man — I prayed for him to find his dream. I thought of Candida and the doubts she had about the meaning of her suffering.

After a final blessing and another hymn sung by Theresa, we gave each other the Kiss of Peace. This was a spontaneous and light-hearted conclusion to the ritual. When I got to Matilda and told her about the bottles of medicine we had placed on the altar, she asked aloud, "And the codeine and morphine? Were they there?" Her eyes were wide with skepticism.

Together we went to the altar and looked. The major pain killers that Candida refused to take were not there. "You see?" said Matilda with a triumphant smile. "The woman will do exactly as she wants.... I refuse to worry about it anymore." I glanced over toward Candida, the tough little lady who had survived over ten years of breast cancer by her method of relating to pain, and shrugged.

When I said goodbye to her sometime later, Candida insisted on giving me a blessing. I bent my neck before her as once I had seen Andy do when he was going out, allowing her prayer for my suffering or conversion or whatever she was offering herself for to wash over me without fear. Clutching my hands in hers, she said with great intensity as though she were the pope, "I . . . pray . . . for . . . you."

"Gracias, Candida . . . and I pray for you . . . Adios." Swiftly we touched cheeks, and I turned and strode toward the door where Juan was waiting. As we shook hands, I asked him how I might get in touch with Andy, and he gave me his son's phone number. I gave him an address out West where I could be reached.

~

Gradually I began to feel myself alternating between intense involvement in the hospice work and a strange feeling of aimlessness, meaninglessness. I wanted to get more involved with my fellow employees, because I was going and I wanted to leave with some significant relationships. Yet at the same time I wanted to withdraw because I didn't want to say goodbye to so many. That would hurt too much. I expected that the ambivalence would increase. It would be a tough time for me and them. It also gave me a clue why our patients begin to withdraw: so they don't hurt themselves so much and maybe so they don't hurt others when they finally leave.

Is there also a parallel with my getting more involved on some levels? Maybe it is like that last little spurt you see in some patients before they die, one that can be misread if you don't know what is happening. One last gasp of choosing life, a "recovery" almost, that quickly becomes a fast slide to the end. Sometimes this is a last trip to their favorite spot, a celebration even. Maybe, as with me, it can even be a depth of relationship with someone because you know you are leaving. One can risk being real, even intimate with another, when you know you will not have to live the rest of your life with that person — the way you might sometimes be with a stranger you meet on vacation.

A few days later I got a message: "Isha wants to see you." When I called, Eloise put her on the phone. It sounded like a little girl's voice. "Me sick, me die," she said. "You come see me?" I went over that afternoon, hiding behind my back a bunch of daffodils as I caught my breath outside her door at the top of the fourth flight of wobbly stairs.

Lilianne was home from work, and she welcomed me with a bright smile. I gave her the flowers for Isha, who was in her bedroom. After she arranged them in a vase, Lilianne and I sat on the sofa and talked. Her pixie figure, which was clad in black leotards, gave a hint of what Isha must have looked like when she was younger.

"My mother has trouble swallowing now, and she hears voices, someone saying 'Hi!' — voices of our deceased relatives, especially her brother." But Lilianne's cheerful expression told me she was not yet ready to go into this in depth, and soon we went into Isha's room.

"Mommy, look what Father Paul brought you!" Lilianne presented the flowers with a flourish. Isha was expressionless. She asked if we would hoist her up into a sitting position, and we did so with great difficulty. After bringing me a wooden chair to sit facing her mother, Lilianne left us alone. We joined hands. Isha seemed quite depressed, and when I tried to converse, she indicated she didn't want to talk.

The room was dimly lit, with few possessions evident. A tattered rug lay beneath Isha's feet, which were swollen grotesquely now. A tableful of medicines was off to the side. As we sat there wordlessly, now and then a plaintive bird-like cry would come out of her. Once she gestured heavenward. With all my heart I wished that I could do something to relieve her pain.

Suddenly there was music! Rock and roll poured out of a clock radio that had just clicked on by the side of her bed. "What the . . . ?" I got up to turn it off. But instead I remembered Ruby saying "Hey, sexy!" and the laughter that had brought out of Isha. So I left the music on and sat down again. Isha, in agony, continued to stare straight ahead.

Without thinking about it, my shoulders began to move. Rotating from side to side as though I were dancing, they kept time to the bass that was thumping out its rhythm. Holding Isha's hand, I ignored her sickness and thought of Lilianne in the black leotards and Isha herself dancing for joy in a photo she had showed me in an album a while back. I rocked in my place as though we were dancing.

> One two three o'clock, four o'clock rock! . . .
> five six seven o'clock, eight o'clock rock! . . .

Slowly Isha's face turned toward me, the whites of her eyes about all I could make out in the darkness. "Chair-dancing," I explained with a straight face, "it's chair-dancing!"

... Nine ten eleven o'clock, twelve o'clock rock!
We're gonna rock, around, the clock tonight! ...

From out of that sunken, dark face like stars twinkling in a winter night sky, Isha's eyes began to dance! Without any other movement from her scrawny, pained body, she matched that rhythm with me, played with her eyes in a way that I could scarcely believe.

"When the clock strikes five, six and seven,
you and I'll be in Seventh Heaven ... "

Good God! Our bodies shrivel and die, but something deeper won't. Something inextinguishable. Forgetting my body movements, I just let my eyes play back and forth with hers. It was grand. After a while I turned the radio off and we fell back into silence. She gripped my hand, which was unusual.

"Isha," I began softly, "you told me on the phone ... 'Me sick, me die. ... '"

Turning toward me, she said weakly, "Cows die, me die, God die, never mind."

I thought of what she had told me about her country. All the famine there, and the cows and people dropping over. Another time she had tapped on her palms with her fingers to show me how Jesus had been nailed to a cross, her face awed by the mystery. I suppose I wanted to pull her out of her despondency. "Do you ever cry about it?"

"No ... Lilianne good, she have good job ... me have enough food, why cry?"

Laughing at her simplicity, I protested, "But sometimes I cry when things hurt me, even though other things are good."

Isha just sat there and gave a little shrug.

My reserve broke. "Oh, Isha, you are such an incredible woman. ... I'm going to miss you so much!"

"Me ... your sister," the tiny voice said.

"I'll never forget you, Isha, you taught me so much." I pulled her hand close to my chest and she squeezed it.

I gazed into the dark, squinting eyes; she had some wisdom I needed. "Isha, do you believe you will be at peace someday, resurrected with Jesus?"

"Maybe."

Maybe! Isha said this in the way she did when she "looked up" in her prayers, with that creaturely look at the beyond that claims nothing and just believes. By just being herself this little lady made me grapple with my faith more than anyone else.

We kissed each other on the cheek and I settled her down in bed, tucking her in like a baby. On the way out, I reminded Lilianne of my home number and asked her to call me if her mother got worse, "...or if you want to talk sometime." The next time I saw Isha—the last time—she was in the hospital.

~ Grieving ~

EVERYTHING seemed to be tumbling in at once. Kate called me into her office one morning to inform me that Natalie wouldn't last much longer. She suggested that I call Dominic. Natalie, the middle-aged Jewish woman with the brain tumor, was semi-comatose the last time I had seen her. Her husband, the histrionic Italian who raised hell with God, had finally begun to converse with us about his wife's eventual death, though still not in front of her. Closing my office door for privacy, I held my head in my hands for some moments in silence, trying to compose myself for what lay ahead before dialing the familiar number.

Dominic answered. "Father Paul!" he cried, "I think Nattie just died this minute...Oh, God!" It was as if he had been stabbed; a storm set loose. At times like this I hated the telephone because words wouldn't do.

"Dominic, Dominic, I'm so sorry... Natalie was such a vivacious woman..."

"Don't rub it in," he pleaded. "Can you come over?"

"Yes... in about two hours." I was thinking of an appointment I had scheduled that would arrive any moment, as well as the subway ride up to their apartment.

"Please hurry..." His voice broke again.

I promised to do so and hung up, but I was stalling to protect myself from being sucked into the pit Dominic was in. I could hear the grief and panic in his voice.

"So, Natalie, you've finally gone!" The clown on the wall looked down and mocked me. Shutting my eyes, I prayed, "Eternal rest grant unto, her O Lord, and let perpetual light shine upon her. May her soul, and the souls of all the faithful departed, through the mercy of God, rest in peace. Amen."

Shortly after two-thirty, the Filipino doorman nodded grimly and signaled me into the lobby of the apartment house. By now he knew me, and the look on his face told me he knew what had happened.

The door with the mezuzah attached to its side was partly ajar. I tapped on it and pushed it open. Many strangers milled about — finely attired professional men, their ties loosened; attractive women in silk blouses and slacks, some in stocking feet. Some of them Natalie's family I presumed.

Someone called Dominic. He was wearing rumpled dark trousers and a dishevelled white dress shirt open at the neck. A gold crucifix was matted in his chest hair. There was a look of having been robbed on his face.

"Dominic, I . . . "

"Thanks for coming, Father Paul." He let me wrap my arms around him and then led me into the bedroom where Natalie lay in her usual position. A flowered pink sheet was pulled up to her neck. On a folding chair with her back to us and her slim shoulders slumped, a lone woman sat watching. Natalie's eyes were open; she wasn't breathing.

"Everyone come in here!" Dominic shouted, "Father Paul is going to say a prayer." One by one the folks from the living room trailed in, though most hung back in the vestibule out of sight of Natalie's body. Discomfort was evident on some of their faces, and given Dominic's previous statements about his wife's family, I began to wonder if I weren't being used.

Stuttering, I faked through the best Jewish prayer I could come up with. "God of . . . Abraham and Sarah . . . and of Isaac and Jacob and David and Ruth . . . " I scrambled through my Old Testament memory, " . . . your daughter Natalie suffered so long . . . may she now be at peace in your bosom."

All of us stood in silence, awkwardly aware of Dominic's highly emotional state. Soon he stooped down beside the bed. With an effort he pulled Natalie's swollen body up into the crook of his arm. Then while he stroked her face, with a quaking voice he spoke aloud of his loss, his pain, and his undying love for his beloved wife.

Wide-eyed with the others in disbelief — or was it disgust

and rage at a display meant to mock their supposed love? — I trembled by the foot of the bed as Dominic went on.

"Nattie was the greatest person that ever lived! I would rather have been shot myself, have my arms cut off, anything!...if it could have saved her." Tears rolled down his cheeks unashamedly onto her nightgown. I didn't know whether to laugh or scream at this claustrophobic drama.

Red-faced, Dominic suddenly turned toward me. "And tell that jerk, God!...that he can go screw himself for such a wicked, damn..." He broke off, whimpering like a child. The rest of us began to shift uneasily, our own feelings or lack of them laid bare by this outburst.

Dominic laid Natalie back down on the pillow and kissed her, and some folks began to drift toward the door. The seated woman stood and folded her chair. But when Dominic dropped his unshaven face down a few inches from Natalie's as though to get one last look at her, our embarrassment finally melted into pity.

"Baby, baby!" he slapped her lightly on the cheek, "give me a sign, will ya? Blink your eye, please? Anything! Just show me you're okay!" Some of us in the room traded smiles when he so accurately characterized his wife, "If anyone can make a deal with God, Nattie, you can!"

"Dominic, Dominic...would it be okay to read a psalm?" I broke in, thinking this might bring some closure.

"Yeah, okay." It seemed to crash through to his normal self and pull him back to reality.

After the psalm, Dominic asked that we leave the room. Gratefully we began to make our exit. "Except for Father Paul," he announced. The others trooped out and the bedroom door clicked shut.

Without another word, and as though I were invisible, Dominic lay down on the king-size bed and rolled over next to his wife's body. Embracing her, he began to converse tenderly as though she were still alive. Intimate things bubbled up from his heart, endearments maybe never before expressed, or maybe never so clearly uttered all the months he clung to the hope she'd get better.

I felt as if I had stumbled upon a couple making love. I wanted to escape, but the Buddhist meditation came to mind.

Maybe this was just an Italian version of it. Taking a deep breath, I sat on the bed by their feet. Trying to imagine the fiery ball that was Natalie's soul, I prayed that her lingering spirit could depart.

"I love you, baby, I love you!" Dominic was murmuring. In my mind, a voice was singing, "Then somewhere near Salinas, Lord, I let her slip away, lookin' for the home I hope she'll find...," and words filtered back from countless marriage vows I had witnessed, "I promise to love you both in good times and in bad times, whether for richer or for poorer, whether in sickness or in health...."

It seemed so bizarre at first, but when Dominic whispered "You'll always be my sweetheart, Nattie...I'll miss you so much," I suddenly felt very blessed to be witnessing this parting act of love between Dominic and his beloved Natalie.

The feelings we have when someone dies cover a whole spectrum: guilt for having caused it somehow, or for being left alive when a loved one goes; maybe anger at the person for leaving us, or even a secret relief that the person is finally "at peace" — and so, praise God, are we!

We may experience grief for feeling we did not do enough — "if I had only..." — or an instinct to blame someone for what seems so unjust — the doctor, a relative, God, even the lost loved one. These feelings emerge in their own time and will hit us in waves. One of the feelings may predominate for a while, while at other times they are all mixed up together.

The most persistent feeling at first might be a cloud of numb depression, accompanied by an aching hole in one's life where this loved one used to bring so much life. Incessant tears can spring up at the most inopportune times, for instance, when we see someone who reminds us of the person. Or we may wish for the release of tears and they do not come. The worst thing we can do is to deny our feelings; the best thing we can do is to acknowledge whatever feelings we have. We need to honor our feelings of grief, even the ones that don't seem nice, and find friends who will simply let us be with them. Our grief proves we are alive and have loved. If we trust it, it will lead us to new life.

We need to take our own unique time to go through this bereavement period. It will teach us some of the most important lessons in our lives: that life is like a river and to be happy we must flow with it; that once we have loved someone, that person will always be a part of us — we just have to discover how. This is our beautifully human way to mourn and to heal and, when we are ready, to begin to live again.

In many cultures the boundary line between the visible world and the spirit-world is more permeable than it is in our culture. Whatever our mourning traditions, grieving those we have lost is one of the bridges to this invisible world, which all of us must finally acknowledge when we die. Because we are human, we grieve our deceased loved ones. We miss them in their flesh and blood. Yet as St. Paul says, "we must not grieve like those who are without hope" (1 Thess. 4:13). Hope in what? That we will see them again or, for those who do not believe in a resurrection, that our loved one is in peace.

Stephen Levine, the author of *Who Dies? An Investigation of Conscious Living and Conscious Dying,* says that grief "tears open the human heart" in order that we may understand our true selves in a way much deeper than we have done so up to then. Only when we lose those things that we have based our identity on, he explains, do we begin to get a glimpse of the "I AM" beneath these things, the One who will live on when even "I" have died.* This knowledge doesn't take away the pain or the grief until the process has run its course, but it can help us to bear with our own and others' grieving and trust that it is teaching us something profound.

One of these lessons is described by the fifth-century African bishop St. Augustine of Hippo, whose beloved classmate had died suddenly when they were twenty-one. Twenty years later he wrote in his *Confessions:*

> I wondered that other mortals should live when he was dead whom I had loved as if he would never die; and I marvelled still more that he should be dead and I his other self living still. Rightly has a friend been called "the half of my soul." For I thought of my soul and his soul as one soul in two bodies; and my life was a horror to me because I

---

*Stephen Levine, "Opening Your Heart to Yourself," tape #8 of Living/Dying Lecture Series, Warm Rock Tapes, P.O. Box 108, Chamisal, NM 87521.

would not live halved. And it may be that I feared to die lest
thereby he should die wholly whom I had loved so deeply.

(Book 4)

Augustine discovered that his friend, in order to live on, needed
him to live.

" ... The Lord gave, and the Lord has taken away ... Blessed
be the name of the Lord!" (from Job 1:2). When I finished reciting the Kaddish prayer over Natalie's body, Dominic and I joined
the others in the living room. He introduced me to Natalie's
daughter, Rochelle, by a former marriage. A brunette in her early
twenties, she had a striking figure like her mother's before her
sickness. Rochelle's husband grasped my hand warmly and told
me he appreciated the prayers. An older man with a shock of
white hair pulled me aside. This uncle recounted how close he
had been to Natalie, noting bitterly that one of her aunts had left
less than a week ago for a Caribbean cruise. Also milling about
the room were a crowd of Natalie's colleagues from the theater,
bright-looking women and men who appeared devastated and
hung together in small groups.

Dominic's sister came up and told me, "The undertaker's
in the lobby. Will you keep my brother occupied at the bar?"
Dominic was chatting with Cindy from Long Island, who was
bartending. She offered me a cocktail of grapefruit or cranberry
juice with vodka when I sat down, but I declined.

A couple of the actors placed a brocaded dividing screen between us and the vestibule. "Keep his back to the door," one of
them whispered to me. I'll try, I thought, but felt panicky. What
if Dominic turns around and sees them, even runs after the body
with his emotional style?

"Changed my mind!" I motioned to Cindy with a grin. "I'll
have one of those drinks after all."

"Go for it, Father Paul!" said Dominic.

I had gulped a third of it down when I noticed a commotion
behind the screen. "These are good, Dominic ... you sure you
don't want one?"

He stared at me with his wrecked face. "Later ... I'll get drunk
later." As they zipped up the remains of his wife into a body bag
in the next room and hustled it out the door behind us, Dominic philosophized, "Can you believe it? ... we come into life

all pink and cuddly, and in the end they take us out like a pile of garbage!" I gagged on my drink, laughing at his outrageous imagery. Cindy and he got napkins while I choked and fussed until the door closed.

Quickly the screen came down and an air of relief settled over the room. Some lit up cigarettes. The group of young people piled next to each other on the long white sofa. The talk became more animated and even included some soft laughter. At one point, Rochelle slipped up and whispered something in Dominic's ear and he nodded. Soon long-stemmed glasses were being handed out to everyone and a bottle of champagne was poured. "Nattie's favorite," mumbled Dominic.

I wasn't sure what was happening, but accepted a glass when it was offered. Everyone stood, including Dominic. With arms wrapped around each other, everyone lifted their glasses high as Rochelle led us in a toast: "As Mom would say," she announced with a firm voice, 'Here's to those who wish us well, and all the rest can go to hell!' " Her slender arm shot into the air while applause erupted, including shouts of testimony to Natalie's vitality and love of life. We clicked our glasses and sipped. Yes, not to Death, their defiant faces taught me, not to Death do we drink, but to *Life! L'Chaim!*

Later that night before retiring, I went up to the fourth floor solarium in our rectory in the Bronx. I wanted to think of Natalie and lit a candle in the dark. Dominic's words came to my ears, "Give me a sign, Baby!" The next moment — the connection frightened me at first — a clap of thunder struck right above my head! This was followed by brilliant bursts of lightning. Over and over they crackled around me right outside the windows, lighting up the sky as though it were noonday.

I shook in my place until the thought came: *It's Natalie's sign!* When was the last time a tornado hit New York City? It felt as if it were Natalie's spirit taking off. Not easily would she go. No, this lady would light up the sky with her life, even on the day she said goodbye. "Baby, give me a sign that you're okay!" Dominic pleaded. I wondered what he believed when he heard the tornado.

~

During my last week with the hospice program I was thrust headfirst into another struggle of faith. Peggy, the spunky, intelligent office manager for all of the nursing programs, was struck with a personal tragedy. It wasn't the terrible pain of watching a loved one gradually waste away from cancer or AIDS that confronted her at the age of forty-three. With four children to support, three from her first marriage, the most recent a little girl born to her and her new husband, Jack, Peggy received word at work that he had collapsed and died of a heart attack.

Gradual or sudden death — which would you choose for yourself or a loved one? Each has a unique effect on the survivors. Peggy showed me this in a way I had not known before.

After Kate announced Peggy's loss to the team, she asked if I would be willing to speak with her when she returned to work. Peggy's family background was Polish, and Kate felt it might be helpful if a priest reached out to her even though she was seeing a counselor.

I didn't know Peggy well; I had only said hello to her on occasion when we passed in the front office. Mostly I knew of her reputation for being hard-nosed with her co-workers. Occasionally you could hear her giving loud-mouthed directions to those under her as though she were some kind of general.

One afternoon I had come in from a patient visit. There was a commotion going on in a far corner of the office. Glancing over, I saw the back of Peggy's head and noticed some of the nurses and office staff huddled around her. An unmanageable scene and I wanted no part of it, but went over to the group anyway. Someone stood aside and Peggy, weeping uncontrollably, went straight into my arms. The advice of a colleague came to mind, "When you don't know what to do, dedicate it to God and just be yourself." I led Peggy into her office and closed the door behind us.

As I faced her on a folding chair, she put her head against me and wailed like an animal. "Oh, Paul, Jack is dead . . . I can't believe it! In the middle of a touch football game with my sixteen-year-old he grabbed his chest. He died before they got him to the emergency room."

"Peggy, oh, Peggy . . . " My arms cradled her.

"I can't let go, I can't let go . . . I've lost my faith." She sobbed into my shoulder.

Her little daughter, only two years old, and her three boys by a former marriage — seventeen, sixteen, and fourteen — are destroyed by this, she cried. "The baby asks 'How?' rather than 'Why?' when I tell her her daddy is dead and taken by God." Peggy leaned back, dabbing her eyes with her fingers, brushing strands of hair aside.

"Paul, it breaks my heart...my little girl runs to comfort me when I start breaking down at home...'Mama's got a boo-boo in the head,' I tell her...'I hold Mommy and you get better,' she says." With a groan, the tough-talking little general burrowed into my shoulder again.

"Oh, Paul, I can't believe in an afterlife...it feels like Jack is only dust now...I desperately need to believe he is still with me somehow, that I'm not all alone with our kids to raise. But I can't sense that...." Her tears poured down and soaked the front of my shirt.

In the clutter of her desk I searched for a tissue and some words of consolation for her. "He will be with you in a new way; maybe you won't see it right now."

Peggy clung to the words and my hands like a life preserver. "Oh, Paul, I need to believe that, I do...even if I only believe 10 percent."

"Good!...your 10 percent, my 30 percent, and Ruby's 60 percent will do." A little laugh burst through her tears.

"We were married for almost four years and were so happy. But I told the other nurses that it couldn't last, because we're not supposed to be this happy here. 'See?' I told them when this happened."

But God does want us to be happy! My own faith felt rocked by her plight. Looking up, I prayed, "O Lord, hear Peggy's weeping. Be with her now. And let her and her children know Jack's presence...Please!" Never had I prayed so desperately in front of anyone before.

Peggy calmed down after a while. Gritting her teeth, she spoke with more of her normal brassy anger about how Jack's son from his first marriage had cared so little for him. "But he left a $30,000 annuity to him — can you believe it? Because he had been in such good health, Jack never got around to changing it to me and our baby!"

"It could be worse," a friend told her at the wake.

"Sure!" Peggy snapped bitterly, "I could be homeless and without a job, but still living on the streets with my husband and children."

"No," the friend responded, "you could be in the box yourself!"

Peggy said she realized then that it could be worse, certainly for her kids, whom her husband really wouldn't have been able to care for. Yet none of these thoughts could alleviate her loss. "God damn!" she muttered. A trace of acceptance was in her voice though. Moments of silence passed during which we sat with our heads bowed. It was as though a tidal wave had plowed through the room.

"I did bring my little girl into the wake," Peggy said, her voice soft now as she looked up and dabbed her eyes with the tissue. "When it was almost over I said to her, 'Say goodbye, honey.' My baby looked up at the closed coffin and without knowing what was in it said, 'Bye-bye.' She's all I have of him now." Peggy smiled bravely. "She has my looks, thank God, but Jack's personality."

Letting go of me, she looked around the office while I made a joke about the piles of patient records and pink message slips.

"Yeah, I came in here just to get away from the thoughts at home, but I can hardly do anything... I'm such a mess."

"We're all with you in this, Peggy," I offered, and when she looked up, I said, "God is too. He's as close as your own heart, you know. Talk to him whenever you want. Tell him just how you feel. I'm sure he is with you in this and wants to know."

We stood. I would have done anything for her. Her pain made any of mine seem like nothing.

"We love you so much, Peggy."

"Thanks, Paul."

"If it's okay, I'll ask you how you're doing now and then. I don't want to bug you, but if you want to talk..."

"Okay." But she knew that when all is said and done she was on her own with her grief. Peggy was shuffling papers on her desk when I left for the team meeting.

When I returned to the rectory later that afternoon, I threw some cold water in my face, grabbed a cold beer, and headed up to the roof to unwind a bit before dinner. The sun was still blazing so I pulled a chair over into the shadow of the chimney and leaned back against the wall. Two pigeons were strutting along the parapet. When they saw me they scrambled upward in a flurry of wings and divebombed out of sight.

Street sounds from below made me grateful today — the police sirens, the shouts of the children on the summer evening, even the usually maddening jingle of the ice cream truck parked by our front door: Life roars on. I swigged the beer.

The events of the day crowded in anyway. Earlier I had visited a lady in Queens who said she had no faith in God though she always wished she could believe. And there is the 101-year-old Buddhist man whose daughter said he *is* Buddha! Then Peggy, her faith so wrecked by the tragedy of her husband's death. People's faith is so fragile — my faith is! What do I believe, anyway? On a day like this I hardly knew.

Poor Peggy! The unanswerableness of her "why?" to a God who often seems capricious or cruel. Even impotent. She and Jack didn't even get to say goodbye.

My mother was never able to say goodbye either. Is that why all these years I've been so caught up in helping others to do so? Realizing from this experience how crucial such partings are, I suppose I've wanted to help others have these goodbyes so they do not pine away for a word or gesture left unspoken. The hospice ministry has been a way of healing myself too.

What would Mama have said if she had the chance to say goodbye? Oh, she would have organized the family during that last week, made sure we knew how to buy the groceries, work the washing machines, pay the telephone bills on time, get to church, water the plants. Chuckling at her penchant for taking care of everyone, I choked on the beer.

And what would she have said to *me* if she could have said goodbye? With a start I bolted upright in the chair, my last image of her in the hospital vivid in my mind. But you did say something at the end, Mama! I had forgotten it until now.

The beer tingled at the back of my throat as her words filtered up from my unconscious: "Paul, you're just like me, a chip off the old block, always taking care of everyone. Don't wait until you are ready to die, like I did, to let someone hold you. Do it now, Paul, before it's too late."

No, that's impossible! It's just my imagination! No matter, I silently absorbed this message from Mama, let it become clear and present in my mind. The most amazing thing was that she had "said" these words to me while she lay in a coma fifteen years before. In any case, I heard these words from her now more deeply than if she had screamed them to me the morning she had died.

A jetliner broke through the cloud bank in front of me, and rocked the neighborhood with its deafening roar. When the sound subsided, I strolled over to the edge of the roof and gazed down at the people five stories below.

The message from Mama had been engraved on my heart years ago. More than I could know, it had colored my life and my way of ministry ever since. Was I following her advice? Like her I was taking care of all these people — Peggy, Isha and Lilianne, Natalie and Dominic, Candida and Andy, Henri, Elmo...*my* children. Sparky, Marianna and Eddie, Alberto and his family, on and on and on....But at least in the way I was taking care of them I was halfway to letting myself be held, wasn't I?

Is this such a bizarre thought: my interaction with hurting people is as much their holding my hand as my holding theirs? As much their giving to me as my giving to them?[14] The sick and the dying have nothing to be ashamed about in their helplessness and pain if they "hold" the rest of us in it; through their suffering they can draw us out of our petty isolation and selfishness into love — before our brief time is up.

A kaleidoscope of images came to me: the "last breakfast" with Dominic and Natalie; Elmo's love of comics; Henri's confession that he had wasted his life; Uncle Sparky's childlike reaction to the back rub; Alberto's refusal to let go of my hand; Isha's bright-eyed "chair-dancing" even while she knew she was close to the end; Candida's indomitable faith and her son's fight to escape from it; Teddy's prayer for his wife's dog; Marianna's heartrending scream when her father died; even Peggy's "God damn!"

I may have held all of these people...yes, surely I did. But God in his wisdom knows how they held me by their love and courage in the midst of the most difficult challenge of their lives. For all it may appear otherwise, I have been learning that ministry doesn't go just one way. One of the reasons priests are ordained is to help people know their own power to forgive and bless, not to take this from them and keep it ourselves, no matter what wonders this may permit.

Finishing my drink, I went down to my room and threw on some shorts and a T-shirt. Carlos was engrossed in homework, but I talked him into a walk through the park before the sun went down.

~ Closure ~

WITH ONLY A FEW DAYS LEFT before I was set to leave the program, it wasn't clear whether Isha or I would depart first. She was failing fast, but that had happened before. The team joked about her being the hospice record-holder: Isha had been with us for over two-and-a-half years now! Because of pain that we couldn't seem to regulate at her home, Doc was planning to admit her to the hospital. I was going to wait until the next day to make a visit, but decided to call the office for an update after finishing earlier than I expected with a patient in Chinatown.

It wasn't quite eleven o'clock when I emerged from the pagoda-shaped phone booth near Canal Street into streets bustling with Asian people. It might have been Shanghai unless you knew that the suspension bridge at the end of the street led from Manhattan to Brooklyn. Something caught my eye as I waited on the corner for the light to change. About three blocks away, at an intersection of two streets that came together in a V-shape, a large statue was sheltered beneath a red and gold canopy. It seemed to be some kind of shrine, probably one of those fat and happy-looking Buddhas! Since I wouldn't be getting down this way again, I decided to have a look.

Peering out inscrutably at something off in the distance was none other than Confucius himself! For some moments I stood and gazed up at this ancient religious figure I had heard about but had never investigated. His dates said he lived five hundred years before Christ. When an old man arose from the sunny spot where he was reading his paper, I was able to ponder the inscription on the statue's base:

223

When the Great Principle prevails, the world is a Commonwealth in which rulers are selected according to their wisdom and ability. Mutual confidence is promoted and good neighborliness is cultivated. Hence, men do not regard as parents only their own parents, nor do they treat as children only their own children. Provision is secured for the aged till death, employment for the able-bodied, and the means of growing up for the young. Helpless widows and widowers, orphans and the lonely, as well as the sick and disabled are well cared for. Men have their respective occupations and women their homes. They do not like to see wealth lying idle, yet they do not keep it for their own gratification. They despise indolence, yet they do not use their energies for their own benefit. In this way, selfish schemings are repressed, and robbers, thieves, and other lawless men no longer exist, and there is no need for people to shut their outer doors. This is the Great Harmony — Ta Tung.

Ta-Tung! I wonder what Confucius would think of modern-day New York. How close were we to living the Great Principle? It got me thinking of the various faith traditions of our patients. Wang, whom I had just seen, was Buddhist, and Isha, whom I was about to visit, was Orthodox Christian. We had just buried Natalie, a Jew, while her husband Dominic was Catholic. Sparky and Elmo were Baptists; Peggy, the office manager, was Roman Catholic. All of them so different, yet all brought together somehow by the experience of death.

As a child I had been educated in Roman Catholic schools and taught that we were the "one true faith," that if we were baptized and died in the state of grace we would go to Heaven where God was. There we Catholics would be perfectly happy with the Beatific Vision, though as a boy what I really got excited about was the promise of having all the ice cream you could ever want — twenty-eight flavors too!

We knew that all the non-Catholics — except the ones we contributed our nickles and dimes for so the nuns could buy them as "pagan babies" — would go somewhere else when they died. Limbo or Hell, we weren't sure. Someday I hoped to meet one of these pagan babies.

I remembered my brother Shawn, an ex-Marine, phoning me

a few years before and asking if I could recall baptizing one of his daughters. She was now fifteen years old and about to make her Confirmation. He said that they couldn't find her baptismal record in the book at their parish rectory. Had I forgotten to register it? Shawn had four daughters, and I remembered baptizing one of them years ago, but couldn't remember which. It was embarrassing, but we figured out the year and decided it must have been so. That led us to reminisce about our childhood Catholic education.

"What was it that happens to you if you die without being baptized?" Shawn inquired.

"You go to Limbo."

"Limbo! Oh, yeah. What is that, anyway?"

"Limbo is where you are perfectly naturally happy," I explained the theological idea, "and where you don't know that you aren't supernaturally happy."

"Hey, Limbo sounds pretty good. I'll take it!" The two of us laughed over that in a way we hadn't done in years.

The experience in hospice work had taught me something important: everyone's faith — not just Catholicism or Christianity — is a way to God. Yahweh or Buddha or Allah is the image of God for other believers the way Jesus Christ is for me. If this is so, then Yahweh will meet Jews, Buddha will meet Buddhists, Allah will meet Muslims, and Jesus Christ will meet Christians at the moment of death. If we can manage to meet each other with mutual respect for our different expressions of faith, surely God must do the same!

Being so close to so many different people at the moment of their deaths had made me see more of what God's way might be. Not to make the world Christian — or Buddhist, Muslim, Hindu, or Jewish for that matter — but for believers everywhere to go deeper into their own faith no matter what it is. This is what ecumenism must mean: deep down in our roots is where we will all meet the one true God.[15]

It was early afternoon by the time I found a parking space near Gramercy Park, a few blocks from Cabrini Hospital. Lunch had already been served on the hospice ward and the carpeted corridors were quiet. Bright splashes of watercolor paintings on the walls lifted my spirits. At the far end of the hallway the nursing station was visible, but I spotted the number of Isha's room first. The door was slightly ajar.

No one was with her and my first thought was, "My God, Isha's dead in her bed!" With her head thrown back against the pillow and her mouth open, not a muscle stirred. Her eyes were glazed and unseeing. The sunny, shiny room accentuated the dark, emaciated body — as though a strange and terrible jewel had been placed upon an inviting silken cushion.

But no, Isha wasn't dead yet. As I crept closer I could see her feeble, erratic breathing. Though it still hit hard to see my friend's familiar face now almost a skeleton, I had prepared myself for the past few months and was even glad that her release was so close at hand. I was going to be a part of it.

Amazingly, when I got into her line of sight Isha recognized me. Even from her semi-coma, a little sound of greeting escaped from her throat. When her bony hand stirred, I took it. A nurse looked in on us and asked Isha if she were in pain. She nodded.

"I'm her priest," I explained, though I felt more like family. The nurse allowed me to remain while she gently rolled Isha on the side and gave her a morphine injection in her pitifully thin backside.

I thought it would probably be our last visit together. What followed was the sweetest time I ever spent with a patient, perhaps because I was listening for what she needed and also voicing what I did. The deepest communication happened in the silent spaces between us.

It is striking how at the end everything takes on such deep significance; perhaps if we never died we wouldn't really value the preciousness of life. In the last hours the slightest gesture feels momentous.

At first, since she was facing the wall, I pulled Isha's bed out diagonally from it and drew up a chair so we could be close. She was too weak even to hold her eyes open, and the morphine made her doze off and on. I held her hand, wanting to be in whatever emotional space she was in. I read her the scripture passage in which Jesus is shown crying out on the cross, "My God, my God, why have you forsaken me?" (Mark 15:34).

"Isha, maybe you feel like this too?" The little head nodded. Wanting to encourage her in her faith, I read a Resurrection passage too.

"Jesus went before us through the doorway of death," I said, "so we wouldn't be so afraid ... don't be afraid, Isha." The feeble breaths came slower now. A tiny heave of the chest, and then long moments until the next. "If you want to go, you can," I told her. "We'll stay in touch with Lilianne.... If you want to stay, that's okay too."

For five or ten minutes, it's hard to remember, I sat holding her hand. Once I began to play as we had in the past — chair-dancing — but Isha shook her head.

What did I want to say to her before it was too late? Glancing behind me first to make sure we were alone, I asked if she would kiss again the wooden cross I wore around my neck. It symbolized my commitment to Christ and I wanted her blessing of that. With my face bent down over hers, I placed the cross on her cracked lips and she kissed it. A deep gratefulness surged up in me.

"Isha, what a wonderful woman you are! ... I will never forget you." The words sounded cheap. When I told her she would always be my favorite patient, her lips moved. Catching my breath, I leaned closer. My dear friend was saying a profound word that I could hold in my heart forever. "What was that? ... Oh, Isha, what?"

There was barely a sound, but if I strained with all my might I could grasp what syllables she was trying to utter. "I ... screem ... "

What? ... please! "ICE ... ?" Oh, for God's sake! It came to me — ICE CREAM! "Isha, you want some ice cream!"

Despite the serious moment, I couldn't help laughing aloud. I swear a faint smile crept up on her face too. You devil, Isha! Zapping me like that even on your way out! I went and got some vanilla ice cream from the nurse and fed her in minuscule spoonfuls.

After I had been there an hour-and-a-half, Isha uttered a great sigh. It was a deep and earthy moan that came all the way up from her toes, as though it summed up everything. This seemed like a natural moment to part, and I asked her if it were all right for me to go. Yes, she nodded. Slowly I gathered my things up. For a moment I stood over her and then leaned down and kissed her on the forehead. "Isha, my friend ... goodbye." Letting go of her hand, I moved toward the door. Turning for one more look,

I heard Isha say with great difficulty, "Thank you . . . " Her voice trailed off into nothingness.

I gave a little bow toward this woman, the shell of her anyway, who had taught me so much about patience and love and the ability to suffer and die with such grace. Quickly I went down the stairway and out through the revolving doors into the August sunlight.

It was only later when I talked with a friend about Isha that I realized what she had been for me. "Whatever you had to offer her was always good enough, wasn't it?" Yes, Isha. What a wonderful gift your love was for me and that you let me love you back so freely!

The next morning, Saturday, was my day off. Sleeping late, I saw the red light on my answering machine when I got up to go to the bathroom. When I pressed the message button it was Ruby's voice, "Hi, Paul! I hate to have to tell you this way, but Isha died at seven-thirty this morning. Would you call Lilianne? I'll catch you later . . . "

Sleepy-eyed, I knelt down before an ikon of the black Jesus and prayed. "Goodbye, Isha . . . please don't forget me." An era had ended. Now I could leave the hospice program in peace.

I was unable to reach Lilianne, but she finally phoned me on Monday evening. "Father Paul?" Her voiced was subdued but not devastated. "Would you assist at the graveside on Wednesday?"

"Of course, I'd be honored. . . . How are you doing, Lilianne?"

"I'm doing okay. I was with my mom on the last night from one o'clock on. I'm glad you were with her that afternoon; Ruby was there a little later too. I'm glad Mom wasn't alone."

Alone, that's how Lilianne is now, I thought as I hung up. She could also be relieved. Two years is a long time in a young woman's life.

On the day of Isha's burial, Ruby, Yolanda, and I took the subway up to Cooke's Funeral Parlor at Seventy-second Street on the West Side of Manhattan. We didn't go to every patient's funeral, but we did for those who by some combination of needs had become special to us. We needed the closure ourselves, and rituals allowed us to see with our eyes and accept with our bodies that indeed such a person was gone. It enabled us to begin to let go so we had room in our hearts for the next group of patients who were waiting in the wings to meet their Maker.

It was a hot and hazy day. The subway itself would be an air-conditioned blessing but the platform on which we waited was a furnace of hell. The train came quickly, however, and when Ruby suggested we stop for a bite to eat at the food stand on the corner of Broadway, we welcomed the respite. I wolfed down a large papaya juice and two hot dogs smothered in sauerkraut and relish while the women each nursed a small juice.

It had been a long journey with Isha for the three of us, and without saying so we knew we had gotten sustenance from each other. Ruby in particular, as close as she was with patients, rarely showed her deep feelings about them. Instead she would mask the pain in a matter-of-fact bravado about death. Over the years she had let me see cracks in this toughness. It had helped me let down my own guard to acknowledge my feelings. Yes, we would miss Isha for many reasons. We were stalling, wanting to savor some of the experience we had had with her on this day before we bid her a final farewell.

I told them of my plans for the service. I had brought Isha's picture with me, the one with her praying with the medicine as she looked up, and asked if they thought it would be all right to show this to the mourners.

"Ask Lilianne," said Yolanda.

"I'm planning to say a few words," I informed them. "Would either of you want to?"

"If I feel up to it," Ruby said, but Yolanda, her eyes glistening, declined.

Rounding the corner, we spied a limousine and a few old cars lined up alongside the curb of the funeral parlor. This would be the Budget Special: no viewing of the body and no actual service at the funeral parlor; the friends of the departed would only be allowed to mill about in the narrow corridor inside the front door until the body was brought out to the hearse.

In the group of a dozen or so people in the hallway, we met Lilianne, who was clad in black and looked somber.

"Father Paul, would you mind riding with the hearse?" she asked.

"That would be fine." I didn't tell her I would rather not be separated from her and the other people. Pointing at my briefcase, I mentioned the picture of her mother. "Could I hold it up at the service, Lilianne, to show the people your mother's faith?"

"That would be okay, Father Paul," she said softly. Lilianne looked like a little girl. I wanted to gather her to me, pull her into my arms, tell her I would stand by her forever. I gave her a hug.

It took us over an hour to get to the cemetery in New Jersey that handles these poverty-level funerals. With the hearse leading the way, the little caravan of cars into which Lilianne and her friends had piled was strung out behind us with their headlights on, just one of many similar processions in New York that day. Despite the Holland Tunnel and the turnpike traffic, they stuck close behind us. When we turned through the gates of Rosewood Memorial Gardens, a pair of crusty gravediggers glanced at us from beside a mound of dirt fifty yards away and turned back to their shoveling. When they had finished, they stood off to the side watching.

When the cars had all disgorged their passengers and the plain pinewood casket had been laid in place at ground level, the funeral director motioned for us to gather closer. Standing next to Lilianne, and with Ruby and Yolanda right behind us, I placed a stole around my neck. I glanced up at the withering sun, stepped beside the casket, and began: "Dear Lilianne, and dear friends of Isha..."

I cannot remember precisely what I said, except that I reminded those gathered of Isha's faith — how Christians believe that life is not ended by death, only changed. While I held her picture above my head, I told them, "This is a view of Isha that we should all take into our hearts. It represents her faith, a gift from God that she has given to me too." I remembered Isha's response to my asking her if she believed in the resurrection: "Maybe..."

Usually at events like this, I find it easy to slip into the personable but controlled persona of a pastor. It's a way to keep my emotions in check. This day my hands were shaking as I spoke to the little band of Isha's friends. In the huge barren lot they looked so pitiful. With the red clay dust swirling around us in the blazing afternoon heat, it could just as well have been Ethiopia. Placing the picture of Isha at the foot of her casket, I opened a Bible and read in a loud voice from the Book of Revelation:

Then I saw new heavens and a new earth. The former heavens and the former earth had passed away, and the sea was no longer. I also saw a new Jerusalem, the holy city, coming down out of heaven from God, beautiful as a bride prepared to meet her husband. I heard a loud voice from the throne cry out: "This is God's dwelling among men. He shall dwell with them and they shall be his people and he shall be their God who is always with them. He shall wipe away every tear from their eyes, and there shall be no more death or mourning, crying out or pain, for the former world has passed away." The One who sat on the throne said to me, "See, I make all things new!" (Rev. 21:1–4)

When I had finished, Lilianne introduced another minister, a heavy-set, bearded man in a gray suit and tie, with a large gold crucifix hung by a chain in the middle of his chest. From his severe expression, I was not sure how he felt about me. It was only when he began to speak with a high-pitched passion in his voice, in what I presumed to be Ethiopian, that it occurred to me the majority of the people may not even have grasped what I had said.

Oh, well, that's Lilianne's problem, I told myself, and glanced back at Ruby, searching for a clue to what she wanted to do. She had her stolid public face on and didn't look my way; her eyes were fixed forward and she looked very sad. When the minister had finished a few minutes later, she went forward without any coaxing.

Ruby stood partially facing us, partially turned to the side toward the casket. Reaching into her pocket, she read slowly from a crumpled funeral parlor brochure:

> In tears we saw you sinking,
> and watched you fade away.
> Our hearts were almost broken,
> we wanted you to stay.
> But when we saw you sleeping,
> so peacefully, free from pain,
> how could we wish you back with us,
> to suffer again?
> It broke our hearts to lose you...

Ruby's voice faltered. For a moment she peeked up at us and then finished quickly...

> . . . but you did not go alone.
> For part of us went with you,
> the day God took you home.

Ruby rolled up the paper and stared out at us with her sol-
dier's expression. For a few seconds all you could hear was the
lonesome wind blowing the dust across the treeless landscape.

"No more pain!" Ruby announced almost defiantly. "Free at
last!" She leaned in the direction of the casket and in a tenderer
voice murmured, "Goodbye, Isha." A single tear ran down her
cheek. Ruby! I couldn't believe it.

It was time to go. I asked if we could hold hands and say the
Lord's Prayer. We did so, each in our own language, after which I
sprinkled holy water on the casket and offered a final blessing.

The funeral director came forward and told the people it was
time to pay their last respects. He handed each person a red
carnation from a bouquet he had retrieved from a neighboring
gravesite. Each placed the flower on Isha's casket in silence; Lilianne, held on either side by Yolanda and Ruby, was last. Though
she wept softly, I had the feeling she would be okay.

The crowd began to drift back toward the cars for the ride
home. When I noticed Ruby quietly press some money into Lilianne's hand, I did the same. All of a sudden there were screams
back at the graveside. The women shouted one last protest as
the gravediggers lowered Isha's casket into the trench. Used to
this, the workmen continued to shovel the dirt onto the coffin.
Soon only an occasional sob punctuated the raspy sound of steel
against dirt, dirt against wood. The last thing I remember is the
slight figure of Lilianne, standing by herself with her dark hair
flying, gazing back at her mother's remains.

~

My car seemed to direct itself by memory across the Triboro
Bridge toward home. It was my last day with the hospice program. The sun was going down over the familiar Manhattan
skyline in a gold and orange blaze. On the horizon up ahead I
could see a thunderstorm approaching.

At the toll booth, I flipped a token into the machine for the
last time. No more traffic jams and subways — thank God!

A pang of loss hit me. Never mind, there's a token on the dashboard I can keep as a souvenir.

So many people, so much pain and loss. It's a wonder the world doesn't explode from it all. Looking up through my sunglasses into the stormy black clouds sweeping in from the north, I was glad the other drivers couldn't see my eyes. Let the tears speak for me. Let them speak for Lilianne and Isha and for all the others as well.

Yes, let them speak to our God whom we cannot feel at times, but in whom we somehow believe even in all this sadness. Let them speak to the One whose eternal spirit dwells within each of us and is stronger than our body's demise. Whatever we call ourselves, it is in holding each other's brokenness that we express a living faith.[16]

You too, God — with your heart of flesh and blood — I bet you've been holding me through these suffering ones of yours. How else could I feel such peace even while the tears flow? Whatever "almighty" name we call you, you are holding us through these wounds, bearing our pain along with us. This is the way we receive the forgiveness we need, and the way you receive ours when we are ready to offer it.[17]

Such faith is a wonderful gift. It isn't the kind of gift you can just give away to others as though it were your possession. Rather, it is a gift to "hold" others and trust that God will give to them in God's own good time. Maybe this happens through our prayers, or at least by our lifting up these dear human beings' lives. If my experience during the years in hospice ministry has taught me anything, it is that God's eyes must stream with tears over his children's losses at least as much as ours do.

~

The night before I left the hospice program and New York City, I called Andy Perez at the number in Connecticut where he was staying. An older man's voice answered. Somewhat suspiciously he inquired who I was and then put Andy on.

"Andy, it's Father Paul! How're you doing?"

"Oh, hi!" In an aside I heard him respond to someone and laughter ensued. "What's up?" he said back into the phone. A more mature voice than I remembered.

"I wanted to tell you that I am going away for awhile, Andy.

. . . I won't be seeing your mother anymore." Or you, I wanted to say, but didn't. I felt strange to myself and wondered why I was telling him this.

"Really?"

"Yeah, I was wondering about you, how you've been doing up there."

"Fine, I'm doing real fine, Father Paul. I've been painting houses, and I'll be coming home at the end of the summer." An awkward silence hung in the air.

I wanted to say I would miss him, that I really was glad to have gotten to know him, that I wished he felt the same and that maybe we could stay in touch. "Well, I'll be leaving town tomorrow, and I just wanted to say goodbye . . . "

"Oh, thanks. Good luck wherever you're going."

"Thanks Andy . . . goodbye."

"Goodbye." I waited until I heard a click.

About three weeks later, after I had driven 3500 miles across the country by myself, sometimes shedding tears for no special reason and saying to myself, "Let it go, let it go . . . " I received a card in the mail.

> Father Paul, Thank you for everything you did for Candida and us. She is now closer than ever to God and she won't forget you, because you were so nice to her. Angel is doing very well, and Candida knew in advance that he was going to change. Thanks again from all of us.
>
> *The Perez Family*

It didn't dawn on me at first — not until I read the enclosed holy card with her dates on it — that Candida had died! It was less than a week after Andy had returned home. Laying my head back on my chair, I said a prayer for her and imagined how she must have finally allowed herself to go. I thought of how Candida had made an art of offering her pain up, of the manipulation in it, of the barely mentioned doubts, and of Juan's enigmatic way of saying she had died.

What a unique ritual it is when children leave their parents. In this case God seemed to have used Candida's offering to do the opposite of what she had prayed for — drive Andy away rather than bind him close. Yet when Candida believed his going away was good, she was finally able to die.

And Andy and Juan? On their own now. No more excuses, no more blaming anyone else for their choices. The same goes for me.

My mother was similar to Candida in her devotedness to God. You might even say to "prove" this faith to herself and to God she had given birth to fourteen children. Their close-binding love was a similar kind of mothering, yet my mother's death was the opposite of Candida's in a way. In a coma after her brain operation, Mama had felt no pain, unless a person in a coma can suffer from some barely conscious desire to be awake with those she loves. So it was we who sat helplessly in her room night after night praying to God, wiping the tears from our eyes. Mama didn't really have a choice; it was we who finally had to let go. We weren't aware then that her dying would be a gift to us — a challenge to grow up and stand on our own.

~

One evening about a week after the anointing service we had in the ICU with the whole family present, Mama's sister Anne, the little nun, whispered to me in the corridor that she wanted to talk. I took her elbow and we swung down the corridor past the nurse's station, she in her black habit and veil, I in slacks and a sport shirt. We strolled past rooms with half-open doors where patients were hooked up to their machines. Most of them were unconscious or asleep; some had visitors on whose faces you could read the prognosis. I could hear Aunt Anne breathing heavily at my side. She was the other one in the family with a religious vocation like myself. We gave one another support in our chosen path though we were of different generations. Yet I resisted her too. I didn't want to be the goody-two-shoes priest she, like my mother, wanted me to be.

At sixty, younger by four years than her sister Nora, Anne reminded us all of Mama by her looks, voice, and mannerisms. The two of them had been very close growing up, and even more so when Anne went into the convent and needed a "home" to come back to after their parents had sold their house and moved in with our family in 1950. On Saturdays, Aunt Anne would come over to our house from the school for the deaf in Philadelphia where she taught. She and Mama would "chew the fat," as Daddy called their sisterly chats, while they folded mountains of laundry on the dining room table. During the past week, Anne had realized with unspeakable pain that she was losing her dearest friend.

Turning to me in an even more intense way than her usual manner, Aunt Anne gripped my two hands in hers and locked my gaze into hers.

"What is it, Aunt Anne?" I held my composure.

"Paul, Nora's waiting for something, isn't she?" she whispered hoarsely. The precise lip movement of those who work with the hearing-impaired added even more gravity to her voice. "She's waiting for something, and I think I know what it is."

"What is it? . . . What do you mean?" I glanced back down the corridor toward a few of the family members who were sitting outside Mama's room.

"Has everyone seen her?" She stared up at me as though pleading for me to see the connection.

"I think so . . . no, wait a minute, I don't think Richie has."

"That's it!" Her grey eyes gleamed. "Nora's waiting to go, but she won't until she says goodbye to everyone."

All of us had been in and out to see Mama so often the past week — except Richie, at nineteen the youngest of the brothers. The last he had seen her was when he and Daddy had discovered her collapsed on the floor of her hospital room the night she had to be operated on. Since then he had only slipped in and out of the house like a shadow.

"Promise me you'll speak to him," Aunt Anne said, gritting her teeth.

"I will."

"Okay, old top." Only then did she release her grip. We walked back to the others while I wondered how Mama could say goodbye when she was in a coma.

The next night after dinner, before I went to the hospital, a few of us were relaxing in the living room at the family home on Copley Road, watching the news. The back door slammed. Moments later Richie rushed past us up the stairs.

"Richie!" I called after him, "I want to talk to you before you go out again." No answer. The bathroom door on the second floor closed. In a few minutes he was back down the stairs again. Halfway through the dining room, he paused and looked back over his shoulder toward me.

"Whaddaya want?" He sounded brittle and scared.

I got up slowly from the rug and walked over toward him. "Come down to the basement with me; I want to talk about something with you." I placed my hand on his shoulder, but he was looking away. We went down through the dark basement where we had celebrated many parties through the years. I remembered the time Richie had asked me and Shawn to buy a case of beer for him and his teenage buddies. They had drunk so much that we had to pour black coffee down their throats so they could make it home.

The laundry room door was ajar. I pushed it open. With its buckling linoleum floor and a single bare light bulb dangling off a ceiling full of cobweb-covered pipes, it was the only place in the three-story house you could hope to have a private conversation.

Richie pulled the light on while I grabbed two old kitchen chairs and pulled them up to face each other. We weren't used to talking like this. My siblings and I were much more convivial in groups than we were with just two of us. Our father never seemed comfortable one on one, so the brothers especially hadn't learned to communicate like this.

I sat down first, then Richie. With his eyes glued to the floor, he seemed ready to burst. "Richie..." I straddled his legs between mine, "everyone's concerned about you, wondering what you are feeling these days.... Can you tell me?"

For an instant he glanced up at me and croaked in a tight voice, "I'm okay." Then he let out his breath with a whooshing sound. My hands were on his knees and we sat in silence.

"You don't look okay to me. It is a tough time for all of us. What do you think is happening to Mama?"

"She's in a coma.... Will she get better?" His eyes were filled with fright.

"We don't know yet. But you know what I've been thinking? You haven't seen her since the operation, right? If she doesn't get better..." I paused to let the idea sink in, "you're going to wish you had said goodbye." His thigh muscles tensed, but I still wasn't prepared for the explosion that followed.

Throwing his hands to his head, Richie screamed "NO! NO! NO! NO! NO!..." His body lunged back and forth convulsively as he roared, "O LORD! LORD! LORD!...CHRIST! CHRIST! CHRIST!" As he tapered off into a helpless plea, "...please,

please, *nooooo!*" I wrapped my arms around his contorted face and hugged him to me. His tears soaked the front of my shirt. I rocked him while he cried for all of us. "Yes, yes . . . it hurts so much doesn't it?"

It seemed that we were there like this for a long time before I noticed Richie's sobbing had quieted. He gave a deep sigh and pulled free from my embrace. He shook his head as if it were a bad dream and slumped back into the seat.

"Would you do something for me?" Richie didn't move. "Would you come in to see Mama with me tonight? You can just stay a few minutes, but it will be good for you and for her." He shivered as though he were shaking leaves off his back but nodded his head that he would.

"Thanks, Richie. Sally and I will be driving down to the hospital in about a half hour."

"Okay, bro." We stood and gave each other a hug.

After I turned the light out, I shivered in the darkness too. It was a roller coaster the family was on now, heading wherever it wanted. It was the last day of September 1975.

As we crossed through Cobbs Creek Park into Philadelphia, Sally turned to Richie and said softly, "It'll be a bit strange when you first see Mama, Richie. She's got bandages on her head and all. But just remember that it's her under all those machines and you'll be okay." Through the rear view mirror I could see him looking out the window. It wouldn't have surprised me if the door had flown open and he had bolted at the next red light.

When we had parked the car and were walking toward the entrance, I stopped and turned to Richie, who was a step behind us. The shadows from the street lights played across his face, more masculine than mine with a jaw like Daddy's.

"Richie, since Mama is in a coma, that means she is basically unconscious. She won't be reacting or talking back to you. We don't know for sure, but it is likely she can hear us when we talk to her. So that's what we'll be doing. Just go in, say hi, and whatever else you want. It doesn't have to be long, okay?"

"Yeah!" he muttered into the darkness. We wove our way through the maze of doors and elevators into the old hospital until we were outside the Intensive Care Unit. Sally said she would wait outside.

As casually as I could I walked straight through the door

with Richie, went up to Mama, and addressed her limp body, "Mama, guess who's here to see you tonight... your favorite son!" I grinned over at him while he hung back by the curtain. "Come on over by the bed, Richie." I motioned to him. Got to keep it light, I thought.

"Mama, Richie says if you come home he won't complain about putting the garbage out anymore!" My chuckle sounded hollow, while Richie looked even more distressed with his hands jammed into his pockets. But he took a few steps closer.

Mama's hands caught my gaze. With the intravenous tape and their yellowish, lifeless look, they weren't pretty hands. I let my fingers stroke the one nearest me.

Mama's hands — had I ever seen them at rest during my entire life? Always in motion — cutting vegetables in the kitchen when we arrived home from school, washing sinksful of dishes without a dishwasher, dusting venetian blinds, changing babies' diapers. On the coldest winter days, those hands would wash endless hampers of laundry and hang them out on the clothesline to dry. Unpacking groceries, watering plants, bandaging cuts — if those hands stopped moving the world would stop! Or she would anyway. Even at the end of the day, before Mama went up to bed at night, her hands would be mending socks while, to reward herself at last, she'd be indulging in a few Oreo cookies she had hidden in the oven.

There were age spots on Mama's hands, and her nails were unpolished and broken in a few places. Not pretty hands, not the kind you'd see in the TV advertisements or imagine tenderly stroking your face. In fact, I couldn't remember ever being lovingly held by those hands... oh, maybe when I was a baby I was washed in the kitchen sink.

Mama's hands were too busy working to hold you or to be held. Yet now somehow in their ugliness they seemed beautiful to me. I would give anything to see them flutter to life again; I would reach out to her more myself if I had another chance. I took one and cradled it in my palm.

"Richie, why don't you just thank Mama for everything." He searched my face quizzically. "If Mama needs to go, it'll help her if we can thank her for all she's given us."

Mechanically he came a few steps closer, stared down at her and said in a strangled voice, "Thanks, Mama."

We stood there awkwardly until I said, "Why don't you come over here and hold her hand? We could say a Hail Mary." Richie did so, gingerly touching her arm at first and then letting his calloused fingers slide down to her hand.

We knelt down on the terrazzo floor with Mama between us and recited the old prayer we knew by heart. "Hail Mary, full of grace, the Lord is with you. Blessed are you among women, and blessed is the fruit of your womb...." As we watched the closed eyelids, the incessant gasp of the respirator was the only sound we could hear.

I didn't think to ask Richie if he wanted to be alone with her or if he wanted to say anything else; I just remembered what Aunt Anne had told me as we stood to go. Richie looked like he might wail "I'm sorry," "I love you," even "I hate you" or any of the other things pent up inside. As we edged toward the door, at the last moment he turned his head and said, "Goodbye, Mama." Quickly we exited to the corridor.

Half asleep, Sally had her feet propped up on a chair. She stretched lazily and asked, "Want a soda or something?"

"I need more than a soda!" said Richie. His eyes were filled up but he looked relieved.

"Come over here, brother," said Sally, mussing up his hair. She gave him a hug and he plopped down beside her. I went to hunt for a soda machine. Then the three of us passed the time in small talk until about 10:00 p.m.

"I'm heading home," Richie announced suddenly.

"Are you okay?"

"Yeah, I'll be fine... and I've got to work tomorrow, not like you lazy bums just hanging around here."

"Want a ride?"

"No, I'll take the subway. Can't trust your driving!" He was back in his sassy style. I punched him on the arm.

"Thanks, Richie. I'll see you at home."

He grabbed my shoulder. "Later, man." Sally kissed him and he quickly strode away. We watched him turn the corner at the end of the corridor, grimacing at one another after he was out of sight. A clock tolled the hour on a building outside.

Sally took a turn with Mama while I dozed. Every two hours we alternated. To stay awake during my turns I read Scripture aloud to Mama, even sang to her and babbled about all sorts of things.

On my last shift, during that hour just before dawn when everything is so quiet, the machines seemed to hum more softly, or maybe my brain had become numb to them by then. Since the patients are asleep or unconscious, only a small crew of nurses covers the wards during these hours, though occasionally you'll see a few family visitors like Sally and me — a sign of the outside world.

This is a strange and mystical time in a hospital. Your own thoughts and breathing are so still that for all you know you could be one breath away from death yourself. Since I thought the respirator would pump on no matter what, the evening before I had sheepishly asked the night duty nurse, "How will we know if Mama has died?" All she had said was a mysterious, "You'll see the change in her; you'll know."

My mother's right hand rested in mine as the first pale shades of dawn appeared on the horizon and filtered through the curtains. Outside the window, the hardy Philadelphia sparrows began to chirp a welcome to the new day. Wondering what the nurse had meant — I wished she had been more definite so we could be prepared — I scrutinized Mama's face. She looked the same. Everyone has said goodbye; maybe tonight's the night.

I spoke aloud to her, "Well, Mama, your beloved son Richie has come to see you. He thanked you and said goodbye. . . . " I imagined her giving a wry smile, saying "It's about time!" Then she would laugh ruefully at the stumbling grief of her youngest and wildest son. Yes, Mama, you did the best you could; Richie will get along fine. What else could she be waiting for?

"So Nora . . . " I got uncharacteristically personal, "if you want to go . . . if it really is your time and you're ready, you can go now." I heard a tremor in my voice, but pushed on. "You won't be abandoning us. We'll miss you a lot, but don't worry, we'll take care of each other. That's what you and Daddy taught us. Thanks for that, and for everything you gave up so that we could have life."

Then to the woman who had brought me into the world, and who had always been there for me, even the times when I couldn't stand her love, I said as though to reassure her, "I'll be okay. I've got good friends who will stand by me." Sliding my hand from hers, I stood and watched for a moment, wishing I could hear a response from her. I leaned down to kiss her forehead.

"Good morning!" Aunt Anne greeted me cheerily when I emerged into the corridor. She and Sally were sipping cups of tea from cardboard containers. After she looked in on Mama briefly, the three of us went up to attend Mass in the hospital chapel. It was the feast day of St. Therese, the "Little Flower," one of Mama's favorite saints.

"The queen is led into the king in robes of gold..." we recited the entrance antiphon together. Aunt Anne looked over at me and smiled. Sometime during that half hour, the only time during the two weeks since the operation that we had left her alone for more than a few minutes, Mama died.

We didn't find out until we had already driven home and I had climbed into bed and was half asleep. Sally poked her head through the doorway. "Paul!...Paul!...the hospital just called about Mama!" Her cheeks were wet and the look on her face told me it was all over. Leaping out of bed, I ran to hold her.

We decided that she and Maura would drive to where Daddy worked part-time in a jewelry shop to break the news to him, and I would go immediately to the hospital. We would meet there. As we divided up the phone numbers to inform the rest of the family members, Sally laughed softly, "She waited until she was alone, didn't she?...so that none of us could say we were her favorite."

Later, I numbly wove my car down Spruce Street to Misericordia Hospital where the fourteen of us had been born. An old Irish love song on a tape kept me company.

> Oh, Danny boy, the pipes the pipes are calling,
> From glen to glen, and down the mountainside,
> The summer's gone, and all the flower's are dying
> 'Tis you, 'tis you must go and I must bide.
>
> But come you back when summer's in the meadow,
> Or when the valley's hushed and white with snow.
> Yes, I'll be here in sunshine or in shadow,
> Oh, Danny boy, oh, Danny boy, I love you so.

And if you come, when all the flower's are dying,
And I am dead, as dead I well may be,
You'll come and find the place where I am lying,
And kneel and say an Ave there for me.

And I shall hear, though soft you tread above me,
And all my dreams will warmer sweeter be,
If you will kneel and tell me that you love me,
Then I shall sleep in peace until you come to me.

~ Afterword ~
A Memorial Service

Come away, O human child!
to the waters and the wild
with a faery, hand in hand,
for the world's more full of weeping
than you can understand.

—William Butler Yeats,
excerpt from "The Stolen Child."

ONCE A YEAR, before the holiday season at the end of the year, the Visiting Nurse Service hospice program in New York City celebrates a memorial service. The idea is that during the holidays when everyone else is celebrating people need some special advice on how to deal with the loss of their loved ones. Because of past memories stirred up, their loss is often felt most poignantly at these festive times. When all the songs are filled with childhood hopes and promises, they can be a depressing contrast with your real life, even if you haven't suffered a recent loss. Those who are experiencing such a loss need special bereavement plans to help them cope.

Though friends sing, "Should old acquaintance be forgot? . . . " the end of the year is a natural time to let go of the hurtful past, with hopes to start the New Year afresh. None of this can be forced. The loss or death that one is grieving may be so recent that it is still impossible to move on. But for the families who are able and for the hospice staff itself, who need to let go of the past year's losses so they can enter those of the New Year, it is a good time to ritualize this letting go.

The first time we planned this service, we wanted to have it in a beautiful place. Given the multiple faith traditions of our hospice families, we also decided to host the memorial service in a nondenominational setting. We found the perfect location: the gorgeous wood-panelled board room of our agency headquarters, located in a townhouse in a lovely midtown neighborhood accessible by car and subway.

We scheduled this gathering for a Sunday in early December. It would take place after Thanksgiving, but a week or so before Chanukah and Christmas. We hoped to involve the hospice staff as much as possible so that the family members who came would feel welcomed by someone they knew. It could be a bereavement experience for the team members too. The Juilliard School of Music, whose student volunteers gave home concerts to our patients throughout the year, offered us an ensemble for this special occasion. We would provide a translator for the Spanish-speaking families.

Printed invitations were sent out to the families who had lost someone during the past year. Notices went out to every department of the Visiting Nurse Service. All the preparations were made. The day arrived, brisk and sunny. The hospice staff gathered anxiously.

The strains of a cello, a flute, and two violins welcomed us into the warm room we had prepared and coaxed the participants back into the tender feelings they had toward their loved ones. Clusters of the various families sat together with spaces between. As they were greeted by the nurses and others who had shared their pain, conversations broke out, sometimes accompanied by tears on both parts. We waited an extra ten minutes after the scheduled starting time and then signalled to the musicians that we were ready to begin.

"Good afternoon, and in behalf of the whole hospice staff, welcome!" voice was a little tremulous. "As the administrator of our hospice program, it is very gratifying for me to see all of you here today. We are conducting this memorial service to provide all of us an opportunity to remember the people that we knew and loved and cared for, those who died during the past year.

"For those of us on the staff, it feels very important to reflect on the patients that we took care of, those whom we touched and whose lives touched ours. And to have an opportunity to see and be with their families and their friends again. For those of you who lost someone this past year, we know that this season is bittersweet with memories and longings and hopes for the future. Our Tree of Life symbolizes healing, and we hope that the opportunity to be together today in this intimate, warm, beautiful old room and to feel the connectedness with each other will be healing and renewing for all of us. Now I'd like to introduce to you Beverly, our social work coordinator."

"I am very glad to be here with you," Beverly began. "Some of you I have met before, some I have not had the opportunity until this moment. First of all, I'd like to talk a little about bereavement and the meaning of bereavement, and then bring it into the holiday season. Bereavement is the grieving experience one undergoes after losing a loved one. The feelings of emptiness and helplessness that accompany this, the sense of loss of control, make bereavement one of the most stressful events in all of one's life. There are approximately eight hundred thousand new widows and widowers every year in this country, and this doesn't even include the loss of siblings, the loss of father or mother, the loss of a child or grandparent. Bereavement is going on all around us.

"Most bereaved people have symptoms of depression, and this depression can last for several months. For some people this depression lifts quickly, and there is a bouncing back of feelings — back and forth. There are many stressful factors in loss. Initially there might be some shock. Right after the person dies there is almost a disbelief, although there might have been a long preparation for the death. The person is finally gone. In some ways, it can lift a burden from the shoulders of some of the caretakers. We have ambivalent feelings when someone dies.

"What do we need when we are going through the shock? Well, we certainly need the support of people close to us, of people who care about us, and of our immediate family members. If we are fortunate to have good friends, these are the people we need to hold us close at such a difficult time. But we have to protect ourselves, and shock is a way the mind protects itself.

"There is a period of numbness that can last several weeks or even several months. There is disorganization when one thinks, 'My God, I must be losing my mind! I can't remember things.

I'm constantly forgetting things, I'm leaving things all over.' You need to seek out people who will permit you to talk about these feelings. It's a very uncomfortable situation for some people to deal with. They cannot listen to your pain; they cannot hear. They think you should be over the grief. But we know you are not over the grief, nor will the grief ever completely leave. The healing process is slow. There will always remain a scar. That's not to say there can't be growth. From past experience we know that people do grow from the grieving process.

"There is a time of reorganization, when things start to fall into place, ever so slowly. Perhaps we can reach out to memories, pictures, look at things, be a part of activities that we thought we'd never be able to be part of again. Perhaps we'll look for new areas in which to develop ourselves. Perhaps go back to school and take a course, perhaps join a group. That group may be a group of other bereaved people. At some point you might consider being a volunteer visitor to other people going through this process. All of this can be part of your healing.

"We know one other thing about the bereavement process. It goes on for different lengths of time for different people. It can go on for months or for years. At this time, during the holiday season, we know those feelings come back again. As Kate said, bittersweet feelings. We need to decide how we want to celebrate the holidays. Maybe you'll say, 'I'm going to pretend it's just like it's always been.' But we know it can't be that way. That special person is no longer here. What can we do to compensate so that we can get through the holiday season?

"Perhaps we'll do things a little differently. Maybe the person who has died had a special task in the family. He or she may have been the one who decorated the tree and did the special cooking, did some special baking. Perhaps people all came to our house. Maybe this year we should go somewhere else, to someone else's home.

"Perhaps we don't want the stresses of the holidays to be as they once were. This year we may need to relax and take it a little slower, maybe not shop as frenetically or have as much company. Or maybe we need to have more company! We need to do what is comfortable for us and not necessarily what is expected of us from others. We have to be comfortable with our feelings and how we want to spend the holidays. Yes, we can be selfish in a nice kind of way and protect ourselves.

"There is something here I want to read you from a woman who has lost two people who were very dear to her in her life. 'No one can tell you how long, or in what manner, you should grieve,' she says. 'Your grief is unique. There are similarities of course — the shock, the numbness, the disorganization, the re-organization. There is that sameness in the grief process, but each grief is unique because we are all separate and individual people. So there are unique qualities to your grief that you must honor, but there are also elements of bereavement that are more or less common to all of us who pass through it. Understanding these common elements, and how others have dealt with them, can be a great help.' I think we would all agree with this woman. It is why we have come together today.

"In closing, I'd like to say that I feel all of us, just by be-ing here, are supportive of each other. We all came for our own needs, our own reasons. But just the fact that you were all able to come is extremely selfless, enough to care for the next person and to help each other. In sharing our grief it becomes a little lighter. Thank you."

The first part of the program concluded with a reading from the Jewish Scriptures.

> On this mountain the Lord of hosts
> will provide for all peoples
> A feast of rich food and choice wines,
> juicy, rich food and pure, choice wines.
> On this mountain he will destroy
> the veil that veils all peoples,
> The web that is woven over all nations;
> he will destroy death forever.
> The Lord God will wipe away
> the tears from all faces;
> The reproach of his people he will remove
> from the whole earth; for the Lord has spoken.
> —Isa. 25:6–8

The musicians began a Bach fugue, and the planning team relaxed. We had gotten over the first threshold, and no one had rushed out yet. The next part would be crucial; Kate looked

over and smiled. After the music and a moment of silence, I
introduced it.

"Good afternoon! Having been with many of you at a special
time during the past year, I am glad to be with you here as we
come together. When my mother died about fifteen years ago, a
friend of mine told me something that I didn't understand then.
She said, 'Paul, tell everyone about her. Tell everyone; it'll be
good therapy.' My friend was telling me to do something that
people of many cultures and traditions do naturally. We remember those we love by telling stories about them. It is the way we
are healed from their loss.

"The Irish, a cantankerous group of people of which I am
one, at our 'wakes' invariably wind up telling stories about the
one who has just died. Of course we embellish the facts a little!
Sometimes it's an anecdote that's a little hurtful, but other ones
even cause us to break into laughter at the unique characteristics
we are all recalling about this person we have loved.

"What are we doing? This storytelling is a natural human
phenomenon. People come alive by our remembering them.
They come alive in our memory first of all, and in more than
our memory if we let them. Native peoples speak of their Old
Ones who have gone to the Happy Hunting Grounds. Christians
believe in the Communion of Saints. Indeed whole cultures ritually remember their ancestors so that they do not live in a time
vacuum. We do this also with our individual loved ones and with
our families. We tell stories about them and invite them around
us again at special moments like this so that they and we can
live.

"So will you do something with me for a minute? Just relax,
close your eyes a little bit, and get back in touch with a memory about that person or persons you love. Let them rise up in
your memory a little. They've been there already today, but now
you might let them come up a little closer. It might be a hurtful
or tender memory from long ago. It could be something even a
little humorous, or an interaction that happened more recently.
Whatever it is, would you all pause for a moment now, and together we'll let these memories come up. It'll be good for us.
[Here we paused for about three or four minutes.]

"Together now, because that is why we have gathered here,
we are going to lift these memories up. We are going to hold

these people up whom we love, and if you feel comfortable doing so, you might even wish to share one of those memories that came to you. You don't have to, but there might be something you would like to share, a brief image or story. . . . "

Beverly stood and spoke first. "This is something that happened to me in a kind of spiritual way. One Thanksgiving I was trying very hard to remember a recipe. Of course, I didn't listen when my mother had tried to teach me! . . . She kept saying, 'Write this down' . . . And I'd say, 'Ma, you're always gonna be here to do it . . . why do I have to write it down?' . . . and she'd always say, 'Write it down' . . . and we'd go through this, and guess what? I just never wrote it down. Mom had died; it was the first Thanksgiving after her death, in fact just a few months later. And I thought about this recipe and said, 'Why didn't I write that down?' Here I am, and I have to make it because she made it and everybody expects it. So I go into the kitchen, and I get together most of the ingredients that I remembered, and suddenly — it became very spiritual — the recipe fell into place! The ingredients, what came next, how long to bake it . . . and everything turned out fairly well. I said, 'My God, I feel her presence!' It was a wonderful feeling."

We laughed softly with Beverly, grateful to her for breaking the ice. Some of the family members then began to voice their memories. Surprisingly, most of them caused us to laugh. Divine humor was percolating up from our wounds to heal us. It was as though our loved ones who had gone before us were gathering around us to say, "We're okay, and you will be too . . . so laugh with us."

A middle-aged black man in the second row began to speak in a muffled voice: "I've got a lot of nice memories . . . but one of the fondest ones of my father-in-law is this: I was going to ask for my wife's hand in marriage, and he said to me, 'You really want to marry her?' . . . I said, 'Yes, I do', and he started to laugh. . . . I said, 'Is that very funny?' He said, 'No, no, it's not very funny. You see, my daughter has a very expensive foot . . . and now all her problems are going to be yours!' " The crowd broke up on hearing this, including his wife with the expensive foot who was dabbing her eyes next to him.

"What's his name?" I asked.

"Leon."

"God bless Leon!"

A woman in the back of the room had her hand raised. "I had a son whom I lost when he was only twenty years old. . . . He drowned. When he was about five, his older brother, Leo, was getting ready to make his First Communion, and I let Patrick go over to confession with him one Saturday evening, to get him out from under my feet. So he went downstairs, but then came back up because he wanted to ask me questions about it first. I explained to him, 'When your brother goes into the confessional box, you wait outside in the pew; don't move. When he comes out, he'll go up to the altar rail to say his penance, and then he'll come back and pick you up to take you home.' Patrick looked at me with his big blue eyes and said, 'I want to ask you something, Ma. . . . Suppose the priest opens up the bottom of that confessional box, and takes Leo right down to hell!' " Again the room exploded in laughter.

"Thank you, Patrick!"

It was amazing how we could walk into these very difficult feelings of loss and grief and touch on them, releasing something pent up by our laughter. I could see the contorted faces relaxing. I wondered about anger though, the rage someone might feel about the one who died?

"An emotion that is sometimes hard to deal with is anger," I told them. "Recently I was talking to the wife of one of our patients who died and was asking her about how she felt. When we had been talking a while, she confided, 'I feel angry that I've been left alone.' We were discussing how she expressed this when she said, 'I never got angry with my husband when he was alive.' In mid-sentence she stopped suddenly: 'Oh, yes, I did!' Grinning, she explained, 'Quite a while ago we got into an argument one evening. I wanted to watch TV and my husband wanted to hear the stereo. We were in the living room, and I turned on the TV and then he got up and turned on the stereo. Then I got up and turned down the stereo and he got up and turned it up again. The two of us sat there steaming, not able to hear either the TV or the stereo. Finally, I had it. I got up and left and came back to the room with a pair of scissors. I went over and *SNIP!* . . . I cut the cord!' "

"Oooh!" The roomful of grievers caught their breath as one. This was followed by nervous giggles.

"Somehow, after her husband had died, it gave this woman a sense of joy to remember this, this little event that meant something about her and him. We chuckled about it before I left her house that day. When I was driving home, I wondered if this ability to remember her anger allowed her not to feel simply like the victim of his death. After all, she had cut the cord first!"

A reflective silence followed. The time seemed ripe to move into the ritual part of our ceremony. We would be reading the names of the deceased aloud and placing their pictures on the Tree of Life. (We had asked everyone to bring a picture of their loved one and be prepared to hang it on a ficus tree, which we would keep in our office until the next year.)

"There will be lots of moments to share one of your stories during the refreshment period afterward. You might feel more comfortable sharing your memory with just one or two persons rather than the whole group. In any case, stay in touch with it yourself, because it is beautiful. These are the kinds of memories of our loved ones we are going to be holding through the holidays, but especially in the next moments when we walk up and place their pictures on the tree here. We will be placing some of our memories on the tree as well."

What followed was one of the most powerful liturgical experiences I've ever participated in. Without any fuss, Doc and Ruby stood and took turns reading aloud the names of the dead from what we called our Book of Life. (During a brief ceremony at the beginning of each weekly team meeting, we would inscribe a book with the name and date of death of our patients who had died during the previous week.) This recitation took the form of a litany as the familiar names washed over us.

The family members waited until they were ready or had heard their loved one's name before they came forward and hung a photo — sometimes recent but more likely an earlier one — of a younger and healthier spouse, parent, or child on the Tree of Life. Some were yellowing ancient photographs: a tiny one of a beautiful lady that might have been in a locket, one of a dapper dude under a palm tree, another of a man in shorts, golfing. While the violins played, it was as if they held their dear ones in their hands as they placed the precious pictures on our tree.

Ruby's and Doc's voices wavered at times. A few of the family members needed to be helped to come forward in tears and to let go of their photo, to give their loved one up to the Tree of Life. The last one was a shy little girl who approached the tree with her mother and carefully hung her father's picture on a low branch.

This is what we had hoped and prayed for, that people would find a way to embody their feelings. So many griefs remain all stuffed up inside of us. They keep us stuck in the past because we have no way to acknowledge them in faith. Our losses wound us, but they also invite us to be more fully alive if we dare to believe. The future is as wide open to us as our cracked hearts.

The litany ended. The music diminished to a single violin chord. Each of us sat with our own thoughts. Outside on the pavement we could hear the sound of a woman's high-heeled footsteps fade off into silence. It was time to offer the closing prayer. "Please stand."

O God, Creator of all that is, everything is alive to you. Everything has meaning to you. We lift up our memories and feelings, the hurting ones and the beautiful ones, asking you to bless and heal them today. Thank you for the *life* of the person we have loved: a wife or husband, a mother or father, a lover, child, niece, neighbor, or friend. We thank you for the time we had with them and for the way they are in our hearts even now. Help us through this special time of the year, when songs of hope and joy may remind us of our loss.

But you, O God, are in the loss too. You call out in our pain for the love that even you need. Let us love one another, then, as a way of remembering our dear ones and loving you. Give us confidence in your promise of a time when death will be no more, when every tear shall be wiped away, and when at last we shall understand. Grant us faith and love until then. . . .

And may God bless you and keep you, may the face of God shine upon you and be gracious to you. May God look upon you with favor and grant you peace. Amen.

~ Appendix A ~
Pastoral Notes

Some may choose to use this book as a resource to teach skills in pastoral care. Others may suggest it for their students to open up a discussion on ethics or the meaning of religion. The stories presented here aren't the last word in pastoral interactions, but one man's response to a multitude of specific situations that priests, ministers, and caregivers may encounter. The stories — like role-plays — can allow responses other than mine. What might you have done differently if you were there as a caregiver? How might you have reacted to this pastoral care if you were the patient? The following notes elucidate a few pastoral issues worth discussing.

1. Some sincere religious people believe that homosexual people are bad. In fact, many of their churches or synagogues have taught them so, quoting Bible passages to back them up. What this family showed me is that God reveals himself in whomever he wishes and shows the magnitude of his love by the love of the people around us. "By their fruits you will know them." (Matt. 7:16) It is not possible for God to hate homosexuals while revealing his presence in their love for one another.

2. To me, the best ministry is the most wholistic. People seem to be healed as much from human touch as from medicines and talking. That is why all of the Christian sacraments have a *sensible* component to them. In fact, the priesthood was attractive to me precisely because it was a way of life in which a man could express human affection. However, one's touch is not always understood; a gesture may need to be explained, with permission granted beforehand.

3. There is a risk in using a pastoral gesture, which has a sacred significance in one religion, toward those who are considered externs. It could scandalize members of the religion who see the gesture as an exclusive sign for them. I knew, however, that anointing with oil is a human and even sacred rite that predates Christianity, so I was willing to suggest this ritual to anyone who would appreciate it. Also, I was beginning to experience myself as a priest ordained for all, an ecumenical priest. When I explained this rit-

255

ual and it was welcomed by a dying person, it became a symbol of this new understanding.

4. There are two reasons I no longer believe it is my task as a priest to save souls. First, to save "souls" is too otherworldly. It suggests that a priest — and God — is disconnected from the world of bodies, blood, sweat, semen, wombs, earth, nations, cosmos. "My kingdom is not of this world," Jesus said (John 18:36), but he healed people's physical infirmities and fed them; he held them and wept with them and forgave their sins. In other words, his love for them was embodied. Second, to "save" souls is usually understood by people as doing their work for them, for example, making verbal faith statements that are supposed to take away people's doubts instead of helping them work through them to real faith: *"Your* faith has saved you" (Luke 7:50).

5. At a time when the sexual abuse of children is coming into public consciousness, some priests have been tried and found guilty of this crime. It is a challenging and frightening time to be a professional caregiver since what used to be an innocent gesture can be grounds for suspicion of malintent. I know newly ordained priests who refuse to speak to a teenager in private now because of the climate of suspicion. While caregivers need to develop a genuine carefulness and concern, I am reluctant to surrender one of the greatest roles of trust and healing that a priest historically has been given. In this case however, it would have been wiser for me to explain first to the nurse who I was and how I intended to interact with the patient.

6. The promise of celibacy, which priests are required to take at ordination, is often misunderstood. I used to think it meant to push away one's sexual feelings because this dimension of one's humanity was dedicated to God by its non-use. Now I am more likely to understand a celibate person in a positive way, as a dedicated single person (from the Latin word *coelebs,* meaning single). In this meaning, a celibate is one who spreads his or her sexual love — affective, not genital — out to many people for God's sake: friends, religious community members, people one ministers to, even enemies. In the present age, which glorifies "couple-love" even while it mocks the fidelity that should accompany it, "single-love" can unleash a tremendous reservoir of energy — a nonpossessive affective energy that can be a healing force in the world.

7. As a hospice counselor, it was my responsibility to foster life until a person died. Therefore I could not ignore a patient's suicide threat and should actively intervene if I were able. Frederick's words and behavior suggested that he had the means and a plan. This is a clearer warning signal than simply a random thought about suicide. It required a team response to help Frederick deal with his plight less drastically; I intended to alert them. I believe, however, that there could be circumstances in which a person is determined to take his or her life and I would not ultimately stand in that person's way.

8. The Apostles' Creed states the Christian belief that Jesus Christ "suffered under Pontius Pilate, was crucified, died and was buried. *He descended into hell;* the third day he arose again from the dead...." Traditionally this has meant that after Jesus died, his spirit went down to the realm of the dead

where all those who died before him had been waiting for a savior through the centuries, in order that he might lead those among them who were just into the resurrection. I experience this truth in a more personal way, that Jesus saved us by himself having gone down first into any "hell" we are presently experiencing or by being in it with us at this very moment if we can believe it.

9. According to Vatican Council II, "Extreme Unction, which may also and more fittingly be called Anointing of the Sick, is not a sacrament for those only who are at the point of death. Hence, as soon as any one of the faithful begins to be in danger of death from sickness or old age, the appropriate time for him to receive this sacrament has certainly already arrived." The biblical Letter of the Apostle James is quoted to support this: "Is there anyone sick among you? Let him call for the elders of the Church, and let them pray over him and anoint him in the name of the Lord. This prayer, made in faith, will save the sick man. The Lord will restore his health, and if he has committed any sins, they will be forgiven" (James 5:14-15). To be "healed" means more than to be "cured;" it could even mean to peacefully let go and die if we are ready.

10. As the pastoral care director for the hospice program, I was responsible for supervising the interns who worked with me. Included were Protestant, Jewish, and Catholic seminary students to enable us to be sensitive to our patients' varied religious traditions. Each week they were required to spend an hour individually with me to go over the care they were providing for patients whom I had assigned them. In contrast to what most pastors have available, I had contracted with a pastoral psychotherapist to receive supervision myself. The freer a caregiver felt to bring up any questions to a supervisor without being judged, the better the supervision.

11. People hasten their deaths in many ways, e.g., by not eating or drinking when they have an incurable illness and see no point in lingering on. One's "appetite" for life is naturally declining at such a point, and thus one's appetite for food or drink, involvement with the world, and even conversation with loved ones subsides as well. Currently there is a debate going on about the ethics of removing life-support systems such as respirators and feeding tubes. What is really being wrestled with here is the *quality* of life: who is qualified to determine when "ordinary" requirements for the preservation of life have become extraordinary, and thus a person or caregiver is free to continue them or not? Life is so precious that nations and the various religious traditions make laws to guide us on these matters as each new scientific discovery poses a new question. The Roman Catholic Church would ordinarily guide us this way: "Each human life is *God's* ultimately; thus we cannot actively take our own life or that of another. We *must* take ordinary means to preserve life; we *can* take extraordinary means." Yet with all of these guidelines before us, it is ultimately each of us in our own heart who decides whether to live or die.

12. In various religious traditions, it is assumed that the soul/vital presence of the deceased person does not depart immediately, but hovers around for some time after what appears to be the physical death. In any case, we

may need to say goodbye to loved ones *years* after their physical death. They will truly rest in peace when we can do so.

13. This approach could appear to trivialize or merely psychologize the holy symbol of the Eucharist. Rather than diminish it, if we experience the *human* dimension of this and other signs of God's love, our experience of the divine will deepen.

14. Caregivers may be sent in as professionals, and this role is important. But if caregivers experience themselves only as the givers, it is easy for them to grow proud and to burn out. The patients will recognize this power position for what it is and react accordingly. When caregivers can begin to notice what they *receive* from those they minister to, the caregiving situations become less daunting and more graceful. Then a true blessing takes place and it is experienced as mutual. Caregivers should not be unconsciously preoccupied with meeting their own needs instead of the patients' needs — this is dealt with in supervision as countertransference — but *afterward* they should not be surprised to recognize even the most difficult pastoral encounters as gifts of God served up precisely for themselves.

15. In the present era, when religious fundamentalism on all sides threatens our fragile world order, it seems especially important to respect the truth found in all religions, and if possible seek the common ground, the Spirit, within each of them. As though anticipating this, Jesus once said to a non-Jew who asked him where to worship, "Woman, believe me the hour is coming when neither on this mountain nor in Jerusalem will you worship the Father. . . . God is spirit, and they who worship him must worship in spirit and in truth" (see John 4:19–24). This openness need not make us less a missionary, just supremely respectful of what the religious traditions we encounter have to offer us.

16. In the end, it is not what religion we belong to that determines our holiness, nor how perfect others perceive us to be that will insure us life beyond our body's dying. It is in "bearing one another's burdens" (Isa. 53; Amos 6:4–7; Gal. 6:2).

17. We are not saved by calling God by the right name, whether it be Allah, Yahweh, Ram, or Jesus. Anyone can shout "Lord, Lord!" (Matt. 25:11). Rather, salvation would seem to be the experience of the One we call God holding us in our pain/sin and bearing it along with us. We may thus need to "forgive" God for not making us and the world perfect.

~ Appendix B ~
Criteria for Admission to a Hospice Program

You should consider hospice if:

1. you have an advanced illness with a limited life expectancy (usually six months or less);

2. your physician agrees to your participation in the program (the hospice personnel will negotiate this with the doctor if you prefer);

3. you have tried all curative care and it hasn't worked, and you now want and need supportive care for comfort;

4. you want to be cared for at home (most hospices in the United States are home-based);

5. you have a family member or friend who is willing to assume responsibility for ongoing assistance (the primary care person).

Medicare, Medicaid, and private insurance all pay for hospice care. If you are interested or have a question, call HOSPICE HELPLINE at 1-800-658-8898, and they will direct you to a hospice program in your area. Hospice personnel will work with you to determine whether this is the right program for you.